2ND NATIONAL EDITION

The Employer's Legal Handbook

BY ATTORNEY FRED S. STEINGOLD

EDITED BY BARBARA KATE REPA

NOLO PRESS  BERKELEY

YOUR RESPONSIBILITY WHEN USING A SELF-HELP LAW BOOK

We've done our best to give you useful and accurate information in this book. But this book does not take the place of a lawyer licensed to practice law in your state. If you want legal advice, see a lawyer. If you use any information contained in this book, it's your personal responsibility to make sure that the facts and general information contained in it are applicable to your situation.

KEEPING UP-TO-DATE

To keep its books up-to-date, Nolo Press issues new printings and new editions periodically. New printings reflect minor legal changes and technical corrections. New editions contain major legal changes, major text additions or major reorganizations. To find out if a later printing or edition of any Nolo book is available, call Nolo Press at 510-549-1976 or check the catalog in the *Nolo News,* our quarterly newspaper.

To stay current, follow the "Update" service in the *Nolo News.* You can get a free one year subscription by sending us the registration card in the back of the book. In another effort to help you use Nolo's latest materials, we offer a 25% discount off the purchase of your Nolo book when you turn in the cover of an earlier edition. (See the "Recycle Offer" in the back of the book.) This book was last revised in **February 1997**.

SECOND EDITION	**FEBRUARY 1997**
EDITOR	Barbara Kate Repa
BOOK DESIGN	Jackie Mancuso
COVER DESIGN	Toni Ihara
PROOFREADER	Ely Newman
INDEXER	Susan Cornell
PRINTING	Bertelsmann Industry Services, Inc.

Quantity Sales: For information on bulk purchases or corporate premium sales, please contact the Special Sales department. For academic sales or textbook adoptions, ask for Academic Sales, 800-955-4775, Nolo Press, Inc., 950 Parker St., Berkeley, CA 94710.

Steingold, Fred.
    The employer's legal handbook / by Fred S. Steingold: edited by
  Barbara Kate Repa. --2nd ed.
       p.   cm.
    Includes index.
    ISBN 0-87337-370-7
    1. Labor laws and legislation--United States--Popular works.
  I. Repa, Barbara Kate.   II. Title.
  KF3455.Z9S74 1997
  344.7301--dc21   96-50108
                                 CIP

QUANTITY SALES: For information on bulk purchases or corporate premium sales, please contact the Special Sales department. For academic sales or textbook adoptions, ask for Academic Sales. 1-800-955-4775, Nolo Press, Inc., 950 Parker Street., Berkeley, CA, 94710.

THANK YOU

Several people generously contributed advice and information in the preparation of this book, including:

- James Bruno
- Fred Daily
- Tony Duerr
- Mark Hartley
- Joel Hearshen
- Jon Huegli
- Diane Hunter
- Nancy Keppelman
- Lonnie Loy
- Len Pytlak
- William Simmons, and
- Dave Tiedgen.

Special thanks to Barbara Kate Repa for her superb editorial guidance and to Jake Warner for his excellent additions to the manuscript.

—Fred S. Steingold

CONTENTS

PERSONNEL PRACTICES

CHAPTER 3

WAGES AND HOURS

EMPLOYEE BENEFITS

TAXES

CHAPTER 6

FAMILY AND MEDICAL LEAVE

HEALTH AND SAFETY

ILLEGAL DISCRIMINATION

WORKERS WITH DISABILITIES

CHAPTER 10

TERMINATION

CHAPTER 11

INDEPENDENT CONTRACTORS

Unions

LAWYERS AND LEGAL RESEARCH

APPENDIX

INDEX

CHAPTER

1

HIRING

Many state and federal laws—as well as countless court decisions—set out legal protocol for every phase of the employment relationship, including the hiring process. If you've correctly sensed that many workers today are well informed about their legal rights and are willing to fight to enforce them, you may be concerned about making costly mistakes during hiring.

Fortunately, you can steer clear of most of the legal perils of hiring employees by understanding and following these sensible guidelines:
• avoid illegal discrimination
• respect the applicant's privacy rights
• don't imply job security—unless you mean it
• protect against unfair competition
• observe the legal rules for hiring young workers and immigrants, and
• follow the IRS standards for hiring independent contractors.

Section A of this chapter discusses these key principles—some of which apply throughout the employment relationship and are discussed elsewhere in this book as well.

Sections B through H of this chapter explain how to keep legal risks to a minimum as you write job descriptions, advertise for workers, design job applications, interview applicants, check into their backgrounds and offer them jobs.

(See Chapter 11 for a detailed discussion of hiring independent contractors.)

A. Legal Guidelines for Hiring Employees

Most large companies maintain human resource departments and in-house lawyers to lead them through the intricacies of employment law. But if you run a small or mid-sized company, this is an unaffordable luxury. More likely, you keep a close eye on legal expenses and call a lawyer only when absolutely necessary.

The guidelines discussed here should reduce your need for outside legal help when hiring employees.

1. Avoiding Illegal Discrimination

Federal and state laws prohibit you from discriminating against an employee or applicant because of race, color, gender, religious beliefs, national origin, physical disability—or age if the person is at least 40 years old. Also, many states and cities have laws prohibiting employment discrimination based on marital status or sexual orientation.

These anti-discrimination laws—covered in depth in Chapters 8 and 9—apply to all stages of the employment process: preparing job descriptions, writing ads, conducting interviews, deciding who to hire, setting salaries and job benefits, promoting employees, and disciplining and firing them.

A particular form of discrimination becomes illegal when Congress, a state legislature or a city council decides that a characteristic—race, for example—bears no legitimate relationship to employment decisions. A law or ordinance is then passed prohibiting workplace discrimination based on that characteristic. Courts get involved, too, by interpreting and applying anti-discrimination laws and ordinances.

Obviously, as an employer, you need to know the types of discrimination that are illegal. At the same time, be aware that anti-discrimination laws don't dictate who you must hire. You can exercise a wide range of discretion based on business considerations. You remain free, for example, to hire, promote, discipline and fire employees and to set their salaries based on their skills, experience, performance and reliability—factors that are logically tied to a valid business purpose. You only risk violating the law when you treat a person or a group differently for reasons that legislators and judges have decided don't serve a valid business purpose.

Some illegal practices are obvious—such as advertising a job for people ages 20 to 30 in violation of age discrimination laws, or paying lower wages to women than men for the same work in violation of equal pay laws.

Other types of discrimination are more subtle, but just as illegal. Employment practices that have a disproportionate and discriminatory impact on certain groups are also barred by anti-discrimination laws. For example, if your main means of seeking job candidates is through word of mouth and your workforce consists entirely of white men, the word-of-mouth recruitment can be illegal discrimination; it's likely that few people other than white men will hear about the job openings. The effect of the procedures is what counts.

To avoid violating anti-discrimination laws at the hiring stage:

- advertise job openings in diverse places so they come to the attention of diverse people
- determine the skills, education and other attributes that are truly necessary to perform the job so that you don't impose job requirements that unnecessarily exclude capable applicants, and
- avoid application forms and screening techniques that have an unfair impact on any group of applicants.

Running afoul of anti-discrimination laws can be both time-consuming and costly. An unhappy employee or applicant may sue your business. Federal and state agencies also may take legal action against it. And publicity about a violation of anti-discrimination laws can adversely affect your business reputation, driving down revenues. If word gets out that a company has discriminated against women employees, for example, women customers may avoid dealing with the company for years—even long after the discriminatory practices have been dropped.

2. Respecting Applicants' Privacy Rights

As an employer, you likely believe that the more information you have about job applicants, the better your hiring decisions will be. But there's a potential problem in mounting intensive background checks. Your attempt to assess an applicant by gathering information about the past can conflict with his or her right to privacy—and sometimes violate federal and state laws. To avoid claims that you've invaded an applicant's privacy, obtain the applicant's written consent before you send for high school or college transcripts and credit reports and before you contact a former employer. (See Section G.)

Will It Tell You What You Need to Know?

It's often a waste of time and effort to acquire and review transcripts and credit reports—although occasionally they're useful. If you're hiring a bookkeeper, for example, experience garnered on the job is much more important than the grades the applicant received in a community college bookkeeping program 10 years ago. But if the applicant is fresh out of school and has never held a bookkeeping job, then a transcript may yield some insights. Similarly, if you're hiring a switchboard operator, information on a credit report would be irrelevant. But if you're filling a job for a bar manager who will be handling large cash receipts, you might want to see a credit report to learn if the applicant is in financial trouble.

In addition, laws and court rulings restrict your right to screen applicants through aptitude tests and drug tests. (See Section F.)

Another privacy concern, for which legal guidelines are less clear, is your ability to control what workers do outside of the workplace. Certainly, you can't lay down political tests for hiring and promoting employees; their rights of free speech and free association are protected by the Constitution. Some employers want to limit their employees to people who don't smoke, drink alcohol or use drugs—even off the job—to hold down healthcare costs or to keep a harmonious workforce. The emerging law is that you can't dictate such off the job behavior. (See Chapter 7, Section G for more on smoking and Chapter 7, Section H for more on drug testing.)

3. Avoiding False Job Security Promises

Traditionally, employees have had no job security. Employment has been an at will relationship. If there's no contract for a fixed term of employment, the employee works at the will of the employer and employee; the employer can fire the employee at any time for any reason—or for no reason at all. And the employee is free to quit at any time. That's still the basic law, although you can't fire someone for an illegal reason—because of the color of the employee's skin, for example, or because you prefer to put a younger person in the job.

The at will relationship gives you maximum freedom to fire employees, but preserving your legal right to fire at will can be tricky. Courts in many states have held that if employers are not careful about what they say during job interviews and in employee handbooks, they may lose that right.

- A law firm hired Joan as a receptionist and fired her eight months later. Joan sued the law firm. She claimed that when she was hired, she was assured that she would remain employed as long as she did a good job. The court held that such assurance was sufficient to create a contract that Joan would be fired only for just cause. (*Hetes v. Schefman & Miller Law Office*, 393 N.W.2d 577 (1986).)
- A bingo hall hired Scott as a general manager and gave him an employee handbook. Later, Scott was fired without warning or suspension. He sued, claiming that the handbook stated that the employer could fire an employee only after warnings were given and disciplinary procedures were followed. The court ruled that the employer was required to follow the procedures set out in its own employee handbook and couldn't fire Scott at will. (*Lukoski v. Sandia Indian Management Co.*, 748 P.2d 507 (1988).)

During the hiring process, don't give assurances that you may not be able to honor and that may give an applicant a false sense of security. This restraint can be difficult when you're trying hard to entice an attractive candidate to join your workforce. You'll have a natural tendency to say positive things about your business, the candidate and the future relationship. But those upbeat statements can be turned against you if the employee is later fired.

Your best protection is to make sure your application forms, employee handbooks and offers of employment state that the job is at will—and to have the applicant acknowledge this in writing. Then you'll have an excellent chance of terminating the employment on your own terms and without legal repercussions. Be aware, however, that some judges approach the whole idea of at-will employment with a measure of hostility or skepticism. These judges may disregard even the most carefully worded at-will language if it seems to be contradicted by other oral or written statements you've made to the applicant or new employee.

Here's an example of language you may wish to include in your job application form:

At Will Employment. I acknowledge that if hired, I will be an at will employee. I will be subject to dismissal or discipline without notice or cause, at the discretion of the employer. I understand that no representative of the company, other than the president, has authority to change the terms of an at will employment and that any such change can occur only in a written employment contract.

_____ Initials

TRUTH IN HIRING

Statements you make during interviews and when making job offers may later be treated as binding contracts.

In a leading case, a New York law firm recruited a lawyer who was beginning to make a name for herself in environmental law. The carrot that was dangled in front of her was that she'd head an environmental law department that the firm was starting. She bit—but wound up being assigned to general litigation work instead.

Later, when she was fired as part of a cutback, she sued the firm, claiming she'd been damaged because the firm had thwarted her career objective of continuing to specialize in environmental law. The court of appeals held that she had a valid legal theory. (*Stewart v. Jackson & Nash*, 976 F.2d 86 (2d Cir. 1992).)

The lesson of this and similar cases is that the type of work an employee does can be important. Employees often leave one employer to join another—or turn down opportunities—because a particular job seems to offer a greater chance for career advancement. To avoid claims that you misled an applicant about the nature of the work, stick to what you know the work will consist of rather than what you think the applicant may want to hear.

Similarly, if your company is considering staff reductions in the near future—because, for example, a major account is about to move out of the state—disclose this to applicants. Otherwise, you may find yourself on the defensive end of a lawsuit, especially if the employee left a secure job elsewhere to come work for you.

Consider, for example, the case of Andrew, who held a good job in New York City—a job that paid $120,000 a year. According to Andrew, executives of a Los Angeles company strongly urged him to take a job with them that they said would be secure and would involve significant pay increases. The executives portrayed the company as financially strong, with a profitable future. Brushing aside Andrew's request for a written employment contract, they told him, "Our word is our bond."

That was good enough for Andrew. He quit his New York job, bought a home in California, moved there with his wife and two children, and began working for the L.A. company. Two years later, the company fired Andrew as part of a management reorganization. He sued, claiming that the company fraudulently induced him to give up his old job and move to California. He said that when the company executives induced him to change jobs, they falsely represented the company's financial condition—concealing the fact that the company's financial outlook was bleak and that the company was already planning to eliminate the job for which it was hiring him. The California Supreme Court held that Andrew could sue for both fraud and breach of contract. (*Lazar v. Superior Court (Rykoff-Sexton Inc.)*, 49 Cal. Rptr. 2d 377 (1996).)

4. Preventing Negligent Hiring Claims

The main reason to investigate an applicant's background is to make sure the person will do a good job for you and fit in with other employees on the staff. But sometimes there's an additional, equally powerful reason to make a thorough investigation. When you hire someone for a position that may expose customers or others to danger, you must use special care in checking references and making other background checks.

Legally, you have a duty to protect your customers, clients, visitors and members of the general public from injury caused by employees you know or should know pose a risk of harm to others. If someone gets hurt or has property stolen or damaged by an employee whose background you didn't check carefully, you can be sued for negligent hiring.

Be especially vigilant when hiring maintenance workers and delivery drivers, whose jobs would give them easy access to homes and apartments.

Example: The Village Green, a 200-unit apartment complex, hires Elton as a maintenance worker and gives him a master key. Elton enters an apartment and sexually molests a four-year-old girl while the child's parents are running an errand. Had the company checked before hiring Elton, it would have discovered that Elton had just completed a prison term for a sexual offense. The child's parents sue The Village Green for negligent hiring.

Doing a background check can be a delicate matter, since laws also require you to respect the applicant's privacy. If you hire people for sensitive jobs, you must investigate their backgrounds as thoroughly as possible without stepping over the line and violating their privacy rights. You can be faulted for not looking into an applicant's criminal convictions—but not for failing to learn about prior arrests that didn't result in convictions, since such arrest records are generally protected by privacy laws.

In doing background checks on applicants for sensitive jobs, check for felony convictions and also be diligent in contacting all previous employers. Keep a written record of your investigation efforts. Insist that the applicant explain any gaps in employment history. Consider turning over the pre-hire investigation to professionals who do this for a living. If you choose to follow this route—and can afford it—it can go a long way toward refuting later claims that you failed to use reasonable efforts to learn about the employee's history.

To learn more about negligent hiring cases, see *Employer's Guide to Workplace Torts,* by Ronald M. Green and Richard J. Reibstein (Bureau of National Affairs). It costs $45 and can be ordered by calling 800/372-1033.

5. Protecting Against Unfair Competition

One risk you run in hiring people is that they'll later start a competing business or go to work for a competitor. If so, they may use information they gained at your workplace or contacts they made there to draw away business that otherwise would be yours.

Obviously, you need not be too concerned about the employee you hire to flip hamburgers or the clerk you hire to handle drycleaning orders. But employees who have access to inside information about product pricing or business expansion plans, for example, may pose competitive risks. The same goes for employees who serve valuable and hard-won customers—a salesperson, perhaps, who handles a $200,000 account.

You can help protect your business from unfair competition by asking new hires to sign agreements not to take or disclose trade secrets and other confidential information. You can also ask selected employees to sign covenants not to compete with your business—although such covenants must be carefully written so that a former employee has a reasonable chance to earn a living.

a. Trade secrets

In hiring and working with employees, some business owners need to protect their unique assets from misuse. Some possibly protectible business assets may include, for example:

- a restaurant's recipes for a special salad dressing and muffin that draw people from miles around
- a heating and cooling company's list of 500 customers for whom it regularly provides maintenance, or
- a computer company's unique process for speedily assembling computer boards.

If they are treated as such, the recipes, the customer list and the assembly process are all trade secrets. Other examples are an unpatented invention, engineering techniques, cost data, a formula or a machine. To qualify for trade secret protection, your business information must meet two requirements.

First, you must show that you've taken steps to keep the information secret—for example, by:

- keeping it in a secure place such as a locked cabinet
- giving employees access to it on a need to know basis
- informing employees that the information is proprietary, and
- having employees acknowledge in writing that the information is a trade secret.

Example: Sue works at Speedy Copy Shop. She has daily access to the list of larger accounts that are regularly billed more than $2,000 per month. Sue quits to open her own competing shop. Before she does, she copies the list of major accounts. One of her first steps in getting her new business going is to try and get their business away from her former employer. Speedy sues Sue for infringing on its trade secret. At trial, Speedy shows that it keeps the list in a secure place, permits access only to selected employees who need the information and has all employees sign non-disclosure agreements. In light of these precautions, the judge orders Sue not to contact the customers on the list and requires her to compensate Speedy for any profits she has already earned on those accounts.

Second, the information must not be freely available from other sources. If the recipe for a restaurant's award-winning custard tart can be found in a standard American cookbook or re-created by a competent chef, it simply isn't a trade secret. On the other hand, if the restaurant's chef found the recipe in a medieval French cookbook in a provincial museum, translated it and figured out how to adapt it to currently available ingredients, it probably would be considered obscure enough to receive trade secret protection. That's because the recipe isn't readily available to other American restaurants.

In addition to the requirements that a trade secret must be guarded information that is somewhat obscure, judges sometimes look at how valuable the information is to you and your competitors and how much money and effort you spent in developing the trade secret.

For more information on the legal nuances of trade secrets, see:

Trade Secrets, by Roger M. Milgrim (Matthew Bender & Company), available at many law libraries.

"Can Your Client Keep a (Trade) Secret?" by Daniel J. Gleason and Michael J. Engelberg, *The Practical Lawyer,* March 1994. A single issue of *The Practical Lawyer* costs $7.75. An annual subscription, consisting of eight issues, costs $35. Call (215) 243-1640 or write to: 4025 Chestnut Street, Philadelphia, PA 19104-3099.

b. Covenants not to compete

To prevent an employee from competing with you after leaving your workplace, consider having him or her sign a covenant not to compete. In a typical covenant, the employee agrees not to become an owner or employee of a business that competes with yours for a specific time and in a specific location.

The best time to secure a covenant not to compete is when you hire an employee. An employee who is already on the payroll may be more reluctant to sign anything—and you'll have less leverage to negotiate the agreement.

Battles over the legality of these agreements must usually be resolved in court. Judges are reluctant to deprive people of their rights to earn a living, so the key to a legally enforceable covenant not to compete is to make its terms reasonable. In evaluating whether a covenant not to compete is reasonable, focus on three questions—each of which relates to the specific job and the specific employee.

- *Is there a legitimate business reason for restricting the future activities of the particular employee?* There probably is if you expect to spend significant time and money in training a high-level employee and plan to entrust him or her with sensitive contacts on lucrative accounts. Such an employee could easily—and unfairly—hurt your business by competing with you. This would motivate a judge to find that you have a legitimate business reason for the covenant. On the other hand, if you require a new receptionist or typist to sign a similar covenant, a judge would probably find that you have no valid business purpose for restricting the employee's ability to work elsewhere.

- *Is the covenant reasonably limited in time?* A one-year limitation may be reasonable for a particular employee. A three-year limit might not be.
- *Is the covenant reasonably limited as to geographical scope?* A 50-mile limit may be reasonable for a particular employee. A limit spanning several states might not be deemed reasonable.

Example: When Mary hires Sid to be the office manager for her profitable travel agency, she realizes that Sid will have access to major corporate accounts and daily contact with the corporate managers who make travel arrangements. Mary also knows that she'll spend considerable time in training Sid and invest more than $4,000 in specialized seminars that she will require Sid to attend. She has Sid sign a covenant not to compete in which Sid promises that while working for Mary and for two years afterwards, he won't work for or own a travel agency within 50 miles of Mary's agency. After six months, Sid quits and starts a competing agency one mile from Mary's. The judge enforces the covenant not to compete by issuing an injunction forbidding Sid from operating his new business and by awarding damages to Mary as well.

While it's important for you to tailor a covenant not to compete to the specific needs of your business, the sample below may be a good starting point.

COVENANT NOT TO COMPETE

In consideration of XYZ Company hiring me as an employee, I make the following covenant:

While I am employed by XYZ Company and for one year afterward, I will not, directly or indirectly, engage in or have a financial interest in any business which would compete with the business of XYZ Company within the counties of Lincoln and Washington.

I will not disclose or use at any time, except as part of my employment with XYZ Company, any secret and confidential information pertaining to the business of XYZ Company. This includes, but is not limited to, the Company's sales and profit figures, its customer lists, its trade secrets, its relationship with its contractors, customers or suppliers and opportunities for new or developing business. I acknowledge the unique and secret nature of this information and the irreparable harm that will be caused to XYZ Company if I violate this covenant.

Dated _____

Signature _____

For more on covenants not to compete, see "A Corporate Counsel's Primer on Restrictive Convenants," by David Lawrence Hankey, *The Practical Lawyer*, January 1993. A single issue of *The Practical Lawyer* costs $7.75. An annual subscription, consisting of eight issues, costs $35. Call (215) 243-1640 or write 4025 Chestnut Street, Philadelphia, PA 19104-3099.

6. Hiring Young Workers

There are federal and state laws that restrict your right to hire workers who are under 18 years old. These laws limit the type of work for which young people may be hired and the hours they may work. (See Chapter 3, Section F for more information.)

7. Hiring Immigrants

Federal law prohibits hiring undocumented aliens. You and each new employee are required to complete INS Form I-9, Employment Eligibility Verification. (See Section K of this chapter for details.)

INDEPENDENT CONTRACTORS: BEWARE OF LABELS

The IRS believes that many small businesses are labeling some workers as independent contractors instead of employees to avoid withholding payroll taxes—and that the agency is collecting less money than it's entitled to. Acting on this belief, the IRS is vigorously investigating and challenging how businesses classify workers.

Before you classify a worker as an independent contractor for purposes of taxes and benefits, read Chapter 11. Making a mistake, however innocent, can be costly.

B. Job Descriptions

Write a job description for each position. Listing the skills and attributes you're looking for in applicants will help make the hiring process more objective. It will also give you ready standards to measure whether or not applicants are qualified—and which ones are most qualified. Current employees can often help you write job descriptions. They know how the business operates and the kind of skills that are needed.

In writing job descriptions, be careful not to violate the laws that prohibit discrimination in employment and that seek to assure employment opportunities for people with disabilities.

Basically, you can't discriminate against applicants on the basis of their race, skin color, gender, religious beliefs, national origin, physical disability—or age if the applicant is at least 40 years old.

1. Necessary Elements

A well-drafted job description usually contains these components:

- *Qualifications, such as necessary skills, education, experience and licensure.* Be careful in setting requirements for education and experience. If set at an unnecessarily high level, your requirements may have the unintended effect of excluding a disproportionate number of women or applicants who are part of other groups protected by anti-discrimination laws.
- *Essential job functions.* The Americans With Disabilities Act (ADA) has forced employers to take a fresh look at job descriptions—and to decide what really is the core of each job. (For more on the ADA, see Chapter 9.) To help eliminate unfair discrimination against people with disabilities, the ADA seeks to make sure a person isn't excluded from a job simply because he or she can't perform some marginal duties listed in a job description. Suppose your job description for a file clerk includes answering the phone, but the basic functions of the job are to file and retrieve written materials. Other employees usually answer the phone. Someone whose hearing is impaired may have trouble handling phone calls but be perfectly able to file and retrieve papers. Phone answering isn't an essential job function and shouldn't be listed as such.
- *Nonessential job functions.* You may wish to specify functions and duties that are desirable but not required for a particular job. Suppose you're seeking a receptionist. If you never or seldom require the receptionist to type, typing isn't an essential function. Listing an unnecessary or marginal skill such as typing would unfairly disqualify a person with a paralyzed or missing left hand from the receptionist job. You could, however, mention typing as a desirable function if you made it clear that it's not required.

2. Permitted Discrimination

Anti-discrimination laws recognize that in a few—a very few—instances an employer may have a legitimate reason to have job qualifications that normally would be illegal. These are called bona fide occupational qualification (BFOQ) exceptions. Religion, sex or national origin can be a BFOQ only if it's a reasonably necessary qualification for the normal operation of a business or enterprise—and it almost never is.

Here are some guidelines.

Religion. Obviously, religion can be a job requirement where the job involves performing religious duties. The law recognizes, for example, that being Catholic is a valid qualification for performing the duties of a Catholic priest and being Jewish is a valid qualification for performing the duties of a rabbi. But beyond that, religion rarely can be a BFOQ. A court has allowed a Jesuit university to limit teaching jobs in its philosophy department to Jesuits. (*Pime v. Loyola University of Chicago,* 585 F. Supp. 435 (N.D. Ill., 1984).) But a school established under a will that required all teachers to be Protestant couldn't enforce that restriction as a job requirement; the school wasn't teaching religion. (*EEOC v. Kamehameha Schools/Bishop Estate,* 990 F.2d 458 (9th Cir. 1993).)

National origin. National origin can sometimes, but rarely, be a BFOQ. An American subsidiary of a Japanese company involved in international trade might be allowed to make Japanese nationality a job requirement because of the need for language proficiency, cultural background and acceptability to trading partners of customers. (*Avigliano v. Sumitomo Shoji of American, Inc.,* 638 F.2d 552 (2d Cir. 1981).) Aside from such a narrow situation, you can't use national origin as a BFOQ.

Gender. About the only time that gender can be a BFOQ is for jobs affecting personal privacy—restroom attendants, security guards required to search employees and acting and modeling jobs.

C. Job Advertisements

You may write a great job description, then get tripped up in summarizing the job in an advertisement. This can easily happen if you let someone write your ad who's not familiar with the legal guidelines. Nuances in an ad can be used as evidence of discrimination against applicants of a particular gender, age or marital status.

There are a number of semantical pitfalls to avoid in job ads.

Don't Use	Use
Salesman	Salesperson
College Student	Parttime Worker
Handyman	General Repair Person
Gal Friday	Office Manager
Married Couple	Two-Person Job
Counter Girl	Retail Clerk
Waiter	Wait Staff
Young	Energetic

Requiring a high school or college degree may be discriminatory in some job categories. You avoid problems by stating that an applicant must have a "degree or equivalent experience."

Help Wanted ads placed by federal contractors must state that all qualified applicants will receive consideration for employment without regard to race, color, religion, sex or national origin. Ads often express this with the phrase An Equal Opportunity Employer—which makes sense even if you're not a federal contractor.

Probably the best way to write an ad that meets legal requirements is to stick to the job skills needed and the basic responsibilities. Some examples:

"Fifty-unit apartment complex seeks experienced manager with general maintenance skills."

"Mid-sized manufacturing company has opening for accountant with tax experience to oversee interstate accounts."

"Cook trainee position available in new vegetarian restaurant. Flexible hours."

D. Job Applications

Develop a standard application form to make it easy to compare applicants. Limit the form to job-related information that will help you decide who's the best person for the job. Consider including the following information in the form:

- Name, address and phone number
- Are you legally entitled to work in the United States?
- What position are you applying for?
- What other positions would you like to be considered for?
- Can you work overtime?
- If you are hired, when can you start work?
- Education—high school, college, graduate school and other (including school names, addresses, number of years attended, degree and major)
- Employment history—including name, address and phone number of each employer, supervisor's name, date of employment, job title and responsibilities and reason for leaving, and
- Special training or achievements.
  In designing a job application, keep two legal principles in mind:
- It's unlawful for you to seek certain information, as discussed in Section 1, below.
- You can use the application to inform the applicant about employment terms and to get the employee's permission to gather background information, as discussed in Section 2, below.

1. Avoiding Unlawful Questions

The chart below outlines the type of information that you can ask for in applications and during job interviews. Follow the chart to comply with federal laws. The chart may also be sufficient for complying with the laws of your state. To be sure, doublecheck with your state's civil rights department.

In addition to the areas covered in the chart, the Americans With Disabilities Act (ADA) prohibits any pre-employment questions about a disability. Before you make a job offer, you may ask questions about an applicant's ability to perform specific job functions. You may not, however, inquire about the nature or severity of a disability, ask about medical history or treatment or require any medical exam. These rules apply to application forms, job interviews and background or reference checks. (See Chapter 9 for more on the ADA.)

The Rules Change After You've Made a Job Offer

After you make a conditional job offer and before an applicant starts work, you're free to gather more details. You can at that point require a medical exam or ask health-related questions—but only if you require this for all candidates who receive conditional offers in the same job category.

PRE-EMPLOYMENT INQUIRY

Subject	Lawful Pre-employment Inquiries	Unlawful Pre-employment Inquiries
Name	Applicant's full name	Original name of an applicant whose name has been changed by court order or otherwise.
	Have you ever worked for this company under a different name?	
	Is any additional information relative to a different name necessary to check work record? If yes, explain.	Is any additional information relative to a different name necessary to check work record?
		Applicant's maiden name.
Address or Duration of Residence	How long have you been a resident of this state or city?	
Birthplace		Birthplace of applicant.
		Birthplace of applicant's parents, spouse or other close relatives.
		Requirements that applicant submit birth certificate, naturalization or baptismal record.
Age	Are you 18 years old or older? This question may be asked only for the purpose of determining whether applicants are of legal age for employment.	How old are you? What is your date of birth?
Religion or Creed		Inquiry into an applicant's religious denomination, religious affiliations, church, parish, pastor, or religious holidays observed.
Race or Color		Complexion or color of skin.
Photograph		Any requirement for a photograph prior to hire.
Height		Inquiry regarding applicant's height.
Weight		Inquiry regarding applicant's weight.

Subject	Lawful Pre-employment Inquiries	Unlawful Pre-employment Inquiries
Marital Status	Is your spouse employed by this employer?	Requirement that an applicant provide any information regarding marital status or children. Are you single or married? Do you have any children? Is your spouse employed? What is your spouse's name?
Gender		Mr., Miss or Mrs. or an inquiry regarding gender. Inquiry as to the ability to reproduce or advocacy of any form of birth control. Requirement that women be given pelvic examinations.
Disability		Inquiries regarding an individual's physical or mental condition which are not directly related to the requirements of a specific job and which are used as a factor in making employment decisions in a way which is contrary to the provisions or purposes of the Civil Rights Act.
Citizenship	Are you a citizen of the United States? If not a citizen of the United States, does applicant intend to become a citizen of the United States? If you are not a United States citizen, have you the legal right to remain permanently in the United States? Do you intend to remain permanently in the United States? To avoid discrimination based on national origin, the questions above should be asked after the individual has been hired even if it is related to the federal I-9 process.	Questions below are unlawful unless asked as part of the federal I-9 process. Of what country are you a citizen? Whether an applicant is naturalized or a native-born citizen; the date when the applicant acquired citizenship. Requirement that an applicant produce naturalization papers or first papers. Whether applicant's parents or spouse are naturalized or native born citizens of the United States; the date when such parent or spouse acquired citizenship.

Subject	Lawful Pre-employment Inquiries	Unlawful Pre-employment Inquiries
National Origin	Inquiry into language applicant speaks and writes fluently.	Inquiry into applicant's lineage; ancestry; national origin; descent; parentage, or nationality. Nationality of applicant's parents or spouse. Inquiry into how applicant acquired ability to read, write or speak a foreign language.
Education	Inquiry into the academic, vocational or professional education of an applicant and public and private schools attended.	
Experience	Inquiry into work experience. Inquiry into countries applicant has visited.	
Arrests	Have you ever been convicted of a crime? Are there any felony charges pending against you?	Inquiry regarding arrests which did not result in conviction. (Except for law enforcement agencies.)
Relatives	Names of applicant's relatives already employed by this company.	Address of any relative of applicant, other than address (within the United States) of applicant's father and mother, husband or wife and minor dependent children.
Notice in Case of Emergency	Name and address of person to be notified in case of accident or emergency.	Name and address of nearest relative to be notified in case of accident or emergency.
Organizations	Inquiry into the organizations of which an applicant is a member, excluding organizations the name or character of which indicates the race, color, religion, national origin or ancestry of its members.	List all clubs, societies and lodges to which you belong.

The Equal Employment Opportunity Commission (EEOC) sets out examples of questions employers may not ask on application forms or in job interviews as prohibited by the ADA.

- Have you ever had or been treated for any of the following conditions or diseases? (Followed by a checklist of various conditions and diseases.)
- List any conditions or diseases for which you have been treated in the past three years.
- Have you ever been hospitalized? If so, for what condition?
- Have you ever been treated by a psychiatrist or psychologist? If so, for what condition?
- Have you ever been treated for any mental condition?
- Is there any health-related reason you may not be able to perform the job for which you are applying?
- Have you had a major illness in the last five years?
- How many days were you absent from work because of illness last year? However, you may provide information on your attendance requirements and ask if the applicant will be able to meet those requirements.
- Do you have any physical defects which preclude you from performing certain kinds of work?
- Do you have any disabilities or impairments which may affect your performance in the position you are applying for?
  It's OK to ask about the applicant's ability to perform specific job functions, with or without a reasonable accommodation—a concept covered in depth in Chapter 9.
- Are you taking any prescribed drugs?
- Are you a drug addict or an alcoholic?
- Have you ever been treated for drug addiction or alcoholism?
- Have you ever filed for workers' compensation insurance?

For additional information on legal protocol during the intake process, see the *Technical Assistance Manual on the Employment Provisions (Title I) of the Americans With Disabilities Act,* available from the Equal Employment Opportunities Commission.

GUARDING AGAINST DISABILITY DISCRIMINATION

Focus on the applicant's ability to perform the job—not on a disability. You can ask questions to determine whether an applicant can perform specific job functions, but you must do so carefully.

Consider attaching a job description to the application form with specific information about the essential job functions. Or describe the job to the applicant during the interview. Then ask the applicant whether he or she can perform the job. This approach gives an applicant with a disability necessary information to request any accommodation needed to perform a task.

You might ask: "Are you able to perform these tasks with or without an accommodation?" If the applicant says that he or she can perform the tasks with an accommodation, you could go on: "How would you perform the tasks, and with what accommodation?"

Section E below includes more suggestions for dealing with disability matters during a job interview.

2. The Legal Effect of Job Applications

A well-written application form can help get the employment relationship off on a solid legal footing. Since it's filled out very early in the process, you can use the form to let the applicant know the basic terms and conditions of the job and the workplace. And, because the applicant signs the application, it can be a valuable piece of evidence if a question comes up later about what you actually promised about the job. (See Chapter 2.)

Section A3 includes language to add to your job application form emphasizing your right to fire an employee at will—that is, without having to give any reason to justify the firing.

You can also use the job application to obtain the employee's consent to having you conduct a background investigation and reference check. If the applicant consents to your investigation, he or she will have a tough time later claiming an invasion of privacy.

Authorization. I authorize XYZ Company to obtain information about me from my previous employers, schools and credit sources. I authorize my previous employers, schools that I have attended and all credit sources to disclose to XYZ Company such information about me as XYZ Company may request.

_____ Initials

Impress on the applicant the need to be honest and accurate in completing the form. Lying or giving incomplete information on an application can be a good legal reason to fire an employee if the correct story later surfaces. So serious is application fraud—or resume fraud as it's sometimes called—that some courts have allowed employers to use this to justify a firing even though the employers didn't even know of the fraud at the time of firing.

Example: Dolores, age 42, applies for a job as a land surveyor with Progressive Engineering Consultants (PEC). In her application, Dolores states that she has a civil engineering degree from a prestigious college and is licensed by the state. The application form warns that false information will be a cause for immediate discharge. Relying on the application, PEC hires Dolores. Six months later, PEC becomes dissatisfies with Dolores's work and fires her, replacing her with a 30 year-old man. Dolores sues, claiming that the firm discriminated against her based on age and gender. PEC belatedly looks into her application statements and discovers that Dolores has neither the degree nor the license she said she had. Because of Dolores's lies, the judge dismisses the case without getting into the discrimination charges.

Including the following language in an application form can help you establish that you clearly told the applicant about the consequences of lying.

> **Accuracy.** I verify that the statements I have made in this application are true and complete. I understand that if I am hired, any false or incomplete statements in this application will be grounds for immediate discharge.
>
> _____ Initials

A few unscrupulous applicants have actually taken home an application form and asked other people to fill it out for them. This can increase the risk of the form being used as an exercise in creative and deceptive writing. To safeguard against such abuses, require applicants to complete the application form on your premises where you can keep an eye on them.

E. Interviews

Before you begin to interview applicants for a job opening, write down a set of questions focusing on the job duties and the applicant's skills and experience. Some examples:

"Tell me about your experience in running a mailroom."

"How much experience did you have in making cold calls on your last job?"

"Explain how you typically go about organizing your workday."

"Have any of your jobs required strong leadership skills?"

By writing down the questions and sticking to the same format at all interviews for the position, you reduce the risk that a rejected applicant will later complain about unequal treatment. It's also smart to summarize the applicant's answers for your files—but don't get so involved in documenting the interview that you forget to listen closely to the applicant. And don't be so locked in to your list of questions that you don't follow up on something significant that an applicant has said, or try to pin down an ambiguous or evasive response.

1. Interviewing Protocol

A good icebreaker is to give the applicant some information about the job—the duties, hours, pay range, benefits and career opportunities. Questions about the applicant's work history and experience that may be relevant to the job opening are always appropriate. But don't encourage the employee to divulge the trade secrets of a present or former employer—especially a competitor. That can lead to a lawsuit. And be cautious about an employee who volunteers such information or promises to bring secrets to the new position; such an employee will probably play fast and loose with your own company's secrets, given the chance.

Also, keep your antennae tuned carefully to the applicant who spouts a litany of complaints against former employers. Hire that person and your business may well become the next object of the applicant's invective. And employees with a ton of gripes also tend to have an appetite for litigation.

Give applicants plenty of time to answer questions. Make sure they understand your questions; ask them to let you know if something is unclear. And ask them if they have any questions about your company or the job for which they're applying. Finally, let them know your timeframe for getting back to them with a hiring decision so they won't bug you with premature phone calls.

For additional suggestions on interviewing, see *Stay Out of Court: The Manager's Guide to Preventing Employee Lawsuits,* by Rita Risser (Prentice-Hall). Price: $18.95.

2. Legal Restrictions on Questions

The Rules of Etiquette once dictated that you avoid discussing sex, religion or politics in a social setting. While that standard has been relaxed, it still applies to job interviews—along with similar cautions about focusing on an applicant's age, ethnicity, birthplace and personal finances. In fact, such inquiries are not only bad manners; they're illegal.

During an interview, stay focused on job requirements and company policies. Suppose you're concerned that an applicant with young kids may spend too much time talking with them on the phone. You can't ask: "Do you have children?" or "Who watches the kids when you're at work?" But you can say to the applicant: "We don't allow personal phone calls during workhours. Do you have a problem with that?" The applicant then knows the ground rules and can let you know if a problem exists. Just be sure you apply your phone policy to all employees.

Review the legal restrictions on what you can and can't ask in a job application. (See Section D.) The same guidelines and restrictions apply to interviews. As with job applications, the focus of your interviews should be to find the best person for the job based on skill, experience, education and other qualifications needed to perform the job.

During an interview, you can obtain specific information about the applicant's ability to perform job tasks and about any needed accommodation. You'll be walking a fine line here, so take some time to avoid potential legal problems. Remember to focus on the ability of the applicant to do the job—not on disability.

Example: Zack, who has only one arm, applies at ABC Industries for a job that requires driving. The interviewer avoids asking Zack if or how this disability would affect his driving. Instead, to comply with the law, the interviewer asks: "Do you have a valid driver's license?" "Can you drive on frequent long distance trips, with or without an accommodation?" The interviewer continues: "At least 80% of the time of this sales job must be spent on the road covering a three-state territory. What is your outside selling experience? What is your accident record?" All are permissible questions.

You can describe or demonstrate the specific job tasks. Then ask whether the applicant can perform these tasks with or without an accommodation. If you're interviewing an applicant for a mailroom job, you can say: "The person in this job is responsible for receiving incoming mail and packages, sorting the mail, and taking it in a cart to many offices in two buildings, one block apart. The mail clerk must also receive boxes of supplies weighing up to 50 pounds and place them on storage shelves six feet high. Can you perform these tasks? Can you perform them with or without an accommodation?"

You can ask an applicant to describe or show how he or she will perform specific job functions—if you require this of everyone applying for a job in this category.

Example: PhoneSale, a telemarketing firm, requires all applicants to demonstrate selling ability by taking a simulated telephone sales test.

Be mindful that some applicants with disabilities will need accommodations to participate in the interview process. For example, you may need to provide an accessible location for an applicant in wheelchairs, a sign interpreter for a deaf person, or a reader for a blind person. (See Chapter 9 for an extensive discussion of the ADA requirements.)

F. Testing

Pre-employment testing—which includes skills testing, aptitude testing, honesty testing, medical testing and drug testing—is most common in larger businesses. But even if your business is small or mid-sized, you should know the legal limitations.

1. Skills Tests

Most small businesses—especially new ones—operate on a slim profit margin and need to know that employees will be up to speed from day one. If you're hiring a typist, you may want to test the applicant for typing speed and accuracy. If you're hiring a person to be a clerk in your bookstore, you may want to test the applicant's knowledge of literature. If you're hiring a driver for a delivery van, a road test would be appropriate—and a cooking test for a chef is quite reasonable. As long as the skills you're testing for are genuinely related to the job duties, a skills test is generally legal.

Surprises Are Not Appreciated

It's courteous to let applicants know in advance that they'll be tested.

To avoid discriminating against applicants protected by the Americans With Disabilities Act (ADA), be sure your tests measure actual skills and abilities needed to do a job—for example, a typing test or a sales demonstration test. (For more on the ADA, see Chapter 9.)

Avoid tests that reflect impaired mental, sensory, manual or speaking skills unless those are job-related skills that the test is trying to measure.

Example: A written question-and-answer test for a job as a heavy equipment operator might screen out an applicant with dyslexia or other learning disability, even though the applicant has the necessary skills to operate heavy equipment.

2. Aptitude Tests

Some employers use written tests—usually multiple choice tests—to get additional insight into applicants' abilities. Others attempt to probe the applicants' psyche.

These tests are going out of fashion, and for good reason. A multiple choice aptitude test may discriminate illegally against minority applicants, because it really reflects test-taking ability rather than actual job skills. A personality test can be even riskier. Besides its potential for illegal discrimination, such a test may invade an applicant's privacy—by inquiring, for example, into religious beliefs or sexual practices. (See Section A2 for more on privacy concerns.)

If you do decide to use aptitude or personality tests, proceed cautiously. Make sure that the tests have been screened scientifically for validity and that they are correlated to job performance. Review them carefully for any questions that may intrude into the applicant's privacy.

Be aware, too, that the Americans With Disabilities Act (ADA) sets special requirements when you test people who have impaired sensory, speaking or manual skills. Sensory skills include the abilities to hear and to see and to process information. If the applicant wouldn't have to use the impaired skill on the job, you must design your tests so that he or she doesn't have to use the impaired skill to take the test.

Example: Joe is applying for a position as a food handler which requires hardly any reading. Because of dyslexia, Joe has a very difficult time reading. He should be given an oral rather than a written aptitude test. By contrast, if you were interviewing Joe for a proofreader job—which clearly requires the ability to read without help—a written test would be appropriate and legal.

TESTING RUN AMOK

One large department store recently used a psychology test to screen applicants for security guard jobs. The test was based on the Minnesota Multiphasic Personality Inventory which has been used for decades and was widely accepted. Included in the test were hundreds of true or false questions, including:

I feel sure there is only one true religion.

My soul sometimes leaves my body.

I believe in the second coming of Christ.

I believe that there is a Devil and a Hell in afterlife.

My sex life is satisfactory.

I am very strongly attracted to members of my own sex.

I have often wished I were a girl.

I have never indulged in any unusual sex practices.

I like to talk about sex.

A group of applicants in California sued the store, claiming that the test violated their rights to privacy and was discriminatory. The California Court of Appeals agreed, ruling that the questions were not job-related. The court held that the job applicants were entitled to a legal order prohibiting the store from using the test. (*Soroka v. Dayton Hudson Corp.*, 235 Cal. App. 3d 654 (1991).)

3. Honesty Tests

Lie detector or polygraph tests—rarely used by small businesses anyhow—
are virtually outlawed by the federal Employee Polygraph Protection Act.
With just a few exceptions, you can't require job applicants to take lie
detector tests and you can't inquire about previous tests. The only private
employers who can use lie detector tests to screen applicants are businesses
that offer armored car, alarm and guard services or that manufacture,
distribute or dispense pharmaceuticals—and even in those situations there
are restrictions on which applicants can be tested and how the tests must be
administered.

About the only time a typical employer can use a lie detector test is
when an employee is reasonably suspected of being involved in a workplace
theft or embezzlement.

You must post a notice of the Employee Polygraph Protection Act
where employees and job applicants can readily see it. For a poster containing the required notice, contact the local office of the Wage and Hour
Division. Look in the telephone book under U.S. Government, Department
of Labor, Employment Standards Division.

Some employers use written honesty tests to screen job applicants.
Because these tests are often inaccurate and can sometimes invade an
applicant's privacy or have a discriminatory impact on some minority
groups, the legality of the tests is doubtful in most states. While honesty
tests are not yet prohibited or restricted by federal law, Congress is considering possible legislation against them.

Limit honesty tests to situations in which you have a legitimate business
reason to be concerned about workers' honesty—such as in hiring workers
who will be handling cash. Before using a test, ask to see scientific back-up
establishing the test's accuracy. And to protect yourself against charges of
illegal discrimination, test all applicants for a particular job.

4. Medical Tests

To avoid violating the Americans With Disabilities Act (ADA), don't ask the applicant about his or her medical history or conduct any medical exam before you make a job offer. You can, however, offer a job conditioned on the applicant passing a medical exam. If you do require such a post-offer exam, be sure you require such exams for all entering employees who are doing the same job.

Example: Cornerstone Corporation has openings for construction crane operators. It offers Bill a job conditioned on a medical exam showing he doesn't have a disability such as uncontrolled seizures which may be risky to other workers. Cornerstone requires such exams for all the crane operators it hires.

If you require medical exams only for people with known disabilities or those who you believe may have a disability, you'll violate the ADA. But the scope of medical exams needn't be identical for all employees. You can give follow-up tests or exams if further information is needed. Suppose, for example, that your restaurant requires a blood test for all prospective kitchen workers. If one person's test indicates a problem that may affect job performance or is a direct threat to health and safety, you can require further tests for that person.

After making a conditional job offer, you may require a full physical exam and you may ask questions that you couldn't ask at the pre-employment stage—for example, questions about previous illnesses, diseases or medications. You can probe to find out if the person has the physical or mental qualifications needed to perform the job—or to determine if a person can perform the job without posing a direct threat to his or her health or safety or that of others.

If you withdraw a conditional job offer made to a disabled person based on results of an exam or inquiry, you must be able to show that:

- your reasons were job-related and consistent with business necessity, or the person was excluded to avoid a direct threat to health and safety, and
- no reasonable accommodation could be made or such an accommodation would cause undue hardship. (For more guidance, see Chapter 9, Section E.)

To avoid claims that you discriminated against a person with a disability, carefully document all medical inquiries and the responses to them. If you reject the prospective employee, be prepared to show how the medical facts relate to the person's ability to perform the job or how the medical facts revealed a direct threat to health and safety.

The Equal Employment Opportunity Commission, the enforcing agency of the ADA's employment provisions, has set out a number of examples of post-offer employment decisions that are likely to be permitted under the law.

- Alex's medical history reveals that he has suffered several serious re-injuries to his back doing similar work. These have progressively worsened his back condition. XYZ Corporation decides not to hire Alex because of the strong risk that he would further re-injure himself on this job.

- Hannah's workers' comp history indicates she has filed several claims in recent years—all of which have been rejected. ABC Company has good reason to suspect that Hannah has submitted fraudulent claims. ABC withdraws its job offer. The withdrawal wouldn't violate the ADA because ABC's decision isn't based on a disability. But be careful. You could easily run afoul of state laws that specifically prohibit an employer from discriminating against employees or applicants because they've filed workers' comp claims.

- Kendra's medical exam reveals an impairment that will require her to frequently be away from work for lengthy medical treatment. The job requires daily availability for the next three months. The company doesn't hire Kendra. This is permissible under the ADA because Kendra isn't available to perform the essential functions of the job, and no accommodation is possible.

5. Drug Tests

You have a legal right to insist on a drug-free workplace. The only problem is that testing to weed out drug users may conflict with workers' rights to privacy. The laws on drug testing vary widely from state to state and are changing quickly as legislators and judges struggle to strike a balance between workers' rights and the legitimate needs of businesses.

The ADA Restricts Timing of Drug Tests

The Americans With Disabilities Act (ADA) forbids you from testing an applicant for drugs until you've made a conditional offer of employment.

Some state statutes allow you to test employees only in a narrow range of jobs, such as those concerned with safety. (See the chart below.) Fortunately, even restrictive states generally allow you much more leeway in screening job applicants than in testing employees who are already on board. If your state permits testing applicants or employees and you plan to do such testing, use the application form to inform applicants of this policy. State law may also require you to give applicants a written policy statement that's separate from the application. When applicants are told up front about drug testing, it's harder for them to later claim that they expected more privacy on drug testing results.

Once an applicant becomes an employee, drug testing gets stickier. Testing is usually permitted when employees have been in an accident or you've seen them bring illegal drugs to work. Your legal right to test at random and without prior notice is unclear—and questionable.

In any drug testing, treat all employees consistently, being careful not to single out any one group. And consult with competent drug testing experts to assure that your test procedures are as accurate as possible.

For help in developing a drug policy, contact The National Institute on Drug Abuse, 5600 Fishers Lane, Rockville, MD 20857; (301) 443-6245.

STATE DRUG AND ALCOHOL TESTING LAWS

The following is a summary of state laws that affect employers in the private sector.

Alabama	To qualify for a reduction in workers' compensation rates, you must require testing of all new hires and may perform tests on some applicants. You may test if there is a reasonable suspicion of illegal drug or alcohol use, may use regularly scheduled and random tests and must test if the employee is involved in an injury-causing accident at the workplace. You must have an employee assistance program or provide a resource file on employee assistance programs. Ala. Code §§25-5-330-340
Alaska	No statute
Arizona	No statute
Arkansas	No statute
California	If you employ 25 or more people, you must reasonably accommodate any employee who enters an alcohol or drug rehabilitation program, unless the employee's current alcohol or drug use makes him or her unable to perform work duties or do a job safely. You're excused if this accommodation would impose an undue hardship on you. You must take reasonable efforts to safeguard the privacy of an employee who's enrolled in a treatment program. Cal. Lab. Code §§1025 and 1026
Colorado	No statute
Connecticut	You may require a drug or alcohol test when there's a reasonable suspicion that an employee is under the influence and job performance is or could be impaired. You may test randomly when authorized by federal law, the employee works in a dangerous or safety-sensitive occupation, or the test is part of a voluntary employee assistance program. Job applicants may be required to submit to test. Conn. Gen. Stat. §31-51t through 51aa
Delaware	No statute
District of Columbia	No statute
Florida	You may test for drugs and alcohol upon reasonable suspicion that an employee is under the influence, as a pre-employment screening, during routine fitness-for-duty examinations and as a follow-up to participation in a drug treatment program. Fla. Stat. Ann. §440.101
	Employees who voluntarily seek treatment for substance abuse can't be fired, disciplined, or discriminated against, unless they've tested positive or have been in treatment in the past. Fla. Stat. Ann. §440.102
Georgia	The state may not enter into any contract with a private contractor unless the contractor certifies that its workplace or site is drug-free.

	You must post your policy and report any employee convictions for illegal drug use to the state agency with which you've contracted. The statute doesn't establish drug testing by the you. Ga. Code Ann. §50-24-1
Hawaii	You may test employees or job applicants for substance abuse as long as the following conditions are met: you pay all costs; the test is performed by a licensed laboratory; the individuals tested are given a list of the substances they are being tested for and a disclosure form for the medicines and legal drugs they are taking; and the results are kept confidential. Haw. Rev. Stat. §329B-1 and following
Idaho	No statute
Illinois	No statute
Indiana	You may implement reasonable policies, including drug testing, designed to insure that an employee is no longer using illegal drugs. Ind. Code §22-9-5-6
Iowa	You can't request random drug testing of employees or require employees or job applicants to submit to a drug test as a condition of employment, pre-employment, promotion or change in employment status, except as part of a pre-employment or regularly scheduled physical examination under certain restrictions. You may require a specific employee to submit to a drug test if there is a reasonable suspicion that the employee's faculties are impaired on the job, or if the employee is in a position where such impairment presents a danger to the safety of others or if the impairment is a violation of one of your known rules. Iowa Code §730.5
Kansas	No statute
Kentucky	No statute
Louisiana	You may require all job applicants and employees to submit to drug testing as long as certain procedural guidelines are followed and the specimens are collected with due regard for the individual's privacy. La. Rev. Stat. Ann. §49:1001
Maine	You may require an employee to submit to a drug test when there is probable cause to believe the employee is impaired. Random testing is permitted when substance abuse might endanger co-workers or the public or when it is permitted by a union contract. Job applicants may be tested only if offered employment or placed on an eligibility roster. Me. Rev. Stat. Ann. tit. 26 §§681-690
Maryland	You may require testing of employees, contractors or other people for job-related reasons for alcohol or drug abuse as long as certain procedural guidelines are followed. Md. Code Ann. Health Law §17-214.1
Massachusetts	No statute
Michigan	No statute
Minnesota	You may require employees to submit to drug or alcohol testing if there is a written and posted testing policy and the test is performed by an independent licensed laboratory. Random tests may be given

only to employees in "safety-sensitive" positions. Job applicants may be tested if they've been offered the job. Specific individuals may be tested when there is a reasonable suspicion that the employee is under the influence of drugs or alcohol, has violated rule against use, possession or distribution of drugs or alcohol on the job, has caused an injury or accident at work. Minn. Stat. Ann. §§181.950 to 181.957

You may refuse to hire, or may discipline or discharge an employee who refuses or fails to comply with the conditions established by a chemical dependency treatment or aftercare program. Minn. Stat. Ann. §181.938(3)(4)

Mississippi	You may require employees to submit to drug or alcohol testing if the policy is posted and certain prescribed procedures are followed. Testing is authorized when there is a reasonable suspicion that an employee is abusing drugs or alcohol. Random testing is also authorized. You may also test as part of routine fitness-for-duty examinations or as part of follow-up to a rehabilitation program. Job applicants may be tested if they're warned when they apply for the job. Miss. Code Ann. §71-7 and following
Missouri	No statute
Montana	No person may be required to submit to a blood or urine test unless the job involves hazardous work or security, public safety, or fiduciary responsibilities. Mont. Code Ann. §39-2-304
Nebraska	If you employ more than six employees , you may require employees to submit to drug or alcohol testing if certain screening procedures are met. Refusal to undergo a test can be grounds for discipline or discharge. Neb. Rev. Stat. §48-1901
Nevada	No statute
New Hampshire	No statute
New Jersey	No statute
New Mexico	No statute
New York	No statute
North Carolina	You may test applicants and employees for the presence of controlled substances as long as they follow specified procedures, including the preservation of the test sample so that the applicant or employee may perform his or her own test. N.C. Gen. Stat. §§95-230 to 235
North Dakota	No statute
Ohio	No statute
Oklahoma	You may test applicants and employees as long as you adhere to statutory procedures and issue a written workplace policy. An applicant may be tested as long as all applicants are tested; an employee may be tested if you have a reasonable suspicion that the employee has violated the written policy. Random testing is allowed for certain employees only, including those whose jobs directly affect the safety of others. Standards for Workplace Drug and Alcohol Testing Act, Okla. Stat. Ann. tit. 40 §§551-565

Oregon	You may not require any employee or job applicant to submit to any breathalyzer alcohol test unless there is a reasonable suspicion that the employee is under the influence of alcohol. Or. Rev. Stat. §659.227
	Employees may be required to be tested for drugs if the laboratory utilized is licensed by the state and certain procedural safeguards are employed. Or. Rev. Stat. §438.435
Pennsylvania	No statute
Rhode Island	You may require employees to submit to drug or alcohol testing when there is reason to believe that the use of controlled substances is impairing the employee's ability to do the job, the test sample is provided in private, the testing is part of a rehabilitation program, positive results are confirmed by the most accurate method available, the employee is given reasonable notice that the test will be given and the employee is given a chance to explain the results. R.I. Gen. Laws §28-6.5-1
South Carolina	No statute
South Dakota	No statute
Tennessee	No statute
Texas	No statute
Utah	If you test for drugs, you must have a written policy regarding the methods used, and management must submit to regular testing as well as employees. A positive test result may be used as grounds for suspension, discipline or discharge. Employees who test positive are not to be considered "handicapped" within the state's anti-discrimination law. Utah Code Ann. §§34-38-1 to 15
Vermont	You may require employees to be tested for drugs or alcohol if there is a probable cause to believe the employee is using or is under the influence on the job, the employer provides a rehabilitation program and the employee who tests positive is given a chance to participate in the rehabilitation program rather than being fired. Employees who have already been through rehabilitation and who again test positive may be fired. Job applicants may be tested when they have been offered the job conditioned upon passing the test, if they are given advance notice of the test and the test is given as part of a comprehensive physical examination. Applicants and employees must be given the opportunity to re-test a sample that has tested positive. Vt. Stat. Ann. tit. 21 §511
Virginia	No statute
Washington	No statute
West Virginia	No statute
Wisconsin	No statute
Wyoming	No statute

Adapted from *Your Rights in the Workplace*, by Barbara Kate Repa (Nolo Press).

PROTECTION FOR RECOVERING ADDICTS

After you've made a conditional offer of employment and as part of a pre-employment medical screening, you may discover that the applicant had a drug problem in the past. The Americans With Disabilities Act (ADA) prohibits you from discriminating against people because of past drug problems. This includes people who no longer use drugs illegally and are receiving treatment for drug addiction or who have been rehabilitated successfully.

To make sure that drug use isn't recurring, however, you may request evidence that a person is taking part in a drug rehab program. You may also ask for the results of a drug test.

You can refuse to hire someone with a history of alcoholism or illegal drug use if you can show that the person poses a direct threat to health or safety. You must show that there's a high probability that the person will return to the illegal drug use or alcohol abuse, and a high probability of substantial harm to the person or others—harm that you can't reduce or eliminate through a reasonable accommodation. Unfortunately, the EEOC offers no guidance on the type of evidence that would suffice to show the high probability of a problem arising.

G. Investigations

Since some people give false or incomplete information in their job applications, it's a good idea to do some investigating to verify their application information. You might find out, for example, that an applicant doesn't have the work experience or occupational license that he or she claimed to have in a job application—or that the applicant didn't really leave the last job voluntarily. What's more, you might learn that the applicant has a history of violent behavior or even a criminal record that would disqualify him or her from a job that may put members of the public or other employees at risk.

Your need to investigate a job applicant is legitimate, but if left unbridled, can conflict with the job applicant's legal right to privacy. The best way to reduce the risk of an invasion of privacy claim is to inform the applicant in the job application that you will be requesting information from former employers, schools, credit reporting sources and law enforcement agencies.

Ask the applicant to sign a consent form as part of the application process. This can either be a part of the application form itself or a separate document. The advantage of having the applicant sign a separate document is that you can easily photocopy it and send it to the people from whom you're seeking information. (See Section D2 for sample language.)

1. Former Employers

Some job applicants exaggerate or even lie about their qualifications and experience. So be sure to contact as many former employers as possible to try to get the inside story.

Former employers are often reluctant to say anything negative for fear that if they speak frankly, they may be hit by a lawsuit for defamation. They're hesitant to do anything more than to verify that the former employee did in fact work there and to give the dates of employment. The fact that some former employers may be more restrictive than they need to be makes it hard to get an accurate picture of an applicant's job history. As mentioned, it may be helpful to send the former employer a copy of the applicant's signed consent to a full disclosure of employment information. (See Chapter 10, Section K for suggestions on giving evaluations for former employees when you're the one being asked for information.)

In speaking with former employers, learn to read between the lines. If a former employer is neutral, offers only faint praise or overpraises a person for one aspect of a job only—"great with numbers" or "invariably on time"—there's a good chance some negative information is hiding in the wings. Ask former employers: "Would you hire back this person if you could?" The response may be telling. To help put the applicant in perspective, you might ask: "What are this person's greatest strengths—and greatest weaknesses?" Since no one is perfect, this may lead to a candid evaluation of the applicant.

If a reference isn't glowing and doesn't take in all aspects of the job, check several other references—and perhaps call back the applicant for a more directed interview.

For more details, see *Reference Checking Handbook,* published by the Society for Human Resource Management. Call (612) 885-5588 for price and ordering information.

Reference Checks May Become More Informative

Responding to the problem of unhelpful reference checks, states are starting to pass laws that allow employers to speak more frankly about their former employees. Under a Kansas law, for example, an employer is presumed to be acting in good faith when answering reference checks. To collect damages in Kansas, a person must show by "clear and convincing evidence" that the former employer acted in bad faith in providing job-related information.

Find out if your state has a similar law. If so, don't assume that the former employers you call for reference checks know about it. Telling them about the protection they have under your state's law may allow you to get a fuller picture of a prospective employee.

2. School Transcripts

On-the-job experience generally is much more relevant to employment than an applicant's educational credentials. Still, you may have good reasons for requiring a high school diploma or college degree for some jobs. If so, you may want to see proof that the applicant really received the diploma or degree or took the courses claimed in the job application.

If you wish to see these records, ask the applicant to sign a written release acknowledging your right to obtain them. Most schools won't turn over the records without such a release—and many won't deliver them to anyone except the former student. This can, of course, complicate your verification, since it creates the possibility of forgery or tampering.

3. Credit History

Credit information usually isn't relevant to employment, but it does come into play when you hire someone who will handle money. Someone with large debts may be especially tempted to skim money from your business. And an applicant who can't keep his or her personal finances in order is probably not a good choice for a job requiring management of your company's finances.

In most other situations, however, a credit check is an unnecessary intrusion into an applicant's private life. What's more, unless you have a good reason for doing a credit check for a particular job, you may run afoul of anti-discrimination laws. According to the EEOC, requiring an applicant to have good credit may subtly discriminate against some minority groups. State laws, too, may limit your use of credit information in deciding whether to hire someone.

Assuming that you have a good business reason to order a credit report on a job applicant, it's courteous to get the applicant's consent first. Some states, in fact, require such consent. A local credit reporting bureau should be able to tell you whether consent is required in your state. However, it's a good idea to verify the law by checking your state statutes; look under credit reports in the index. (For more on doing legal research, see Chapter 13, Section D.)

The federal Fair Credit Reporting Act requires you to let an applicant know if he or she has been denied employment because of something in a credit report. The applicant can then follow up with the credit reporting agency to make sure its information is complete, accurate and current. If you don't make this disclosure, an applicant can sue you for damages, plus court costs and attorneys' fees.

In a concise publication called *Credit Reports: What Employers Should Know About Using Them,* the Federal Trade Commission offers examples to illustrate situations where you must give notice to job applicants. To order the publication, call the FTC's Office of Consumer/Business Education at (202) 326-3650.

For a free copy of *Fair Credit Reporting* which explains the Act more fully, write to the Federal Trade Commission, Public Reference, Washington, DC 20580.

4. Criminal History

Asking an applicant about his or her arrest record or making a hiring decision based on that record can be a subtle form of discrimination that violates state and federal anti-discrimination laws. Many people are arrested and the charges are later dropped or found to be without merit. Asking about arrests can be particularly harmful to black applicants because blacks are arrested disproportionately to their population size. Very rarely is there a legitimate business reason to reject an applicant simply because of an arrest record.

Convictions are another matter. While it can be unlawful discrimination to automatically exclude every applicant who's ever had a conviction, anti-discrimination laws generally do allow you to inquire about an applicant's conviction record and to reject an applicant because of a conviction record that's job-related. If you're hiring a delivery truck driver, for example, it wouldn't violate the anti-discrimination laws to reject an applicant based on a conviction for drunk driving.

State laws may specifically prohibit you from asking about arrest records—and may go even further in restricting your inquiries into an applicants' criminal history. (See the chart below.) In many states, for example, you can't ask an applicant about juvenile records. In some states, you can't ask about convictions for minor offenses or misdemeanors that go back more than five years if the applicant has had a clean slate since that time.

Expunging the Past

Many states have laws that allow individuals to expunge, or seal, their criminal records. When a record is expunged, it is usually not available to anyone other than criminal justice agencies and the courts. If a criminal record has been expunged, a prospective employee is generally allowed to deny that he or she has had one when you ask about it. But states have varying policies on this. Check the following chart for specifics.

STATE LAWS ON EMPLOYEE ARREST & CONVICTION RECORDS

The following is a summary of state laws that affect employers in the private sector.

Alabama	No statute
Alaska	No statute
Arizona	No statute
Arkansas	No statute

California	You may not ask prospective employees to disclose information regarding an arrest or detention which did not result in conviction. You also may not ask about a referral to a diversion program. You may not seek or utilize as a condition of employment any such information, but may inquire as to an arrest for which a current or prospective employee is out on bail or his or her recognizance. Employees and applicants for positions at health facilities and for jobs involving access to drugs and medications may be asked questions regarding certain arrests. Cal. Lab. Code §432.7
	You may not inquire as to marijuana convictions that pre-date January 1, 1976. Cal Labor Code §432.8
Colorado	You may not require that sealed arrest or conviction records be disclosed. Statute does not apply to pleas, convictions or deferred prosecutions for sexual assault offenses. Colo. Rev. Stat. §24-72-308
Connecticut	Information about the arrest record of an applicant may not be available to anyone other than your personnel department or the person in charge of employment. Conn. Gen. Stat. Ann. § 31 - 51i
Delaware	Records of an arrest that resulted in a dismissal or an acquittal, which have been ordered expunged by a court, do not have to be disclosed as an arrest for any reason. Del. Code Ann. tit. 11 §§4371 to 4374
District of Columbia	No statute
Florida	If a background screening or security check is required by law—for childcare, home healthcare and nursing home assistants—applicants and employees must undergo statewide and local criminal records checks, and for persons in positions of trust, checks of juvenile and federal records as well. Fla. Stat. §435.01 and following
Georgia	No statute
Hawaii	No statute
Idaho	No statute
Illinois	You may not inquire about or use arrest information or criminal history record that has been ordered sealed or expunged as a basis to refuse to hire or take any adverse employment action against a current or prospective employee. 775 Ill. Rev. Stat. 5/2-103
	However, certain private organizations can use information from the Department of State Police in evaluating qualifications of applicants or prospective employees. 20 Ill. Comp. Stat. 2630/3
Indiana	No statute
Iowa	No statute
Kansas	No statute
Kentucky	No statute

Louisiana	If you employ a non-licensed person to perform nursing care or health-related services, you must ask the state police to do a criminal record check. The applicant must be told about the check before he or she is offered the job. The statute includes a list of prior offenses which render the applicant ineligible for employment. All information received must be kept confidential and destroyed one year after employment ceases. La. Rev. Stat. Ann. §40:1300.51
Maine	No statute
Maryland	You can't require a job applicant to disclose information regarding criminal charges that have been expunged. Md. Code Ann. art. 27 §740
Massachusetts	If you ask about criminal history, you must include, on the application, advice that an applicant with a sealed record is entitled to answer "no record" regarding prior convictions, court appearances or arrests. Mass. Gen. Laws. Ann. ch. 276, §100A
Michigan	You can't request, make or maintain information regarding arrest or detention that didn't result in conviction. This doesn't apply to felony charges prior to conviction or dismissal. Mich. Stat. Ann. §3.548(205a)
Minnesota	No statute
Mississippi	If you hire employees or volunteers for childcare, treatment, counseling, custody, instruction and entertainment positions, you must obtain sex offense criminal history information from the state. You may not hire people with enumerated prior sex offenses. Miss. Code Ann. §45-31-1 and following
Missouri	No statute
Montana	No statute
Nebraska	No statute
Nevada	No statute
New Hampshire	No statute
New Jersey	You may request criminal conviction and arrest information from the state Bureau of Identification to determine a person's qualifications for work. Requests must be accompanied by a set of fingerprints or the person's Social Security number and date of birth. You must keep the information confidential. New Jersey Administrative Code §§ 13:59 to 13:59-1.6
	If you operate a school, daycare facility or youth center, you must perform criminal history record checks on the federal and state level for all applicants (excluding volunteers) who will regularly come into contact with students under 18 years old. You may not hire applicants with specified convictions unless they can present proof of rehabilitation. N.J. Stat. Ann. §18A:6-7.1

New Mexico	You must conduct a nationwide criminal records check of all employees of childcare and detention facilities. N.M. Stat. Ann. §§32-A-15-1 to 4
New York	If you employ more than ten employees, you can't deny employment to an applicant who has one or more past criminal convictions unless there is a direct relationship between the past offense and the employment sought. You can deny employment if, in light of the applicant's record, the job would involve an unreasonable risk to property or the safety and welfare of individuals or to the general public. N.Y. Correction Law §755
North Carolina	No statute
North Dakota	No statute
Ohio	You may question applicants regarding only those convictions that haven't been sealed by court order, unless the question bears a direct and substantial relationship to the position sought. Ohio Rev. Code §2953.33
Oklahoma	You can't question a prospective employee in any application for employment regarding a criminal record that's been expunged. Okla. Stat. Ann. tit. 22 §19
	Every owner or administrator of a childcare facility or home must arrange for a criminal history investigation conducted by the Oklahoma State Bureau of Investigation for every applicant or, if the applicant has lived in the state less than one year, by the appropriate agency in the previous state of residence. Enumerated crimes bar employment. Okla. Stat. Ann. tit. 10 §404.1
Oregon	Before seeking criminal offender information, you must advise the applicant or employee that such information is being sought. Or. Rev. Stat. §181.555
	You can't discriminate against an applicant because of a juvenile record that has been expunged by law. Or. Rev. Stat. §659.030
Pennsylvania	You may consider felony and misdemeanor convictions only to the extent that they relate to an employee's suitability for a job for which he or she has applied. 18 Pa. Stat. Ann. §9125(b)
Rhode Island	You can't ask prospective employees whether they've ever been arrested or charged with a crime. You may, however, ask whether they have ever been convicted. R.I. Gen. Laws §28-5-7(7)
	Prospective employees who've had a conviction of a crime expunged from their records may state that they've never been convicted of a crime. Employees of early childhood educational facilities are excepted. R.I. Gen. Laws §12-1.3-4
South Carolina	No statute
South Dakota	No statute
Tennessee	No statute

Texas	State-maintained criminal record history information is available to numerous specified employers, including childcare and treatment facilities. Vernon's Texas Code Ann. Government §§411.081 to .128 and Human Resources §135.001 and following
Utah	No statute
Vermont	No statute
Virginia	You can't require an applicant to disclose expunged arrests or charges or to answer questions relating to them. Va. Code Ann. §19.2-392.4
Washington	You may request conviction records from the state of current or prospective employees for these specified purposes only: employee bonding; pre-employment and post-employment evaluation of employees with access to money or items of value; or investigation of employee misconduct which may constitute a penal offense.
	You must notify the employee or prospective employee of the inquiry and make the record available. If you provide services to children or vulnerable adults, you may obtain from the state police the conviction records for employees, applicants and volunteers. The information disclosed is limited to convictions for crimes against children or other people, and does not include expunged records. Wa. Rev. Code §§43.43.815 and .830 to .839
West Virginia	If an employee's or applicant's juvenile records have been expunged—at age 19 or when jurisdiction of the court over the individual has ceased, whichever is later—you can't discriminate against that individual with respect to employment or its terms or conditions. W. Va. Code §49-5-17
Wisconsin	You can't discriminate on the basis of an arrest or conviction record. Wis.. Stat. Ann. §111.321
	However, you may ask about pending charges. You can ask about past arrests or convictions if the position requires bonding. You can deny employment based on pending charges or past record if the applicant is not bondable or if the circumstances substantially relate to the job or activity being offered. Wis.. Stat. Ann. §111.335
Wyoming	No statute

Adapted from *Your Rights in the Workplace,* by Barbara Kate Repa (Nolo Press).

5. Driving Records

When a job requires the employee to drive, it's wise to check on an applicant's driving record. You usually can obtain driving records for a modest cost from the state authority that issues drivers' licenses.

GETTING HELP FROM EXPERTS

Consider entrusting background checks to experts. There are companies that are skilled at obtaining criminal histories and driving records, contacting former employers and rounding up school transcripts. In a sensitive investigation where you want to be as thorough as possible, it's often worthwhile to hire one of these background-checking services.

Of course, be sure to do a reference check on the agency. Get the names of other businesses it has worked for and call to find out if the other businesses felt satisfied with the work done.

H. Making a Job Offer

Be careful what you say orally and in writing when you make a job offer to any applicant. The positive statements you make to an applicant about long-term opportunities can come back to haunt you if you later fire the person. (See Section A3.) A judge or jury reviewing the firing may conclude that your glowing statements were actually a promise—a promise, perhaps, that the applicant's job would be secure for years or that he or she wouldn't be fired without good cause.

You can protect yourself from such misunderstandings by using an employment letter such as the following one.

SAMPLE EMPLOYMENT LETTER

Date _____

Dear _____ :

I am pleased to offer you a fulltime position with our company as__(INSERT JOB TITLE)__
beginning ___(INSERT DATE)___ . Your starting salary will be $_____ per week.

When you applied, I gave you a written list of your job duties which are as follows:
                              (INSERT LIST OF JOB DUTIES)

Also, when you applied, I gave you a copy of our employee handbook. The handbook
sets out our current employment policies and describes your job benefits including
medical coverage, paid vacation and sick leave. It also describes your responsibilities to
the company. Each time the handbook is updated, you'll receive a revised copy.

The company's commitments to you and its other employees are stated in the handbook. The company has made no oral commitments to you. No one at the company is
authorized to make oral commitments regarding employment—either now or in the
future.

While I hope that everything works out here, this is an at will employment. You have
the right to terminate the employment at any time and so does the company.

If this offer of employment is acceptable to you, please sign a copy of this letter and
return it to me within 10 days. I look forward to having you join our staff.

Sincerely,

_____

(Your Name and Signature)

I accept your offer of employment and acknowledge receiving a copy of your current
employee handbook. No oral commitments have been made concerning my employment.

Signature _____

Date _____

Source: The Legal Guide for Starting and Running a Small Business, *by Fred S. Steingold (Nolo Press).*

I. Rejecting Applicants

It's courteous to let unsuccessful applicants know that you've hired someone else for the job. You don't, however, owe them an explanation about why they weren't hired. If pressed, simply tell them that the person you hired is, in your judgment, more appropriate for the job.

There's no ideal way to give someone the news that he or she didn't get the job. The least painful way—which also presents the fewest legal difficulties—is to send a short letter informing the rejected applicant of your decision. Send the letter as soon as you've decided who you're going to hire or when you've narrowed the field down to a few candidates. There's no need to let applicants twist in the wind. Quickly sending your rejection letter will cut down on the number of post-interview calls you get from unsuccessful applicants—calls that are uncomfortable for everyone.

Keep the letter simple and upbeat. And keep a copy in your files, along with the employment application and any information you gathered during the screening process. Lawsuits by rejected applicants are rare, but you can't predict in advance which ones might take that step.

SAMPLE REJECTION LETTER

Date _____

Dear _____ :

Thank you for taking the time to meet with me last Thursday to discuss the _____ position with our company. You were among many fine people who applied. I wanted to let you know that we selected another applicant for the position.

It was a pleasure meeting you and I wish you well in your job search.

Sincerely,

_____

Your Name and Signature

J. Tax Compliance

Your tax obligations as an employer are treated in depth in Chapter 5. Before you hire employees, you must get an Employer Identification Number (EIN) from the IRS—although if you're a sole proprietor, you have the option of using your Social Security Number. To obtain an EIN, file Form SS-4, Application for Employer Identification Number. Some states have similar requirements. (See Chapter 5, Section A, for further information.)

When you hire an employee, have him or her complete Form W-4, the Employer's Withholding Allowance Certificate. This provides you with the number of dependents or withholding allowances the employee is claiming and the employee's filing status—single, married or married but withholding at the higher single rate. Keep a signed Form W-4 on file for each employee. If an employee doesn't complete a Form W-4, you won't know how much income tax to withhold. In that case, you must withhold tax as if the employee were a single person claiming no withholding allowances.

You needn't send the signed Form W-4 to the IRS unless:

• an employee claims more than 10 allowances, or
• the employee earns more than $200 per week and claims exemption from withholding.

The IRS has two free publications that may be useful in helping establish tax procedures for your business. *Circular E, Employers Tax Guide,* containing withholding tables, is updated periodically and mailed automatically to every business that has an Employer Identification Number.

IRS Publication 334, *Tax Guide for Small Business,* covers a wide range of tax issues and is available at your local IRS office or by calling 800/829-3676.

K. Immigration Law Requirements

Immigration laws, enforced by the Immigration and Naturalization Service (INS), prohibit hiring aliens who don't have government authorization to work in the United States. There are specific procedures you must follow when hiring employees—even those who were born and raised in the town where your business is located.

You and the new employee must complete INS Form I-9, Employment Eligibility Verification. This one-page form is intended to ensure that the employee can legally work in the United States and has proof of his or her identity.

For full details, see the free publication, *Handbook for Employers: Instructions for Completing Form I-9,* available from the INS. Call the nearest regional office of the INS to obtain a copy.

The employee completes Section 1 of the form, attesting that he or she is a citizen or national of the United States, a lawful permanent resident alien or an alien with work authorization. Only people in these three categories can lawfully work in the United States.

Section 2 of the form requires you to review documents such as a passport or naturalization certificate presented by the employee as proof of the employee's identity and employment eligibility.

You make a record on Form I-9 of the documents you've examined. It's your responsibility to see if the employee's documents appear valid. The INS advises that you must accept documents that reasonably appear to be genuine and to relate to the person presenting them. To do otherwise could be an unfair immigration-related employment practice and therefore illegal.

It's a good idea to keep photocopies of the employee's documents to prove that you reviewed these papers in case the INS questions your hiring practices in the future. Also, hang on to all Form I-9s for at least three years. If the employee stays with your company longer than that, keep the form for at least one year after he or she leaves. The INS has the right to see your I-9s. You can be fined up to $1,000 per employee if you can't produce them.

PAPERWORK CHECKLIST

Here's a list of documents and forms that you should consider each time you hire someone:

☐ *Employment Letter.* A sample letter is offered above. Modify it to meet your own situation.

☐ *Employee Handbook.* If you have such a handbook and didn't give it to the employee during the application and interview stages, now is the time to do so. Get a written receipt and keep it in the employee's file. (For more on employee handbooks, see Chapter 2, Section B.)

☐ *Covenant Not to Compete.* This is useful if you have employees who could harm your business if they left to work for a competitor or started a business of their own in competition with yours. (For more information and sample language, see Section A5 of this chapter.)

☐ *Confidentiality Agreement.* Use such an agreement if you'll be disclosing trade secrets and other proprietary information to an employee. (The second paragraph of the covenant not to compete in Section A5 of this chapter can be used separately for this purpose.)

☐ *INS Form I-9.* This form, required by the U.S. Immigration and Naturalization Service, is intended to help exclude undocumented aliens from the workforce. (See Section K of this chapter.)

☐ *IRS Form W-4.* Each employee must complete this form so you can properly determine the level of tax to withhold from every paycheck. (See Section J and Chapter 5, Sections B, C and D for details.)

☐ *Employee Benefit Sign-up.* If your business offers employee benefit programs such as health insurance or a 401(k) plan, you may have a sign-up procedure so employees can name their dependents and select options.

☐ IRS Form SS-4: NEW EMPLOYERS ONLY. The IRS requires an Employer Identification Number for all employers except sole proprietorships. (See Chapter 5, Section A.) ■

You can avoid most legal problems in the workplace if you respect employees and treat them well. But no matter how caring you are, there will still be misunderstandings you'll be called upon to handle. Fortunately, the vast majority of job disputes can be resolved within the workplace if you listen patiently to what employees have to say and are prepared to make adjustments when legitimate complaints surface.

However, even though you treat workers fairly, there's always a chance a dispute will get out of hand and that an employee will sue your business for some perceived abuse of his or her rights. Or an unhappy employee may file a complaint with a government agency alleging that you violated a statute or an administrative regulation. If that happens, you'll have to prove to a judge, jury, arbitrator or investigator that you met your legal obligations to the employee. That can be harder than you think. Key paperwork may have been lost—or never prepared in the first place. And witnesses may have forgotten what happened or have moved on and not be locatable.

To maintain a solid legal footing, establish good written policies and then maintain a paper trail indicating how they are implemented. Written policies will help you if you have to defend yourself in a legal proceeding—and, equally important, can nip misunderstandings in the bud before they turn into pitched legal battles. They provide a cogent point of reference when you discuss problems with an employee, increasing the likelihood of reaching an amicable resolution.

The first step for most workplaces is to create an employee handbook that clearly explains company policies and employee rights and benefits. Follow up by keeping records of key employee contacts, including periodic evaluations of how employees are performing their jobs.

Actions Speak Loudly, Too

You must start with sensible and fair policies and apply them with an even hand to all employees. A carefully developed paper trail is important, but if you've violated an employee's rights, the mere fact that you've created good paperwork won't normally shield you from the legal consequences.

A. Employee Files

Create a file for each employee in which you keep all job-related information, including:

- Job description (see Chapter 1, Section B)
- Job application (see Chapter 1, Section D)
- Offer of employment (see Chapter 1, Section H)
- INS Form I-9 and supporting documents (see Chapter 1, Section J)
- IRS Form W-4 (see Chapter 1, Section I)
- Receipt for employee handbook (see Section B)
- Periodic performance evaluations (see Section C)
- Sign-up forms for employee benefits (See Chapter 4)
- Complaints from customers and co-workers
- Awards or citations for excellent performance
- Warnings and disciplinary actions, and
- Notes on an employee's attendance or tardiness.

Employee files can be a two-edged sword. They can provide valuable documentation to support a firing, demotion or other action that's adverse to the employee—but the employee, in turn, can point to indiscreet entries and use them against you. It would be a mistake, for example, to include unsubstantiated criticism of an employee in the file or comments about the employee that are unrelated to job performance and qualifications.

1. Correcting Mistakes

To err is human. To leave an error uncorrected is dumb. It can lead people to conclude that you're callous or unfair or both—not a good impression to leave on those empowered to levy a damage award or penalties against you. And to knowingly keep false information on hand increases the risk of a libel case being brought against you.

> *Example: Joe doesn't show up for work a week after his paid vacation has ended. You put a note in his file documenting this fact. Then you learn that on the last day of his vacation he was in a serious car accident and wound up in intensive care. Put these additional facts in Joe's file. If you don't, Joe will have good reason to be angry with you, and other people who later look at the file won't put much stock in anything else they find there.*

2. Confidentiality

Keep employee files locked up. Make them available only to people in your company who have a legitimate business need to have access to the files—managers, for example, who must make decisions about promotions and discipline. Inform company personnel that the information in the files must remain confidential. While an employee or former employee may have a legal right to see his or her file (see Section 4), no one else does unless they have a subpoena.

3. Medical Information

Special guidelines apply to medical information gathered in the workplace. The Americans With Disabilities Act (ADA) imposes very strict limitations on how you must handle information obtained from post-offer medical examinations and inquiries. You must keep the information in medical files separate from non-medical records, and you must store the medical files in a separate locked cabinet. To further guarantee the confidentiality of medical files, designate a specific person to have access to those files.

The ADA allows very limited disclosure of medical information. Under the ADA, you may:

- inform supervisors about necessary restrictions on an employee's duties and about necessary accommodations
- inform first aid and safety workers about a disability that may require emergency treatment and about specific procedures that are needed if the workplace must be evacuated, and
- provide medical information required by government officials and by insurance companies that require a medical exam for health or life insurance.

Otherwise, don't disclose medical information about employees. Although the confidentiality provisions of the ADA protect only some disabled workers, the best policy to treat all medical information about all employees as confidential. (For more on the ADA, see Chapter 9.)

4. Access by Employees

Many states have laws giving employees—and former employees—access to their own personnel files. How much access varies from state to state. Typically, if your state allows employees to see their files, you can insist that you or another supervisor be present to make sure nothing is taken, added or changed. Some state laws allow employees to obtain copies of items in their files, but not necessarily all items. A state law, for example, may limit the employee to copies of documents that he or she has signed, such as a job application. If an employee is entitled to a copy of an item in the file or if you're inclined to let the employee have a copy of any document in the file, you—rather than the employee—should make the copy.

Usually, you won't have to let the employee see sensitive items such as information assembled for a criminal investigation, reference letters and information that might violate the privacy of other people. In a few states, employees may insert rebuttals of information in their personnel files with which they disagree.

STATE LAWS ON EMPLOYEE ACCESS TO PERSONNEL RECORDS

This is a synopsis of state laws that require private employers to show an employee or former employee his or her employment file.

Alaska	Employees have the right to see their personnel files and make a copy of them. Alaska Stat. §23.10.430
Arizona	No statute
Arkansas	No statute
California	Employees have the right to receive a copy of any employment-related document they've signed. Cal. Lab. Code §432
	You must maintain a copy of the employee's personnel file where the employee reports to work, or must make the file available at that location within a reasonable time after the employee asks to see it. Statute does not apply to letters of reference or records relating to the investigation of a possible offense. Cal. Labor Code §1198.5
Colorado	No statute
Connecticut	Employees have the right to see their personnel files and to insert rebuttals of information with which they disagree. Conn. Gen. Stat. Ann. §31-128b
Delaware	Employees have the right to see their personnel files and to insert rebuttals of information with which they disagree. Del. Code Ann. tit. 19, §§730 through 735
District of Columbia	No statute
Florida	No statute
Georgia	No statute
Hawaii	No statute
Idaho	No statute
Illinois	If you employ five or more people, you must allow them to see their personnel files and to insert rebuttals of any information with which they disagree. Personnel Record Review Act, 820 Ill. Rev. Stat. 40/0.D1
Indiana	No statute
Iowa	Employees have the right to see and copy personnel files, including performance evaluations and disciplinary records, but not references. Iowa Code §91B.1
Kansas	No statute
Kentucky	No statute
Louisiana	Current or former employees, or their designated representatives, have a right of access to your records of employee exposure, medical records and analyses using employee records. La. Rev. Stat. Ann. §23.1016

Maine	Employees have the right to see and make copies of their personnel files, including workplace evaluations. Me. Rev. Stat. Ann. title 26, §631
Maryland	No statute
Massachusetts	Employees have the right to see their personnel files and to insert rebuttals of any information with which they disagree. Employees may take court action to expunge from personnel records any information that the employer knows, or should have known, was incorrect. Statute does not apply to employees of private institutions of higher learning who are tenured, on tenure track or have similar positions or responsibilities. Mass. Gen. Laws Ann. ch. 149, §52C
Michigan	Employees have the right to see and make a copy of their personnel files and to insert rebuttals of any information with which they disagree. Access isn't available to employees whom you're investigating for criminal activity that may cause loss to your business. Upon completion of the investigation or after two years, whichever comes first, you must tell the employee of the outcome and, if no disciplinary action is taken, you must destroy the investigation file. Mich. Comp. Laws §§17(62) and following
Minnesota	If you employ 20 or more people, they have the right to see their personnel files and to insert rebuttals of any information with which they disagree. A former employee may inspect once within the year following termination. You may not use in any retaliatory way any information intentionally left out of the personnel record. Minn. Stat. Ann. §§181.960 to 965
Mississippi	No statute
Missouri	No statute
Montana	No statute
Nebraska	No statute
Nevada	Employees who've been employed at least 60 days have the right to see and copy any records that you used to confirm the employee's qualifications, or as the basis for any disciplinary action. If those records contain incorrect information, the employee may notify you of the errors in writing. You're required to correct the challenged information if you decide it's false. The employee can't inspect confidential reports from past employers or reports from an investigative agency regarding the employee's violation of any law. Nev. Rev. Stat. §613.075
New Hampshire	Employees have the right to see and copy their personnel files and to insert rebuttals of any information with which they disagree. You can't disclose information that relates to a government security investigation or information regarding an investigation of the employee if that disclosure would prejudice law enforcement. N.H. Rev. Stat. §275:56

New Jersey	No statute
New Mexico	No statute
New York	No statute
North Carolina	No statute
North Dakota	No statute
Ohio	No statute
Oklahoma	No statute
Oregon	Employees have the right to see and copy any documents you used in making work-related decisions, such as promotions, wage increases, or termination. Or. Rev. Stat. §652.750
Pennsylvania	Employees and their designated agents have the right to see their personnel files. The files may not be copied or removed. Pa. Cons. Stat. Ann. tit. 43 §§1321 through 1325
Rhode Island	Employees have the right to see their personnel files up to three times per year. A file may not be copied or removed, but an employee may request that specific documents be copied. R.I. Gen. Laws §§28-6.4-1 and 28-6.4-2
South Carolina	No statute
South Dakota	No statute
Tennessee	No statute
Texas	No statute
Utah	No statute
Vermont	No statute
Virginia	No statute
Washington	Employees have the right to see their personnel files and to insert rebuttals of any information with which they disagree. A former employee retains the right of rebuttal or correction for two years. Does not apply if employee is subject to criminal investigation or if the records have been compiled in preparation of an impending lawsuit. Wash. Rev. Code §§49.12.240 to 260
West Virginia	No statute
Wisconsin	Employees have the right to see and copy their personnel files up to twice a year, and to insert rebuttals of any information with which they disagree. The rebuttal must be attached to the record and transmitted with it to any third party. Does not apply if employee is subject to a criminal investigation, to references or recommendations or to records subject to a pending claim in a judicial proceeding. Personnel records include medical records, but if you think that disclosure of these would be detrimental to the employee, you may instead disclose them to a physician designated by the employee. Wis. Stat. §103.13
Wyoming	No statute

Adapted from *Your Rights in the Workplace,* by Barbara Kate Repa (Nolo Press).

5. Informing Employees

Generally, the law doesn't require you to voluntarily tell employees what's in their employee files. You need only disclose information when an employee makes an appropriate request under an employee access law. (See Section 4 above.) About the only exception is that laws in some states require you to tell employees if you're taking adverse action against them because of information in a consumer credit report.

Still, it may be good practice to keep employees informed about what's going into their files. Otherwise, borderline employees may think they're doing fine and be justifiably surprised by a disciplinary action or firing. Admittedly, some employees can get demoralized if they're overwhelmed with negative information about their work, so some discretion is necessary in giving them feedback. But basically, letting employees know where they stand prevents surprises and can lead to improved performance. And if the employee doesn't shape up and winds up being fired, anyone reviewing the facts—a judge or jury, for example—will be more likely to side with you if you've given the employee fair warning about what was wrong.

B. Employee Handbooks

If you have more than one or two employees, consider creating an employee handbook that clearly explains your employment policies.

1. Advantages

An employee handbook can be of practical help in running your business. Once you give it to an employee, there can be no dispute over whether you gave the employee a list of paid days off or explained your vacation policies for new workers. It's all there in writing and everyone is getting the same information. Review the handbook and update it periodically to incorporate changes.

Beyond the practicalities, if your handbook is good, you get a bonus: a measure of legal protection if you're challenged by an employee in a court or administrative proceeding. A handbook that contains clear, reasonable policies—such as one stating that sexual harassment won't be tolerated in the workplace—is the critical beginning of your paper trail if problems develop later. It's an objective piece of evidence that shows you've adopted fair and uniform policies, and that you've informed your employees of exactly where they stand in their employment.

A good handbook should tell your employees how to let you know if they feel unfairly treated or are beginning to have a workplace problem. This in turn gives you a chance to react before a small misunderstanding erupts into a full-blown legal dispute. As another benefit, a well-written handbook may reduce the anxiety that some employees feel about their jobs. Employees will know what the rules and procedures are and where they can turn if they need to discuss an issue.

Even a tiny business with only a handful of employees can benefit from an employee handbook—and you can produce one quickly and cheaply by using a self-help book or software program as a starting point. Modify the sample wording to fit your own needs. Then check with the state department of labor to make sure your handbook complies with the laws in your state. If you have specific legal questions, a brief consultation with a lawyer should be sufficient to clear them up. (See Chapter 13 for more on how to creatively use a small business lawyer.)

If yours is a very small business, keep your handbook short and sweet at the start. At that stage, it's easy to involve all employees in writing it so it accurately covers their concerns. Then, as your business grows, the framework necessary for a more detailed version will be in place.

DON'T INCREASE YOUR LEGAL EXPOSURE

Your handbook may be treated as a contract that can actually limit your right to fire employees. To avoid that result, state in the handbook that:

- employees do not have employment contracts unless they are in writing and signed by the company president, and
- your company reserves the right to terminate employees for reasons not stated in the handbook or for no reason at all.

You might also note that honesty is expected of all employees at all times and an employee found to be dishonest or guilty of excessive absenteeism will be fired. (For a discussion of the at will employment doctrine, see Chapter 1, Section A3.)

Unfortunately, disclaimers in employee handbooks are not always enough to preserve an at will relationship with employees. Courts these days tend to look at the handbook as a whole. They ask: "How would reasonable employees interpret the handbook? Would it be reasonable for employees to conclude that they have been given some rights?" If the answer to the second question is yes, some courts may find the employees do have legal rights to job security despite the disclaimer.

To prevent that result, look closely at each provision in your handbook from the point of view of employees. If employees are likely to conclude you're making binding commitments, fix the language so it's clear you're not.

2. Contents

Here are topics to consider covering in an employee handbook.

Introduction. Begin the handbook by describing your company's history and business philosophy. This helps you set the tone—which can be friendly and welcoming if that's your style. Make it clear to employees from the start that the handbook doesn't cover every possible situation.

Hours. State the normal working hours and how overtime pay is authorized for those employees entitled to it. (See Chapter 3.)

Pay and salaries. Be clear on how pay and salaries are set and how they're raised. In very small businesses, this may be little more than a statement that levels of pay are established and adjusted by the company president taking into consideration past performance, cost of living changes and the ability of the business to pay. But if you do adopt a more formal procedure based on periodic performance reviews, explain how it works—and whether employees may be eligible for bonuses as well as salary increases.

Benefits. Benefits can be nearly as important as salary. Many larger businesses will have a separate publication covering this topic, but most savvy smaller businesses opt to cover it in their employee handbooks. Employee benefits typically include paid vacations, health benefits, sick pay and unpaid leaves for extended illness, pregnancy or family matters. (See Chapter 6 for information on the Family and Medical Leave Act.)

Since the law doesn't require you to provide paid sick days or vacation days, you're free to set the terms under which such benefits are granted—and an employee handbook is the ideal place to inform employees about the rules governing these benefits. Be clear on whether the employee can carry unused sick or vacation days into the next year and what happens to such benefits if an employee quits or gets fired. Finally, describe any 401(k) or retirement benefits you offer.

(See Chapter 4 for an extensive discussion of employee benefits.)

Drug and alcohol abuse. Most businesses have a policy prohibiting employees' use of alcohol or illegal drugs in the workplace. In addition, some businesses offer help to employees in dealing with abuse of these substances—often through an employee assistance program in which the business pays for professional counseling. Spell out your policies.

Sexual harassment. Remind employees that sexual harassment is illegal and violates your policies. (See Chapter 8, Section B for more on sexual harassment.) Let them know that you won't tolerate unwelcome sexual comments or conduct, and that you'll assist those who speak up about it in ending any harassment in the workplace.

Job attendance. Emphasize the importance of good attendance and showing up on time. Tell employees the types of absence that are excused—such as illness, and possibly a family member's death, for example. Also, if you believe it's likely to be a problem, clearly explain that piling up a load of unexcused absences or coming to work late too often can be a basis for disciplinary action or even firing.

PAY CLOSE ATTENTION TO DISCIPLINARY LANGUAGE

The part of your employee handbook dealing with discipline is particularly sensitive. Here's an example of language that may help bolster your legal position in disputes with employees.

Any employee conduct that, in the opinion of XYZ Company, interferes with or adversely affects our business is sufficient grounds for disciplinary action. This action can range from oral warnings to immediate discharge. Depending on the conduct, it is our general policy to take disciplinary steps in the following order:

- *verbal warnings*
- *written warnings*
- *suspension, and*
- *termination*

To decide on the appropriate action, we may consider: the seriousness of your conduct, your employment record, your ability to correct the conduct, actions we have taken for similar conduct by other employees, how your action affects customers and other circumstances.

Some conduct may result in immediate dismissal. Here are examples:

- *theft of company property*
- *excessive tardiness or absenteeism*
- *arguing or fighting with customers or co-workers*
- *using or possessing alcohol or illegal drugs at work*
- *coming to work under the influence of alcohol or illegal drugs*
- *failing to carry out reasonable job assignments*
- *making false statements in a job application*
- *violating company rules and regulations, and*
- *unlawful discrimination or harassment.*

These are only examples. You may terminate your employment at any time; the company reserves the same right.

Discipline. List the kinds of conduct that can get employees in trouble—for example, theft or violence. But again, let employees know this isn't an exclusive list and that you always reserve the right to decide to terminate an employee's employment. (See Section D.)

Employee safety. State that employee safety is a major concern of your business and that employees are expected to heed the posted safety rules and to call to your attention any potentially dangerous conditions. If you have more than half a dozen employees, it's a good idea to set up a safety committee of employees who can help you spot and deal with problems.

Smoking. Most businesses need a written policy for on-the-job smoking. (See Chapter 7, Section G.) And, of course, since many cities and some states now prohibit or restrict workplace smoking, you need to check local ordinances to be sure that your policy is legal.

Complaints. Let employees know what procedures they can follow to resolve complaints. If you have more than a few employees, it's wise to have a grievance committee consisting of employees from various departments who meet informally and make recommendations on employment issues. It's another outlet for upset employees to voice their concerns so you'll be able to address them before minor problems escalate into disciplinary situations and legal crises.

Workplace civility. State specifically that employees at all levels of the business are expected to treat each other with respect and that the success of the business depends on cooperation and teamwork among all employees.

GROOMING AND CLOTHING RULES

If you have a reasonable business purpose for doing so, you can establish on-the-job standards for clothing and grooming as a condition of employment. There's nothing inherently illegal, for example, about requiring all employees to wear navy blue slacks during working hours.

Codes governing employees' appearance may be illegal, however, if they discriminate against a particular group of employees or potential employees. Stay away from imposing different rules on male and female employees. For example, if you have a retail store, you can't require female clerks to wear smocks while allowing male clerks to wear business attire. Courts do, however, allow some latitude in imposing different rules on men and women. For example, a court ruled that a company could lawfully allow women employees to wear jewelry while prohibiting men from doing so.

Several black men have won lawsuits against companies that refused to hire men with beards or that fired men who didn't comply with no-beard rules. Many black men find that if they shave their facial hair too closely, it will cause their curly whiskers to become ingrown and infected. A policy of banning beards might illegally discriminate against black men.

For the sake of creating a uniform company-wide appearance, you may provide workers with some or all of the clothing that they are required to wear on the job. You may even rent suits for your employees to assure that they will be similarly dressed.

Although generally legal, such policies can violate an employee's rights if the cost of the clothing is deducted from the employee's pay in violation of the Fair Labor Standards Act (FLSA). For example, it's illegal under the FLSA to deduct the cost of work-related clothing from an employee's pay so that his or her wages dip below the minimum wage standard. (For more on the FLSA, see Chapter 3.)

3. Documenting Employee's Acceptance

Document that each employee received the handbook. This is also another good chance to reinforce to employees that the handbook isn't an employment contract, that it doesn't guarantee you'll continuously employ them and that you're not obligating your company to continue the current job benefits forever.

To do this, include with your handbook two copies of a statement such as the one below. Then ask each new employee to sign both copies to acknowledge that he or she has received the handbook and is familiar with its terms.

Keep one signed copy of the Employee Handbook Acknowledgment in the employee's personnel file maintained by your business. The employee can keep the other copy. Have each employee sign a similar receipt each time you distribute significant revisions or updates of your handbook.

C. Employee Performance Reviews

Most large companies review and evaluate their employees periodically. This is a sound management practice and one which even small companies should consider—especially for new employees.

EMPLOYEE HANDBOOK ACKNOWLEDGMENT

Welcome to XYZ Company. We hope that you will have a long and productive relationship with our company. To help with this, we are providing you with your own copy of our employee handbook. Please read this handbook carefully. The information in it will acquaint you with company policies and will answer many of your questions.

Please keep in mind that this handbook does not contain all of the information you will need as an employee. You will receive other information through written notices as well as orally. When the company changes a policy, it overrides the past policy.

This handbook is not an employment contract. Unless you have a written employment contract with XYZ Company signed by the president of the company, you legally are an at will employee. This means you or the company may terminate our employment relationship at any time, with or without a reason.

In the future, your status as an at will employee can only be changed through a written contract signed by both you and the president of XYZ Company. No oral statements, promises or contracts regarding the terms and conditions of your employment are valid.

Receipt and Acknowledgment

I have received a copy of XYZ Company's Employee Handbook. I have read the above information and I acknowledge that it is a correct statement of my employment status.

Date:_____

1. Benefits of Evaluations

Evaluating employees periodically gives them a chance to improve if they're not performing well. If you later find it necessary to discipline or fire an employee, it won't come as a surprise to the employee.

By putting your evaluations in writing and saving them in the employee's file, you normally have a credible history of documented problems you can use if an employee claims that he or she was fired for an illegal reason. Legally, you don't have to have a good reason or any reason to fire an at will employee, and you don't have to give notice in advance or afford the employee a chance to improve. (See Chapter 1, Section A3.) However, an employee who is fired may claim, for example, that the firing was based on illegal discrimination (see Chapter 8), so it's not wise to rely solely on your legal right to fire an employee.

You want to stand ready to rebut any possible claim that you fired an employee for an illegal reason such as discrimination based on race or sex. The best way to do this is to preserve in written evaluations and other documents the good reasons you relied on to fire the employee.

Example: Charlotte works at the counter of Parts Plus, a retailer of auto parts. Parts Plus fires Charlotte after she's been there for 18 months. Charlotte sues, claiming that Parts Plus fired her in retaliation for complaining to a state agency about photos of nude women that were posted in the back room where she had to go to retrieve auto parts for customers. At trial, Parts Plus produces copies of written evaluations from Charlotte's file.

Eight months before the firing, Charlotte's supervisor had written: "You must become more familiar with our inventory of parts for imported cars. Also, you need to make fewer errors on the computer system."

Two months before the firing, the supervisor had written: "You're still having problems with imports. We will arrange for you to attend a computer training seminar at the community college at company expense, but you must improve your performance."

Company records separately show that Charlotte attended only one of the six training sessions and that two days before the firing, she mixed up orders for three good customers. The upshot: Because of its thorough documentation of Charlotte's ongoing problems, the judge dismisses Charlotte's case against Parts Plus.

Evaluations have two common purposes—to help employees improve their performances and to protect employers from false claims by former employees. To achieve both ends, thoroughly and objectively evaluate each employee at least twice a year—and more often if an employee is experiencing serious problems. Take the evaluation process seriously and do a careful, conscientious job. In some states, employees have successfully sued employers who used poor evaluation procedures for "negligent evaluation"—the failure of the employer to review employees' work fully and honestly and to warn employees that they faced discipline or discharge if they failed to improve.

2. The Evaluation Process

To keep the evaluation process as consistent and objective as possible, devise an evaluation form that you can use with all employees in the same job category. (See Section C3 below for a sample.) The form should focus on how well the employee has performed the various duties of the job.

Fill in the form before you meet with the employee. Consider these guidelines.

- Give a balanced picture of the employee's strengths and weaknesses.
- Use specific examples of where the employee has met expectations or has exceeded or fallen short of expectations.
- Let the employee know the areas in which he or she must improve. Set objective goals for the employee to meet.
- Where an employee's performance is substantially below par, set a date to meet again with the employee to review his or her progress.
- If the employee's failure to improve may lead to disciplinary measures or discharge, state this clearly in the evaluation.

Leave space on the form for the employee to comment on the evaluation and to acknowledge receiving a copy of it.

Once you've completed the written evaluation, meet with the employee to go over it and to make sure the employee understands it. If you cringe at confronting an employee with criticism, try the sandwich approach: say something positive, something negative, then something positive.

Remember, too, that employees will find it easier to accept criticism—and try to improve their behavior—if you focus on workplace performance and not on the employee's personality. The overall tone of the evaluation should, of course, be as positive as possible because you want the employee to feel motivated rather than resentful.

Whatever your approach, you must tell it like it is. Should you later have legal trouble initiated by a fired employee, a judge or jury won't look at your evaluations in a vacuum. For example, they'll sense that something is wrong if you consistently rate a worker's performance as poor or mediocre—but continue to hand out generous raises or perhaps even promote the person. The logical conclusion: you didn't take seriously the criticisms in your evaluation report, so you shouldn't expect the employee to take them seriously, either.

Just as damaging is to give an employee glowing praise in report after report—perhaps to make the employee feel good—and then to fire the employee for a single infraction. That strikes most people as unfair. And unfair employers often lose court fights, especially in situations where a sympathetic employee appears to have been treated harshly.

If your system is working, employees with excellent evaluations should not need to be fired for poor performance. And employees with poor performance shouldn't be getting big raises.

Once Is Not Enough

Feedback should be an ongoing process. The written evaluation should be a culmination of the feedback you've given throughout the year. Your goal is to have no surprises about how an employee is doing. It's perfectly appropriate, too, to give an employee a written warning between evaluations if the employee is in jeopardy of being disciplined or fired. A copy, of course, should go in the employee's file.

Some employers encourage employees to give their own evaluation of how they're doing—and may also ask employees to rate their supervisors. You'll benefit by making the evaluation process a two-way street. Listen carefully to what the employees say. You'll likely learn a thing or two.

3. Sample Employee Evaluation Form

The following form can be adapted to your needs—to meet your personal style, the set-up of your workplace and the type of work you do.

CONFIDENTIAL
EMPLOYEE PERFORMANCE EVALUATION

Employee name _____

Job title _____

Reviewer _____

Review date _____

JOB PERFORMANCE

(In responding, give specific examples of strengths and weaknesses as often as possible.)

General Quality of Work

(Focus on accuracy, attention to detail, originality, timeliness, organization, degree of supervision needed to accomplish tasks)

_____

_____

Dependability

(Focus on attendance, punctuality, attentiveness, ability to follow instructions, ability to meet deadlines)

_____

_____

Job Knowledge

(Focus on level of knowledge and skills required to master work required, willingness to take the initiative in tackling new tasks)

_____

_____

Personality

(Focus on cooperativeness, decisionmaking skills, ability to work for and with others, ability to handle confrontations)

_____

_____

Communication Skills
(Focus on ability to use language effectively, ability to express ideas clearly and grammatically, command of oral and written language, ability to explain concepts to others)

_____

_____

Management Ability
(Focus on ability to identify problems, ability to creatively solve problems, ability to plan, assign and schedule workload, ability to guide an individual or group to complete a task)

_____

_____

Other Job Requirements
(Focus on specific needs of business or needs for individual improvement: public contact, self-development, quality control, ability to stay within cost guidelines)

PERFORMANCE SUMMARY
What are the employee's outstanding and strongest points?

_____

What are the employee's shortcomings and weaknesses?

_____

Specific accomplishments and changes since last performance review.

_____

_____

GOALS FOR IMPROVEMENT
What can the employee do to be more effective or make needed improvements?

_____

_____

What additional training or equipment would be helpful?

_____

In what ways could your job be changed to make better use of your skills and abilities?

_____

EMPLOYEE FEEDBACK

[To be completed by the employee.)

What are your most important accomplishments on the job over the past year?

_____

What are your weakest job performance areas, or those most in need of improvement?

_____

What steps could you take to improve?

_____

What can management do to support your efforts to improve?

_____

What are your supervisor's strengths and weaknesses in managing your work?

_____

Other work concerns you would like to discuss.

_____

_____

NEXT REVIEW

Date scheduled for next review _____

Particular areas targeted for improvement:

_____

_____

Employee Signature _____

Date _____

_____

Supervisor's Signature _____

Date _____

DEVELOPING AN E-MAIL POLICY

If you provide employees with computers that allow for electronic mail, or e-mail communication, it's smart to develop a written policy so everyone knows the rules. For one thing, you may be assuming that you have the right to see all e-mail messages sent on your equipment, while employees may be assuming they have a degree of privacy. For another thing, you may be assuming that employees are to use your e-mail system only for company purposes, while employees may be assuming they can use it for unlimited personal purposes as well.

You're the sole judge of what to put into your e-mail policy. The important thing is to make the rules clear so that employees can't create legal problems for you by claiming they were taken by surprise. E-mail, of course, is a relatively new means of communication, so the workplace norms are just starting to emerge. Here are some statements to consider when you develop an e-mail policy:

- Our computers and e-mail system are intended to facilitate business communications.
- Our management has access at all times to e-mail communications sent or received on our computers and e-mail system.
- All communications sent or received on our computers or e-mail system are the property of our company.
- Employee privacy doesn't extend to such communications—whether intended for business or personal purposes.
- Employees must provide our management with all passwords and encryption keys.
- Employees may not use our computers or e-mail system for commercial purposes unrelated to our company, or for sending offensive, harassing or defamatory messages.
- Employees who violate these policies may be subject to disciplinary action and may be discharged.

D. Disciplining Employees

Periodic evaluations can work hand in hand with another management strategy—progressive discipline—to keep employees fairly informed of how they're doing and when their jobs are at risk.

Since losing a job can obviously be painful for an employee, some employers make it a practice to fire problem employees only after the workers have gone through a series of less drastic disciplinary moves. A system of progressive discipline may not be right for all businesses—particularly smaller ones. But if you do see fit to have such a policy in place, it can go a long way toward demonstrating your fairness if you eventually have to fire an employee and the employee sues you.

Among the steps you can build into your program are: verbal warnings, written warnings, counseling, probation, suspension and, finally, dismissal. A fired employee's potential wrongful termination claim will be weakened if you can show that the employee knew about the problems that eventually led to dismissal, but he or she muffed repeated opportunities to shape up.

If you follow this approach and generally practice a policy of progressive discipline, make it clear to employees that you reserve the right to fire employees at will—especially for serious infractions—and that your policy of progressive discipline is left to your discretion as an employer. (See Section B2 for an example of language to include in a disciplinary policy.)

Having a policy of progressive discipline can backfire if you create the impression that every employee transgression will be dealt with in that same way. A fired employee, for example, may claim that he or she had a right to be progressively disciplined before being fired.

Obviously, there are times when you may conclude that an employee's conduct is so offensive that decisive action—including immediate discharge—is warranted. To keep an enlightened management policy from turning into a fixed employee right, make it clear that you have the option to dispense with progressive discipline, depending on the situation. (See Section B2 for guidance.) ■

CHAPTER

3

WAGES AND HOURS

A slew of statutes—federal and state—regulate workplace wages and hours, imposing strict requirements on employers. These laws require, for example, that you:

- pay an employee at least the minimum hourly wage unless he or she is exempt from wage and hour statutes (see Sections B1 and A2)
- pay a premium rate for overtime work (see Section B3)
- pay for all the time an employee works (see Section D)
- pay men and women equally for the same work (see Section B2)
- follow special rules if you employ young workers (see Section F), and
- observe legal limits on payroll deductions (see Section H).

For the most part, complying with wage and hour laws is simple and routine: you calculate wages using easy to understand formulas and you retain time and payment records for employees. There are, however, some legal subtleties that can affect your ability to carry out your aims. So in addition to discussing the wage and hour basics, this chapter covers potential problem areas.

A. The Fair Labor Standards Act: Coverage

The main law affecting workers' pay is the federal Fair Labor Standards Act or FLSA (29 U.S.C. §§201 and following) which Congress passed in 1938.

1. Covered Businesses

Your business is covered by the FLSA if you have $500,000 or more in total annual sales. If your business earns less than $500,000 in sales, individual employees may come under the FLSA if their work involves interstate commerce. This includes almost every employee, because courts have interpreted the term "interstate commerce" broadly. An employee of a smaller business is covered by the FLSA if, for example, he or she:

- sends mail to or receives mail from other states
- makes phone calls to or receives them from other states
- keeps records of interstate transactions
- handles goods moving in interstate commerce
- crosses state lines as part of the job, or
- does clerical, custodial or maintenance work for a business engaged in interstate commerce or that makes goods in interstate commerce.

It's possible—but highly unlikely—that your business will fall within a handful of specific exemptions to the FLSA. For example, most small farms are exempt. For specific details on what businesses are exempt, check with the nearest office of the U.S. Labor Department's Wage and Hour Division. (See the Appendix for contact details.)

If you want to research the exemptions to FLSA coverage, you'll find most of them in 29 U.S.C. §213. Look in an annotated edition of the United States Code, which is what your local library is most likely to have. The annotated edition contains summaries of court decisions that will help you understand the courts' rulings about this complex law. In addition, see Title 29 of the Code of Federal Regulations, which goes into great detail on virtually every aspect of the FLSA—but be forewarned that the details can be mind-numbing to the point of incomprehensibility.

INDEPENDENT CONTRACTORS AREN'T COVERED

The FLSA covers only employees—not independent contractors. Whether a worker is an employee for purposes of the FLSA generally turns on the economic realities and not on the IRS definition of an independent contractor.

To determine whether a worker has sufficient economic independence to qualify as an independent contractor under the FLSA, concentrate on:

- the degree to which you control the work
- the worker's opportunity for profit or loss
- the extent of the worker's investment in equipment and facilities
- whether the services require a special skill
- the permanency of the work relationship between you and the worker, and
- whether the worker's service is an integral part of your business.

(See Chapter 11 for a detailed discussion of independent contractors.)

2. Exempt Employees

Even though your business is covered by the FLSA, some employees may be exempt from that law's minimum wage and overtime pay requirements. This is a complex area of law and a source of many misunderstandings. (See Subsection 3b for employees who are exempt only from overtime provisions.)

Most employees who are exempt from the minimum wage and overtime pay requirements fall into one of five categories:

- executive employees
- administrative employees
- professional employees
- outside salespeople, and

- people in certain computer-related occupations.

There are a few miscellaneous categories of workers who are exempt as well.

a. Executive, administrative and professional employees

Generally, these are employees who are paid a minimum weekly salary as specified by law and who spend at least 80% of the workday performing duties that require a measure of discretion and independent judgment. Beyond that, each category of worker has special qualifiers.

An executive, for example, is someone who manages two or more employees within a business or a department, and who can hire, fire and promote employees. An administrative employee performs specialized or technical work related to management or general business operations. A professional employee performs original and creative work or work requiring advanced knowledge normally acquired through specialized study. The exemption guidelines for executive, administrative employees are summarized in the chart below.

Be aware, however, that not all of the legal nuances appear in the chart. Unless an employee fits squarely into the simplified guidelines, your best bet is to dig further. Your state labor department can be helpful, as can the nearest office of the U.S. Department of Labor's Wage and Hour Division. (See the Appendix for contact details.)

Note that there's a long test and a short test for each category. If an employee meets the short test, he or she is exempt and need not meet the long test.

The fine points of these exemptions are explained in a free booklet titled *Regulations Part 541: Defining the Terms—Executive, Administrative, Professional and Outside Sales*. It's available from the nearest office of the Wage and Hour Division of the U.S. Department of Labor—or call (202) 219-8743.

EXEMPTION GUIDELINES

Executive Exemption	Administrative Exemption	Professional Exemption
SHORT TEST		
primarily manages a business or a department	meets the first test described below under "long test"	duties as described below under "long test"
routinely supervises two or more employees	work includes discretion and independent judgment	duties need only include work requiring discretion and independent judgment
earns salary of at least $250 per week	earns salary of at least $250 per week	earns salary of at least $250 per week
LONG TEST		
primarily manages a business or a department	mainly performs office or nonmanual work directly related to management policies	primary duties include work acquired by a prolonged course of specialized intellectual study requiring advanced knowledge
	-or-	*-or-*
		original and creative work stemming primarily from invention, imagination or talent
routinely supervises two or more employees	routinely exercises discretion and independent judgment	work requires consistent exercise of discretion and judgment
can hire, fire or promote workers	routinely assists a proprietor or executive	work is intellectual and varied, not routine
routinely exercises discretion	*-or-*	
	performs technical work under general supervision	
	-or-	
	executes special assignments under general supervision	
spends at least 80% of workday in above activities	spends at least 80% of workday in above activities	spends at least 80% of workday in above activities
earns salary of at least $155 per week	earns salary of at least $155 per week	earns salary of at least $170 per week (doesn't apply

to doctors and lawyers)

The long test requirement that executives and administrators spend at least 80% of the workday in certain activities is reduced to 60% for employees of retail and service establishments. Further, the percentage test doesn't apply at all to an executive who's in charge of an independent business establishment or branch or who owns at least a 20% interest in the business.

Job titles alone don't determine whether someone is an exempt executive, administrative or professional employee. The actual work relationship is what counts. Still, it's possible to make some generalizations about who's exempt and who isn't.

Typical Exempt Jobs

Department Head	Personnel Director
Financial Expert	Executive Assistant
Physician	Lawyer
Credit Manager	Safety Director
Account Executive	Tax Specialist

Typical Non-Exempt Jobs

Clerk	Bank Teller
Errand Runner	Newspaper Reporter
Secretary	Bookkeeper
Inspector	Trainee

Mislabeling Can Be Dangerous

Some employers try to avoid the minimum wage and overtime requirements by labeling all entry level employees Assistant Managers—and then requiring them to work well past the 40 hour workweek with no further compensation. The Department of Labor is well aware of such abuses. Employers who mislabel employees to circumvent the law are playing a dangerous game and may wind up paying stiff penalties.

SALARY TRAPS

One requirement for an executive, administrative or professional exemption is that the employee be salaried. The FLSA treats an employee as salaried only if his or her pay isn't reduced because of variations in the quality or quantity of work performed.

If you dock an employee's salary for personal absences of less than a day at a time, the employee may legally be deemed to be an hourly employee—and no longer exempt from the minimum wage and premium overtime requirements. For example, if a salaried employee misses a few hours of work to take care of personal business, don't reduce his or her salary to make up for that time. If you reduce the employee's salary on an hourly basis, the Department of Labor may conclude that employee is really an hourly worker and not eligible for the overtime exemption.

The reasoning is that salaried workers often put in many hours of overtime without getting paid for it, so it's unfair to reduce their pay if they miss a few hours now or then.

Also, don't deduct for absences caused by jury duty, appearances in court as a witness or temporary military leave. If an exempt employee misses two or three days for jury duty but works the rest of the week, pay the full salary for that week.

b. Outside salespeople

An outside salesperson is exempt from FLSA coverage if he or she:

- regularly works away from your place of business while making sales or taking orders, and
- spends no more than 20% of worktime doing work other than selling for your business.

Typically, an exempt salesperson will be paid primarily through commissions and will require little or no direct supervision in doing the job.

c. Computer specialists

This exemption applies to computer system analysts and programmers who receive a salary of at least $170 a week or who, if paid by the hour, receive at least 6.5 times the minimum wage. That works out to $27.63 an hour.

An employee will likely be exempt from the wage and hour laws if his or her primary duties consist of such things as determining functional specifications for hardware and software, designing computer systems to meet user specs and creating or modifying computer programs.

d. Miscellaneous workers

Several other types of workers are exempt from the minimum wage and overtime pay provisions of the FLSA. The most common include:

- employees of seasonal amusement or recreational businesses
- employees of local newspapers having a circulation of less than 4,000
- newspaper delivery workers
- switchboard operators employed by phone companies that have no more than 750 stations, and
- workers on small farms.

e. Apprentices

An apprentice is a worker who's at least 16 years old and who has signed an agreement with you to learn a skilled trade. Apprentices are exempt from the requirements of the FLSA. But beware that your state may have a law limiting the number of hours you can hire someone to work as an apprentice. State law may also require you to pay the apprentice a certain percentage of the minimum wage. Check with your state labor department for more information. (See the Appendix for contact details.)

Under the FLSA, you must pay an apprentice a progressively increasing wage that averages at least 50% of the journeyman's rate over the period of the apprenticeship.

THE CONSEQUENCES OF BENDING THE RULES

The Wage and Hour Division of the U.S. Department of Labor enforces the wage and hour requirements of the FLSA. Almost always, it is tipped off to investigate a business by an unhappy employee who has complained. Be aware that it's illegal to fire or discriminate against an employee for filing a complaint or participating in a legal proceeding under the FLSA. And many states have similar laws prohibiting such retaliation.

In theory, you can be fined up to $10,000 for violating the FLSA—and even spend time in jail for a second offense if it's willful. But fines and jail time are used in only the most blatant cases.

More typically, you'll be required to pay the employee all unpaid wages including overtime pay, and you may be slapped with a modest fine or penalty. The real cost comes in the time and expense of being involved in enforcement proceedings—not to mention the damage to workers' morale and the animosity that can be created in the workplace, particularly if several employees claim their rights were violated.

B. Pay Requirements

The FLSA and many state laws set a minimum wage and require premium pay for overtime work. In addition, the FLSA requires that men and women receive equal pay for equal work.

1. Minimum Wage

If your business is covered by the FLSA, you must pay all covered employees at least the minimum wage—$4.75 an hour. The minimum wage will
increase to $5.15 an hour on September 1, 1997. Federal law allows you to
pay a training wage of $4.25 an hour to employees under 20 years of age
during their first 90 days on the job.

The law in your state may set a minimum wage higher than the federal
rate. In Alaska, for example, the minimum wage must remain 50 cents
higher than the federal minimum. In the few states that have a lower
minimum, the federal rate controls. As a consequence of the 1996 legislation increasing the federal minimum wage, several states are increasing their
own minimum wage rates. Check with your state department of labor for
increases that may not be reflected in the chart below. (See the Appendix
for contact details.)

In the last few years, some counties, cities and towns have passed their
own wage laws. Check with the law department of your county or municipality if you think that there may be a local wage and hour law.

STATE MINIMUM WAGE LAWS

Alabama	No statute
Alaska	50 cents above federal minimum wage. Alaska Stat. §23.10.065
Arizona	No statute
Arkansas	$4.25. Ark. Code Ann. §11-4-210
California	At least the federal minimum wage. Cal. Labor Code §1182
Colorado	$4.25. By order of the Labor Division, 1515 Arapahoe Street, Tower 2, Suite 400, Denver, CO 80202-2117; 303/620-4700. Authorizing statute: Colo. Rev. Stat. §§8-6-109; 8-6-110; 8-6-111
Connecticut	$4.27, or at least 1/2% above the federal minimum wage, whichever is higher. Conn. Gen. Stat. §31-58j
Delaware	The federal minimum wage. Del. Code Ann. tit. 19 §902a
District of Columbia	Federal minimum wage plus $1. D.C. Code Ann. §§36-220.1 and 36-220.2
Florida	If a manual laborer is paid by the day, week or month, ten hours constitutes a day's work. Hours worked in excess entitle the employee to extra pay, unless you and the employee have otherwise agreed by contract. Fla. Stat. §448.01

Georgia	$3.25. Ga. Code Ann. §34-4-3a
Hawaii	$5.25. Haw. Rev. Stat. §387-2
Idaho	$4.25. Idaho Code §44-1502
Illinois	$4.25. 820 Ill. Comp. Stat. 105/4
Indiana	$3.35, if you employ at least two employees. Ind. Code Ann. §22-2-2-4
Iowa	$4.65. Iowa Code Ann. §91D.1
Kansas	$2.65. Kan. Stat. Ann. §44-1203
Kentucky	$4.25. Ky. Rev. Stat. Ann §337.275
Louisiana	The Secretary of the Department of Transportation and Development must establish a subsistence salary for employees who must spend workdays away from their usual place of residence. La. Rev. Stat. Ann. §48:53
Maine	Same as federal minimum wage up to $5.00. Me. Rev. Stat. Ann. tit. 26 §664
Maryland	At least the federal minimum wage. Md. Code Ann., Labor and Employment, §3-413
Massachusetts	Until 1/1/97: $4.75, unless the commissioner of labor expressly approves of a lesser wage. After 1/1/97: $5.75, unless the commissioner of labor expressly approves of a lesser wage. Labor and Industries Department, 100 Cambridge Street, Room 1107, Boston, MA 02202; 617/727-3452. Authorizing statute: Mass. Gen. Laws Ann. ch. 151, §1
Michigan	$3.35. Mich. Stat. Ann. §17.255(4)
Minnesota	$4.25 for large employers—those grossing more than $362,500 per year. For others, $4.00. Minn. Stat. Ann. §177.24
Mississippi	$4.25. Set by the Employment Security Commission, 1520 W. Capitol, P.O. Box 1699, Jackson, MS 39215; 601/354-8711. Participants in the Work First Program must be paid the federal or state minimum wage, whichever is higher. Authorizing statute: Miss. Code Ann. §43-49-11
Missouri	The federal minimum wage. Mo. Ann. Stat. §290.502
Montana	$4.25 for businesses with gross annual sales of $110,000 or more. For others, $4.00. Mont. Code Ann. §§39-3-404; 39-3-409; Dept. of Labor & Industry Rules §24.16.15104
Nebraska	$4.25. Neb. Rev. Stat. §48-1203
Nevada	$4.25. Notice of the Labor Commissioner. 4/1/91
New Hampshire	Federal minimum wage or the state minimum wage (currently $3.95), whichever is higher. N.H. Rev. Stat. Ann. §279:21
New Jersey	$5.05. N.J. Stat. Ann. §34:11-56a4
New Mexico	$4.25. N.M. Stat. Ann. §50-4-22

New York	$4.25. N.Y. Labor Law §652
North Carolina	$4.25. N.C. Gen. Stat. §95-25.3
North Dakota	$4.25. Commissioner of labor sets the standards of minimum wages, hours of employment and conditions of employment. Labor Department, 600 East Boulevard, Bismarck, ND 58505; 701/328-2680. Authorizing statute: N.D. Century Code §34-06-03
Ohio	$4.25. Ohio Rev. Code Ann. §4111.02
Oklahoma	Not less than current federal minimum wage. Okla. Stat. Ann. tit. 40, §197.2
Oregon	$4.75. Or. Rev. Stat. §653.025
Pennsylvania	The federal minimum wage. 43 Pa. Cons. Stat. Ann §333.104
Rhode Island	$4.45. R.I. Gen. Laws §28-12-3
South Carolina	No statute
South Dakota	$4.25. S.D. Codified Laws Ann. §60-11-3
Tennessee	No statute
Texas	$3.35, except that you are allowed to pay as little as 60% of the minimum wage if the employee's earning or productive capacity is impaired by age, physical or mental deficiency, or injury; of if the employee is over 65 years old. Lower wages may not be paid to agricultural piece rate workers. Labor Code Ann. §§62.051, .055 and .057
Utah	$4.25 for employees 18 and older; does not apply to waitressing. Set by the Industrial Commission of Utah, but may not be more than the federal minimum wage. Industrial Commission of Utah, 160 East 300, Third Floor, P.O. Box 146600, Salt Lake City, UT 84114-6600; 801/530-6921. Authorizing statute: Utah Code Ann. §34-40-103
Vermont	$4.75 or the federal minimum wage, if it is higher. Vt. Stat. Ann. tit. 21, §384a
Virginia	Not less than the federal minimum wage. Va. Code Ann. §40.1-28.10
Washington	$4.90. Wash. Rev. Code Ann. §49.46.020
West Virginia	$4.25. W.Va. Code §21-5C-2a
Wisconsin	$4.25; $3.90 for employees under the age of 18. Set by wage order of the Dept. of Industry, Labor and Human Relations Regulations, P. O. Box 7946, Madison, WI 53707; 608/266-7552. Authorizing statute: Wis. Stat. Ann. §104.02
Wyoming	$1.60. Wyo. Stat. §27-4-202

Adapted from *Your Rights in the Workplace,* by Barbara Kate Repa (Nolo Press).

POSTER REQUIREMENTS

Federal law requires you to display the Federal Minimum Wage poster
prominently in the workplace. It's available at the nearest office of the
U.S. Department of Labor's Wage and Hour Divison. Your state labor
department may also be able to provide this poster as well as any poster
that may be required by state law. (See the appendix for contact details.)

2. Equal Pay for Equal Work

You must provide equal pay and benefits to men and women who do the
same job, or jobs that require equal skill, effort and responsibility. This is
required by the Equal Pay Act—an amendment to the FLSA (29 U.S.C.
§206). Job titles aren't decisive in assessing whether two jobs are equal; it's
the work duties that count. The Act makes it unlawful, for example, for the
owner of a hotel to pay its janitors (primarily men) at a different pay rate
than its housekeepers (primarily women) if both are doing essentially the
same work.

The Equal Pay Act is enforced by the U.S. Equal Employment Opportunities Commission or EEOC. (See Chapter 8, Section A for a discussion of
EEOC enforcement procedures.)

a. Employees covered

The Equal Pay Act applies to the same employees as those covered by the minimum wage and overtime pay provisions of the FLSA. (See Sections A1 and A2.) In addition, the Equal Pay Act applies to executive, administrative and professional employees even though these employees are exempt from the minimum wage and overtime provisions.

The Equal Pay Act doesn't prohibit pay differences based on:
- a seniority system
- a merit system
- a system that pays a worker based on the quantity or quality of what he or she produces, or
- any factor other than the worker's gender—starting salaries, for example, that are based on a worker's experience level.

Example: The Ace Tool and Die Company was founded in 1960. The company initially hired 50 male tool and die makers. Many of those men are still working there. Since 1980, the company has expanded and hired 50 more tool and die makers, half of them male and half female. All of the tool and die makers at Ace are doing equal work, but because the company awards raises systematically based on the length of a worker's employment there, many of the older male workers earn substantially more per hour than their female co-workers who are doing equal work. The pay system at Ace Tool and Die doesn't violate the Equal Pay Act because the pay differences between genders are based on a bona fide seniority system.

If you do base pay differences on seniority, merit, work quantity or quality or worker experience, take a hard look at your practices to be sure that some subtle discrimination isn't taking place.

b. Determining job equality

Jobs don't have to be identical for the courts to consider them equal. In general, two jobs are equal for the purposes of the Equal Pay Act when both require the same levels of skill, effort and responsibility—and are performed under similar conditions.

There's room for interpretation, but if there are only small differences in the jobs, they should be regarded as equal.

Example: At a ceramics company, the major difference between the jobs being done by women and men is a weightlifting restriction placed on the women. The women and men are performing equal work because heavy lifting is only a small part of the job. (Schultz v. Saxonburg Ceramics Inc., 314 F. Supp. 1139 (W.D. Pa., 1970).)

3. Paying Overtime

The FLSA requires you to pay non-exempt workers at least one and one-half times their regular rates of pay for all hours worked in excess of 40 in one week. In 1938, when the FLSA was enacted, the nation was just recovering from the Depression. Congress believed that imposing an overtime penalty on employers would induce shorter working hours and help the nation solve its economic problems by spreading work around. The premium overtime rule may have outlived its original purpose—but the law is still on the books, creating headaches for employers.

The FLSA doesn't require you to pay an employee at an overtime rate simply because he or she worked more than eight hours in one day. Generally, you calculate and pay overtime by the week. The workweek may begin on any day of the week and any hour that you, the employer, establish. Generally, in applying the minimum wage and overtime pay rules, each workweek stands alone; you can't average two or more workweeks. And you can't manipulate the start of the workweek merely to avoid paying overtime.

For a full description of the overtime rules, see the publication, *Overtime Compensation under the Fair Labor Standards Act,* available at no charge at the nearest office of the U.S. Department of Labor's Wage and Hour Division. (See the Appendix for contact details.)

The Minimum Is Going Up

The examples used in this chapter assume that the federal minimum wage rate of $4.75 an hour applies. Note that the rate increases to $5.15 an hour on September 1, 1997. Minimum rates set by state law may be higher.

a. Exempt employees

The employees described in Section A2 as being exempt from some FLSA provisions are also exempt from the overtime pay requirements of the Act. In addition, a number of other employees are exempt.

Transportation workers. Taxicab drivers are exempt from the overtime pay requirements of the FLSA. Drivers and other employees of trucking companies are not covered by the FLSA but are subject to the Interstate Commerce Act, which is administered by the Department of Transportation.

Certain commissioned employees of retail or service establishments. An employee of a retail or service establishment will be exempt from the overtime pay requirements of the FLSA if:

- the employee's regular rate of pay is more than one and one-half times the minimum wage, and
- more than half the employee's pay comes from commissions.

Vehicle salespeople and mechanics. The FLSA exempts from its overtime pay requirements employees who sell cars, trucks, trailers, farm implements, boats or aircraft. Also exempt are parts clerks and mechanics who service cars, trucks or farm implements if they're working for a nonmanufacturing business that sells these items.

Newspeople. Announcers, news editors and chief engineers of certain small radio and TV stations are exempt from the overtime pay requirements.

Employees of motion picture theaters. Employees of movie theaters need not be paid for overtime work at the premium rate.

Farmworkers. Farmworkers need not be paid for overtime work at the premium rate.

b. Partially exempt employees

Special overtime rules apply to some employees.

Employees of hospitals and residential care facilities. Those who have agreements for a 14 day work period must receive overtime premium pay for all hours over eight hours a day or 80 hours in the 14 day work period—whichever amounts to more.

Training time. Employees who lack a high school diploma or who haven't finished eighth grade can be required to spend up to 10 hours a week in reading and basic skills programs. These employees must receive their regular wages for time spent in training, but needn't be paid overtime pay for those hours.

c. Computing overtime pay

The U.S. Department of Labor's Wage and Hours Division offers guidelines on how to compute overtime pay.

Hourly rate. If an employee works more than 40 hours during a week, you must pay at least one and one-half times the regular rate for each hour over 40.

Example: An employee whose regular rate is $4.80 an hour works 44 hours in a workweek. You must pay the employee at least $7.20 for each hour over 40. Pay for the week would be $192 for the first 40 hours, plus $28.80 for the four hours of overtime—a total of $220.80.

Piece rate. To obtain the regular pay rate for an employee who is paid on a piecework basis, divide the total weekly earnings by the total number of hours worked that week. You must pay the employee the full piecework earnings, plus an additional one-half times this regular rate for each hour over 40 that he or she works.

Example: An employee paid on a piecework basis works 45 hours in a week and earns $225. The regular rate of pay for that week is $225 divided by 45, or $5 an hour. In addition to the straight time pay, you must pay the employee $2.50 (half the regular rate) for each hour over 40.

Another way to pay pieceworkers for overtime is to pay one and one-half times the piece rate for each piece produced during the overtime hours. However, you and the employee must agree to this payment arrangement in advance. The piece rate must be the one actually paid during regular work hours and must be enough to yield at least the minimum wage per hour.

Salary. To obtain the regular rate of pay for an employee paid a salary for a regular or specified number of hours a week, divide the salary by the number of hours for which the salary is intended as compensation. You and the employee may have agreed to a salary that meets the minimum wage requirement that you pay for whatever number of hours are worked each week. Here, to obtain the regular rate, divide the salary by the number of hours worked. Both the regular rate and the overtime rate will vary, depending on how many hours are worked each week.

Example: You've agreed to pay an employee a salary of $300 a week. If the employee works 50 hours, the regular rate is $6 ($300 divided by 50 hours). So in addition to the salary, you must pay $3 (half the regular rate) for each of the 10 overtime hours—a total of $330 for the week. If the employee works 60 hours, the regular rate will be $5 ($300 divided by 60 hours). In that case, you'll owe an additional $2.50 for each of the 20 overtime hours—a total of $350 for the week.

In no case can the regular rate be less than the minimum wage required by the FLSA.

If a salary isn't paid weekly, you must determine the weekly pay to compute the regular rate and overtime. If, for example, the salary is paid twice a month, multiply by 24 and then divide by 52 weeks to get the weekly equivalent.

ATTITUDES ON OVERTIME ARE CHANGING

In the recent past, most workers loved overtime work. It represented an opportunity to get ahead financially—maybe a chance to buy a boat or start a college fund for the kids.

Many workers still feel that way, but others don't feel driven to amass as much money as possible from their work. Those who aren't thrilled by overtime work may have family responsibilities or may simply place a high value on their private time.

The law allows you to schedule overtime for workers, but it may be a more sound management practice to give them some choice in the matter. Otherwise, the workers who don't relish overtime work may feel abused and will drag down morale in the workplace. If you anticipate that you'll be requiring overtime work for certain positions, put that fact in the job description so workers are aware of that likelihood right from the start. Applicants who abhor overtime work can decide to seek work elsewhere.

4. Compensatory Time

The practice of granting hour-for-hour compensatory time—for example, giving a worker six hours time off one week as compensation for six hours of overtime worked the previous week—isn't usually allowed for private sector employees covered by the FLSA. The rule is different for public employees. Employers and employees are often puzzled when they learn that comp time isn't permitted in the private sector because it seems like a sensible and mutually beneficial way to handle overtime in many situations.

You do, however, have a few options for avoiding premium overtime pay by giving a worker time off instead of money. One way is to rearrange an employee's work schedule during a workweek.

Example: Susan, a paralegal at the law firm of Smith and Jones, normally works an eight-hour day, Monday through Friday. One week, Susan and the lawyers need to meet a deadline on a brief due in the court of appeals. So that week, Susan works 10 hours a day, Monday through Thursday. The law firm gives Susan Friday off and pays her for a 40-hour week at her regular rate of pay. This is legal because Susan hasn't worked any overtime as defined by the FLSA; only the hours over 40 hours a week count as overtime hours.

If an employee works more than 40 hours in one week, it's sometimes possible to reduce the worker's hours in another week so that the amount of the employee's paycheck remains constant. This is legal if:

• the time off is given within the same pay period as the overtime work, and

• the employee is given an hour and one-half of time off for each hour of overtime worked.

Example: Frames and Things, a shop that specializes in framing paintings, employs Jared and pays him $560 at the close of each two-week pay period. Because a week-long street art fair is expected to generate a great demand for framing services, the shop's owner wants Jared to work longer hours that week. However, the owner doesn't want to increase Jared's paycheck. She asks Jared to work 50 hours during art fair week and gives him 15 hours off the next week. Since Jared is paid every two weeks, Frames and Things may properly reduce Jared's hours the second week to keep his paycheck at the $560 level.

Since state regulations may further restrict the use of comp time, check with your state's labor department. (See the Appendix for contact details.) If you allow employees to take comp time, put your policy in writing in the employee handbook so that everyone knows what to expect.

Private Deals Can Be Risky

It's unlikely that a federal or state labor investigator will look into your comp time arrangements unless an employee files a complaint. Knowing this, you may be tempted to work out comp time deals with employees to meet your needs and theirs. This can be dangerous. You never know when a friendly, loyal employee may turn sour and look for some legal technicalities to use against you.

Relief May Be On the Way

Because employers and employees alike feel that the current rules on comp time are too rigid, Congress is working on changes. One plan being considered would allow you to offer employees a choice between receiving overtime pay or one and one-half hours of comp time for each hour of overtime worked.

STATE PAY INTERVAL LAWS

In addition to the wage and hour laws that many states have adopted (such as minimum wage laws shown in the chart in Section B1), some states have pay interval laws specifying how often employees must be paid. The FLSA requires only that the pay period be one month or less. State laws often require shorter pay periods—such as every two weeks. If you have a question about pay periods, call your state's labor department. (See the Appendix for contact details.)

C. Calculating Pay

The FLSA doesn't mandate any specific system of paying employees. You can pay them based on time at work, piece rates or according to some other measure. But in all cases, an employee's pay divided by the hours worked during the pay period must equal or exceed the minimum wage.

Example: Sam, a clerk-typist for Dr. Martinez, works parttime. Dr. Martinez pays Sam $7 an hour for each hour that he works.

Example: Emily is a parts department employee at Import Autos Inc., a car dealership. Import Autos pays Emily $250 a week for 40 hours of work. Even though Emily's wages are based on a week of work, her hourly rate is $6.25 per hour ($250 divided by 40).

Example: Arturo, a roofing worker, is employed by Home Contractors Ltd. Home Contractors pays Arturo $3 for each bundle of shingles he installs. He never installs less than 100 bundles in any 40-hour week. His pay rate is $7.50 per hour (100 bundles x $3 each, divided by 40).

1. Forms of Pay

Under the FLSA, you must pay employees in cash or something that can be readily converted into cash—a check, for example, or other legal forms of compensation such as food and lodging. Coupons or tokens that can only be spent at your store do not count as wages. And if you grant discounts to employees, you can't count these discounts toward the minimum wage requirement.

a. Tips

When an employee routinely earns at least $30 a month in tips, you can pay the employee as little as $2.13 an hour as long as that amount plus tips brings the employee's hourly earnings to the current minimum wage level. If it doesn't, you must pay the employee enough so that the hourly rate plus tips does come up to the minimum wage level.

Example: Alphonse is a waiter at Chez Nous, where he averages $10 an hour in tips. Chez Nous need only pay Alphonse $2.13 an hour because when his tips are added to that hourly rate, his total pay exceeds the minimum wage rate.

b. Commissions

Commissions that you pay people for sales may take the place of wages for purposes of the FLSA. However, if the commissions don't equal the minimum wage, you must make up the difference.

Example: Julia is a salesperson at Electronics Plus. She's paid a percentage of the dollar volume of the sales she completes. During one slow week, she averaged only $2 in commissions per hour. Under the FLSA, Electronics Plus must pay Julia an additional $2.75 for each hour she worked through the first 40 hours of that week; that will bring her total pay up to the minimum wage level of $4.75 an hour.

2. Time Off

The FLSA doesn't require you to pay employees for time off, such as vacation, holidays or sick days. It may be standard practice for you to pay employees for such time spent away from work, but the FLSA only covers payment for time on the job.

Don't Ignore Your Promises or Practices

If you promise paid vacations, holidays or sick days in an employee handbook or other written policy, or if you customarily grant such paid time off, you may be legally bound to give those benefits to all employees.

Some state laws require paid time off for jury duty and voting. In addition, laws in some states require you to give employees time off for National Guard or other military duty—and a set time off to attend a child's school conferences. Most state laws provide that you can't fire or discriminate against an employee for taking such time off.

D. Calculating Workhours

The Portal-to-Portal Pay Act (29 U.S.C. §251), requires you to pay covered employees for any of their time that you control and that benefits you. In general, time on the job doesn't include the time employees spend washing themselves or changing clothes before or after work, or meal periods when employees are free from all work duties.

It's OK to round off records of worktime to the nearest five-minute mark on the clock—but not if it results in paying workers for less time than they actually worked. So if you're going to round off work periods, it's best simply to add time, and not subtract it.

1. Travel Time

You needn't pay employees for the time they spend commuting between their homes and the normal job site; that's not considered on-the-job time. But you do have to pay for commuting time which is actually part of the job.

If you run a plumbing repair service, for example, and require workers to stop by your shop to pick up orders, tools and supplies before going out on calls, their workday begins when they check in at your shop.

Otherwise, just about the only situation in which you must pay workers for commuting time is when they're required to go back and forth from the normal worksite at odd hours in emergency situations.

Example: Neil normally works 9 to 5 as a computer technician at Arbor City Computer and is paid hourly. One day, about two hours after Neil gets home, his supervisor calls him to say that some computer equipment is malfunctioning and preventing the late shift of employees from doing their work—and asks him to go back to the office immediately to help correct the problem. It takes him half an hour to get there, two hours to fix the problem and half an hour to drive home again. Arbor City must pay Neil for three extra hours—two of them workhours and the third the extra hour of commuting time required by the company's emergency.

2. On-call Periods

You must count as payable time any periods when employees are not actually working, but are required to stay on your premises while waiting for a work assignment. If you require employees to be on call, but you don't make them stay on your premises, then two rules generally apply.

- You don't count as payable time the on-call time that employees can control and use for their own enjoyment or benefit.
- You do count as payable time the on-call time over which employees have little or no control and which they can't use for their own enjoyment or benefit.

Example: Medi-Transit operates a nonemergency ambulance service that transports patients from hospitals to nursing homes. The company hires Ryan to drive an ambulance from 8 to 5, Monday through Friday, and also requires him to carry a beeper one night a week so he can handle an occasional assignment after normal working hours. Since Ryan is free to pursue personal and social activities during nonworking hours, Medi-Transit doesn't have to pay him for his on-call time.

Example: AirTec provides mechanical services for small privates planes at a local airfield. The company designates one of its mechanics to be on call each Saturday. A mechanic who is on call must remain at home near the phone and, for safety reasons, can't drink any alcohol. Since designated mechanics aren't free to use their on-call time as they please, it's payable time.

Unless there's an employment contract that states otherwise, you can generally pay a different hourly rate for on-call time than you do for regular worktime. But keep in mind that employees must be paid at least the minimum amount required under the wage and hour regulations.

3. Sleep Time

If you require an employee to be on duty at the worksite for less than 24 hours at a time, you generally must count as payable any time that the employee is allowed to sleep during a shift of duty.

Similarly, if you require an employee to be at work for 24 hours or more, you also generally must count sleep time as payable worktime. But there's a way around this: you and the employee may agree to exclude up to eight hours per day from payable time as sleep and meal periods. However, if conditions are such that the employee can't get at least five hours of sleep during the eight-hour sleep-and-eat period, or if the employee ends up working during that period, then those eight hours revert to being payable time.

4. Lectures, Meetings and Training Seminars

Generally, if you want a non-exempt employee to attend a lecture, meeting or training seminar, you'll have to pay for that employee's time—including travel time if the meeting is away from the worksite.

About the only situation in which you don't have to pay for the employee's time is if:

- the employee attends the event outside of his or her regular working hours
- attendance is voluntary
- the instruction session isn't directly related to the employee's job, and
- the employee doesn't perform any productive work during the instruction session.

5. Meal and Rest Breaks

Nearly half the states have laws requiring employers to provide meal and rest breaks and specifying minimum times that must be allowed. (See the chart below.)

You don't have to pay a covered employee for time spent on an actual meal period. But the key is that the employee must be completely relieved from work during that period so that he or she can enjoy a regularly scheduled meal. If, for example, you require an employee to remain at his or her desk during the meal period or to keep an eye on machinery, you must pay for the meal time.

Similarly, you don't have to pay for rest periods or coffee breaks if the employee is truly free from job duties. If an employee must listen for the phone or watch for merchandise deliveries during the break, it's not free time and you must pay for it.

It's Better Not to Quibble

Most employees today expect to get one or two paid breaks during an eight-hour shift. Such breaks may help employees work more efficiently since they'll return to the job refreshed. It can put a damper on employee morale if you try to avoid paying for that time.

STATE MEAL AND REST BREAK LAWS

State	Legal Provisions
Alabama	You can't require an employee who is age 15 or younger to work five continuous hours without a meal or rest break of at least 30 minutes. Ala. Code § 25-8-38(c).
Alaska	No statute
Arizona	No statute
Arkansas	In your workplace has more than six employees, you must provide separate lunchrooms for the women. If this is impracticable, you must give female employees at least one hour for lunch and permit them to leave your establishment. Ark. Code Ann. §11-5-112
California	Meal—30 minutes within five hours of starting work if workday is six hours or more. If less, waivable.
	Rest—10 minutes per four hour period. Compensated.
	Industrial Welfare Commission Order No. 1-89. (Does not apply to motion picture, agricultural and household occupations.)
Colorado	Meal—30 minutes within five hours of starting work. Optional if workday is not over six hours.
	Rest—10 minutes per four hours.
	Wage Order No. 19
Connecticut	Meal—30 minutes per 7-1/2 hour workday. Given after second hour and before last two hours. Conn. Gen. Stat. §31-51ii
Delaware	Meal—30 minutes for 7-1/2 hour workday. Given after second hour and before last two hours. Del. Code Ann. tit. 19 §707
District of Columbia	No statute
Florida	No statute

Georgia	No statute
Hawaii	No statute.
Idaho	No statute
Illinois	Meal—20 minutes for a 7-1/2 hour workday beginning no later than five hours into the work period. 820 Ill. Compiled Stat. 140/3
Indiana	No statute
Iowa	Employees under the age of 16 who work five or more hours are entitled to a 30 minute break. Iowa Code §92.7
Kansas	No statute
Kentucky	Meal—"Reasonable" meal break between three and five hours into the work period.
	Rest—10 minutes per four hours.
	Statute does not apply to railroad employees.
	Ky. Rev. Stat. Ann. §§337.355 and 337.365
Louisiana	Divers, tunnel and caisson workers who use compressed air must be given open air rest intervals between shifts, as specified in the statute. La. Rev. Stat. Ann. §23:486
Maine	Meal—30 minutes per six hours of work for meals or rest. Me. Rev. Stat. Ann. tit. 26 §§601 and 602
Maryland	No statute
Massachusetts	Meal—30 minutes per six hour work period. Mass. Gen. Laws Ann. ch. 149, §100
Michigan	Minors who are employed more than five continuous hours must be given 30 minutes for a meal or rest break. Mich. Comp. Laws §17.731(12)
Minnesota	Meal—Employer must allow "adequate time" to eat a meal during an eight hour work period. Minn. Stat. Ann. §177.254
	Rest—Employer must allow a "reasonable" amount of time in a four hour period to use the restroom. Minn. Stat. Ann. §177.253
Mississippi	No statute
Missouri	No statute
Montana	No statute
Nebraska	All employees in assembly plants, workshops, or mechanical establishments are required to have at least 30-minute lunch breaks between noon and 1 p.m. without having to remain on the premises unless it operates 24 hours per day. Neb. Rev. Stat. §48-212
Nevada	Meal—30 minutes per eight hours of work.
	Rest—10 minutes per four hours of work.
	Nev. Rev. Stat. Ann. §608.019

New Hampshire	Meal—30 minutes per five hours of work, except it is feasible for the employee to eat while working and the employer allows him or her to do so. N.H. Rev. Stat. Ann. §275:30-a
New Jersey	No statute
New Mexico	Women's working hours are restricted to eight hours per day and 48 hours per week, except for domestic workers and workers in interstate commerce. Those employees must be given a 30 minute rest period, which is not counted as part of the working day. N.M. Stat. Ann. §50-5-4
New York	Meal—Mercantile or similar establishments: 30 minutes;
	Factory: 60 minutes;
	If shift begins before 11 a.m. and extends past 7 p.m., an additional 20 minutes is given to factory and mercantile workers between 5 p.m. and 7 p.m. If shift is more than six hours long and begins between 1 p.m. and 6 a.m., then mercantile employees are to receive 45 minutes and factory employees 60 minutes at a point midway through the shift.
	N.Y. Labor Law §162
North Carolina	No statute
North Dakota	Meal—30 minutes if shift is over five hours. By wage order. Commissioner of Labor sets the standards.
	N.D. Century Code §34-06-03
Ohio	No statute
Oklahoma	No statute
Oregon	Meal—30 minutes for each work period of between six and eight hours within the second and fifth hour worked. Or if work period is more than seven hours, break to be given between the third and sixth hour worked.
	Rest—10 minutes for every four hours worked.
	Or. Administrative Rules §839-020-050
Pennsylvania	No statute
Rhode Island	Meal—20 minutes per six hours of work. R.I. Gen. Laws §28-3-14
South Carolina	No statute
South Dakota	No statute
Tennessee	Meal—30 unpaid minutes for six hour work period, except if your workplace, that by its nature, provides for ample opportunity to rest or take an appropriate break. Tenn. Code Ann. §50-2-103
Texas	No statute
Utah	No statute
Vermont	No statute

Virginia	Any county having the county manager form of organization may establish laws regulating hours and conditions of employment. Va. Code §15.1-658
Washington	No statute
West Virginia	Meal—20 minutes. W.V. Administrative Regulations §42-5-2.6
Wisconsin	Meal—30 minutes close to usual meal time or near middle of shift. Shifts of more than six hours without a meal break should be avoided. Break mandatory for minors. WI Admin. Code, Ind. 74.02
Wyoming	You must give women employees two rest periods of not less than 15 minutes—one before the lunch hour and one after lunch—if the employees are required to be on their feet continuously. Wyo. Stat. Ann. §27-6-101

Adapted from *Your Rights in the Workplace,* by Barbara Kate Repa (Nolo Press).

E. Keeping Records

The FLSA requires you to keep records of wages and hours. If an employee is subject to both minimum wage and overtime provisions, you must keep records for that employee showing:

- the employee's name, address, occupation and gender
- the employee's birthdate if he or she is younger than 19 years old
- the hour and day when each workweek began
- the total hours worked each workday and each workweek
- total daily or weekly earnings
- regular hourly pay rate for any week when overtime was worked
- total overtime pay for the workweek
- deductions from or additions to wages
- total wages paid each pay period, and
- date of payment and pay period covered.

   Different records are required for exempt employees, and you must keep special information for employees to whom you extend lodging or other facilities. You must retain most records for all current employees and for at least three years after an employee stops working for your company.

For details on your recordkeeping duties, get the publication, *Records to be Kept by Employers under the FLSA*. It's available at the nearest office of the U.S. Labor Department's Wage and Hour Division. (See the Appendix for contact details.)

F. Child Labor

The FLSA has special rules for younger workers. Those rules are designed to discourage young people from dropping out of school too soon and to protect them from dangerous work such as mining, demolition and wrecking, logging and roofing. Check with the local wage and hour office of the U.S. Department of Labor for a current list of jobs that are considered to be hazardous to young people. (See the Appendix for contact details.)

State laws may impose additional restrictions on hiring young workers. The rules are different for youngsters in agricultural and nonagricultural jobs.

1. Agricultural Jobs

The FLSA defines agriculture to include:
- cultivating and tilling the soil
- dairying
- producing, cultivating, growing and harvesting any agricultural or horticultural commodities
- raising livestock, bees, fur-bearing animals or poultry, and

- any practices performed by a farmer on a farm as part of farming—for example, forestry, lumbering and preparing items for market.

In agricultural work, the following rules apply:

- You may hire a worker who is 16 years or older for any work, whether hazardous or not, for unlimited hours.
- You may hire a worker who is 14 or 15 years old for any nonhazardous agricultural work outside of schoolhours.
- You may hire a worker who is 12 or 13 years old for any nonhazardous agricultural work outside of school hours if the child's parents work on the same farm or if you have their written consent.
- You may hire a worker who is under 12 years old for nonhazardous work on a farm outside of school hours if the farm isn't covered by minimum wage requirements—but you need the written consent of the child's parents.
- You may hire a worker who is 10 or 11 years old if you've been granted a waiver by the U.S. Department of Labor to employ the youngster as a hand harvest laborer for no more than eight weeks in any calendar year.

If you own or operate a farm, you can hire your own children to do any kind of work on the farm, regardless of their ages.

OCCUPATIONS HAZARDOUS TO YOUNG WORKERS

The U.S. Department of Labor has identified several agricultural occupations that are deemed hazardous for children age 15 and under, including:

- operating a tractor that has more than 20 horsepower
- working in a yard, pen or stall occupied by a bull, a stud horse maintained for breeding purposes or a sow with suckling pigs
- felling timber with a diameter of more than six inches
- working from a ladder or scaffold at a height of more than 20 feet, and
- handling or using blast agents.

For a complete list of hazardous agricultural occupations, contact the nearest offices of the U.S. Department of Labor. (See the Appendix for contact details.)

2. Nonagricultural Jobs

The FLSA sets out a number of restrictions on young workers hired to do nonagricultural jobs.

- You may hire a worker who is 18 years or older for any job, hazardous or not, for unlimited hours.
- You may hire a worker who is 16 or 17 years old for any nonhazardous job, for unlimited hours.
- You may hire a worker who is 14 or 15 years old outside schoolhours in various nonmanufacturing, nonmining, nonhazardous jobs, but some restrictions apply. The employee can't work more than three hours on a school day, 18 hours in a school week, eight hours on a nonschool day or 40 hours in a nonschool week. Also, work can't begin before 7 a.m. or end after 7 p.m., except from June 1 through Labor Day, when evening hours are extended to 9 p.m.

Fourteen years old is the minimum age for most work, but there are a few jobs that workers younger than 14 can perform, including:

- delivering newspapers
- performing in radio, TV, movie or theatrical productions
- working in a nonfarm business solely owned by their parents—if it's not a manufacturing or hazardous job
- gathering evergreens, and
- making evergreen wreaths.

G. Payroll Withholding

Federal law requires you to withhold income taxes and Social Security and Medicare contributions from employees' paychecks. States and municipalities that have income taxes also require withholding—usually under a system that parallels the federal procedures. (See Chapter 5, Section B.)

You may also deduct the cost of meals, housing and transportation, loans, debts owed to you, child support and alimony, payroll savings and insurance premiums. There are exceptions to these rules, and limits on how much you can withhold or deduct.

1. Meals, Housing and Transportation

You may legally deduct from an employee's paycheck the reasonable cost or fair value of meals, housing, fuel and transportation to and from work. But you must show that you customarily paid these expenses and that:
- they were for the employee's benefit
- you told the employee in advance about the deductions from a paycheck, and
- the employee voluntarily accepted the meals and other accommodations against minimum wage.

2. Debts Owed to an Employer

If you loan money or extend credit to an employee, you can withhold money from his or her pay to satisfy that debt. However, it's illegal to make such a deduction if it would drop the employee's pay below the minimum wage.

Example: Roadmaster Auto Parts Store hires Bruce at $5.50 an hour to make deliveries. One morning, the battery in Bruce's car dies. Roadmaster allows him to replace the battery with a new one from the store's stock—and Bruce agrees that Roadmaster can deduct the price, $60, from his paycheck. Under the FLSA, Roadmaster can legally deduct no more than $30 per week (40 hours X $.75) from Bruce's gross pay to cover the battery. To deduct more would drop Bruce's pay rate of $5.50 per hour to below the required minimum of $4.75.

3. Debts and Wage Garnishments

You may be sent an order from a judge requiring your business to withhold money from an employee's paycheck to satisfy a debt the employee owes to someone else. This order is part of a legal process called wage attachment or wage garnishment. Usually, a judge will issue such an order only after a judgment has been signed stating that the employee actually owes the money—but such a judgment may not be necessary for garnishments based on an employee's failure to pay student loans, child support, alimony or taxes.

If you receive a garnishment order, read it carefully because it will specify deadlines you must meet for processing the order. You may have to pay a penalty if you don't comply with the terms and timetables of the garnishment. Procedures vary from state to state, but most likely you'll be required to file a form with the court disclosing how much you owe to the employee for wages. Then you'll be required to send a portion of those wages to the court or, perhaps, to the creditor or creditor's lawyer.

A federal law, the Consumer Credit Protection Act (15 U.S.C. §1673), prohibits a judgment creditor from taking more than 25% of an employee's net earnings through a wage garnishment. A few states offer greater protection to the employee. In Delaware, for example, a judgment creditor can't take more than 15% of an employee's wages. Usually the papers you receive as part of the garnishment order will explain how much of the employee's wage you should deduct and where to send the money.

The Consumer Credit Protection Act also prohibits you from firing an employee because of a garnishment order to satisfy a single debt. But if two judgment creditors garnish an employee's wages or one judgment creditor garnishes an employee's wages to pay two different judgments, you're free to fire that employee. Again, some state laws place stricter limits on your right to fire an employee because of garnishments. In Washington, for example, you can't fire a worker for judgments owed unless his or her wages are garnished by three different creditors or to satisfy three different garnishments within a year. In Connecticut, you can't fire a worker unless you've had to deal with more than seven creditors or judgments in a single year.

Although statutes limit your right to fire employees because of garnishments, you can still fire such employees for cause—or even without cause, if you can establish that the firing wasn't based on the garnishments.

4. Child Support

The federal Family Support Act of 1988 (102 U.S.C. §2343) requires that new or modified child support orders include an automatic wage withholding order. If you receive a copy of such an order, you must withhold a portion of the employee's pay and send it on to the parent who has custody of the child.

You can't discipline, fire or refuse to hire someone just because his or her pay is subject to a child support wage withholding order.

5. Back Taxes

If an employee owes taxes to the federal government and doesn't pay, the IRS can grab most—but not all—of the employee's wages. The amount the employee gets to keep is determined by the number of his or her dependents and the size of the standard deduction to which the employee is entitled.

If you receive a wage levy notice from the IRS, don't ignore it. If you go ahead and pay the employee in full, you'll be liable to the IRS for whatever amount you wrongly pay.

Most state and some municipal taxing authorities have similar power to seize a portion of an employee's wages. ■

CHAPTER

4

EMPLOYEE BENEFITS

Employee benefits are such a common part of the workplace terrain today that many assume these benefits are required by law. But generally, the decision about whether or not to provide such benefits is up to you.

Even though providing benefits is largely optional, enlightened employers generally do offer some type of benefit package. Offering benefits can reflect your commitment to keeping a satisfied workforce and can help you remain competitive in attracting competent workers.

Because the federal tax laws allow an employer to deduct the cost of many employee benefits as a business expense, the financial burden of providing these benefits is greatly reduced. Benefits that qualify for favorable tax treatment include health and dental coverage, term life insurance, disability insurance, approved pension plans, educational assistance programs and dependent care assistance. But if a benefit plan is rigged to favor the owners of a business or employees who receive the highest compensation, the plan may not qualify for a tax deduction.

If you opt to provide healthcare coverage or pension plans, federal laws may impose requirements on these plans. (See Sections A and B.)

For an excellent introduction to the full range of employee benefits, see *J.K. Lasser's Employee Benefits for Small Business,* by Jane White and Bruce Pyenson (Prentice Hall). Price: $12.00.

EMPLOYEES CAN HELP YOU PLAN

In putting together a benefit program, consider taking a survey of employees or setting up a committee of several of them to recommend the benefits they'd most like to have. Then, after exploring the options and deciding on the benefits you'll offer, communicate that decision—and your reasons for the choice—to the employees.

Perhaps some employee suggestions will be too expensive or even impossible to adopt. Others may be left to reconsider in a year. Whatever the situation, when employees go to the trouble of making suggestions, they need to know that their suggestions are taken seriously.

A. Healthcare Coverage

Healthcare coverage is the benefit most employees covet. Medical treatment is expensive today and it's difficult for an individual seeking coverage to find some that's affordable. Of course, employees enjoy the greatest benefits if the employer foots the entire bill. But even if an employer pays none of the cost of coverage—or just a part of it—the employee benefits by being able to participate at relatively low group rates.

Providing healthcare coverage is optional for employers. Hawaii is the sole exception. Its Prepaid Healthcare Act (§393-1 and following of the Hawaii Statutes) requires employers to provide coverage to every employee who earns a monthly wage of at least 86.67 times that state's minimum wage—$5.25 an hour.

1. Types of Coverage

Traditionally, employers who have provided healthcare coverage have done so through an indemnity or reimbursement plan which pays the doctor or hospital directly, or reimburses the employee for medical expenses he or she has already paid. Blue Cross/Blue Shield is a traditional type of plan.

While traditional coverage allowing employees to seek out their preferred medical provider is still widely used, a growing number of employers today provide coverage through the alternatives of a health maintenance organization (HMO) or a preferred provider organization (PPO).

An HMO is comprised of hospitals and doctors who provide specified medical services to employees for a fixed monthly fee. Within the HMO service area, covered employees must use the HMO hospitals and doctors unless it's an emergency or they receive permission to go elsewhere.

A PPO is a network of hospitals and doctors who agree to provide medical care for specified fees. Often the network is put together by an insurance company that also administers it. Employees usually can choose between using the network's hospitals and doctors or going elsewhere.

2. Making the Best Choice

If you choose to provide health insurance coverage to employees, explore all the alternatives: group health insurance policies, HMOs and PPOs. Until you compare, you won't know which arrangement will be least costly to both your business and the employee.

Under some plans, employees pay for a portion of their medical expenses—usually called copayments. The theory is that employees will seek only essential treatment if they're paying some of the cost.

Your business must decide on who will pay the monthly, quarterly or semi-annual premium for healthcare coverage. Among the choices for who pays the tab:

- Your business can pick up the full amount.
- You can split the cost of premiums with the employee—perhaps paying 80% and having the employee pick up the other 20% through a pay-check deduction.
- You can pay in full for the employee's coverage, but require the employee to pay the extra cost of covering his or her dependents.
- You can require the employee to pay the entire charge—although that won't be perceived as much of a benefit by the employee even though the group plan will undoubtedly be cheaper than individual coverage.

Another way to shift some costs to the employee is through a deductible plan which requires the employee to pay a specified amount of medical bills each year—$500 for example—before the plan's coverage kicks in.

Consider Flexible Coverage Arrangements

Depending on where your business is located and the number of employees in it, you may be able to offer several different choices of coverage to employees. For example, some employers opt to pay 100% of coverage under an HMO. If their particular HMO doesn't require all employees to join, some employers allow those employees who wish to do so to buy their own coverage. Then the employers reimburse them at the HMO rate. Depending on the required co-payments, deductibles and other plan features, employees who select a different plan may pay a bit more or less than the HMO rate.

You should decide, too, whether to cover employees who work parttime. You might, for example, provide full benefits for those who work 30 hours or more per week, and prorated benefits for those who work at least 20 hours but less than 30. Such an approach may help you qualify for cheaper group rates.

Children May Have Rights, Too

If you have a group healthcare plan, a child of a divorced employee may have a right to coverage—even if the child doesn't live with the employee or isn't a financial dependent of the employee. An employee's child will be covered if a domestic relations settlement agreement or a court order requires such healthcare coverage and contains specific information required by ERISA. If you receive a copy of such a settlement agreement or court order and are unsure about what to do, check with the plan administrator or an employee benefits lawyer.

3. Coverage Limitations

The Americans With Disabilities Act (ADA) is designed to eliminate workplace discrimination against people with disabilities. (See Chapter 9.) The ADA doesn't require you to offer healthcare benefits to employees, but it does require you to give people with disabilities the same healthcare benefits you offer to others. If your business is covered by the ADA, you may not deny insurance coverage or limit benefits based on a worker's disability.

Your plan will usually violate the ADA if it excludes specific disabilities, such as deafness, AIDS or schizophrenia. Similarly, it's generally illegal to exclude groups of disabilities—for example, cancers, muscular dystrophy and kidney diseases—or to exclude all conditions that substantially limit a major life activity.

Some insurance restrictions that may at first seem to discriminate against disabled workers are allowed under the ADA.

a. Physical condition restrictions

Healthcare plans often provide more liberal benefits for treating physical conditions than for treating mental and nervous conditions. Similarly, some plans provide fewer benefits for eyecare than for other physical conditions. These broad distinctions are allowed by the ADA. They may have greater impact on some people with disabilities, but they're not intentionally discriminatory.

b. Preexisting conditions

There are limits on your ability to offer a healthcare plan that doesn't cover preexisting conditions. A healthcare plan will violate the ADA if it excludes specific preexisting conditions such as blood disorders. In EEOC parlance, such exclusions are "disability based" and therefore not permissible.

A healthcare portability law that takes effect in mid-1997 further limits your right to provide coverage that excludes preexisting conditions. Under the new legislation, a healthcare plan can exclude coverage for preexisting conditions for only 12 months. And if a new employee had 12 months of coverage under his or her prior employer's health plan, then your health plan—if you offer one—can't exclude coverage based on the employee's preexisting condition.

c. Treatment restrictions

A plan that doesn't cover experimental drugs or treatment or that excludes elective surgery doesn't violate the ADA. Similarly, it's not a violation to put a monetary cap on certain types of treatment—for example, to limit payments for X-rays or blood transfusions—even though such a cap may adversely affect people with certain disabilities.

The U.S. Equal Employment Opportunitys Commission (EEOC)—the agency that enforces the ADA—has issued guidelines to help employers determine if a healthcare plan meets the ADA requirements. To order the *Interim Enforcement Guidance on the Application of the ADA to Disability Based Provisions of Employer Provided Health Insurance,* call 800/669-3362.

DISCRIMINATION IN GROUP HEALTH PLANS

Under federal law, a group health plan can't discriminate in eligibilty for coverage or premiums based on an employee's:

- health status
- medical condition
- claims experience
- medical history
- genetic information
- evidence of insurability, or
- disability.

This list applies to the employee's dependents as well.

But the law doesn't require a group plan to cover any given procedure—and a group plan may limit the level of benefits it provides, as long as the plan doesn't discriminate among similarly situated employees.

---

4. Continuing Coverage for Former Employees

A federal law called the Consolidated Omnibus Budget Reconciliation Act or COBRA (29 U.S.C. §1162) applies to your business if you have 20 or more employees and you offer a group healthcare plan. If COBRA applies to your business, you must offer employees and former employees the option of continuing their healthcare coverage if their coverage is lost or reduced because:

- their employment has been terminated for any reason—except gross misconduct
- their hours have been reduced, or
- they've become eligible for Medicare.

Members of the employee's family must also be given the opportunity to continue their coverage. The chart below depicts the circumstances—qualifying events—that trigger an employer's obligation to allow continuing healthcare coverage under a group plan. COBRA gives rights to different people, depending on the qualifying event. How long the benefits must be continued is determined by the qualifying event and whether the covered employee is disabled.

CONTINUING COVERAGE FOR FORMER EMPLOYEES

Qualifying Event	People Entitled to Continue Coverage	How Long
The employee quits or retires	Employee, spouse, dependents	18 months; 29 months for disabled worker
You fire or lay off the employee for reasons other than gross misconduct	Employee, spouse, dependents	18 months; 29 months for disabled worker
You reduce the employee's hours so he or she loses coverage	Employee, spouse, dependents	18 months; 29 months for disabled worker
The employee dies	Surviving spouse, dependents	36 months
The employee divorces or becomes legally separated	Former spouse, dependents	36 months
The employee goes on Medicare	Spouse, dependents	36 months
A dependent loses coverage through marriage or age	Dependent	36 months

The employee must pay for continuing coverage under COBRA, including both your share and the employee's share. You can charge 102% of the premium cost—using the extra 2% to cover administrative costs. The cost to the employee or the employee's family for continuing coverage must be similar to the cost of covering people still on your payroll.

COBRA covers HMO and PPO plans in addition to traditional group insurance plans. COBRA also covers all other types of medical benefits, including dental and vision care and plans under which an employer reimburses employees for medical expenses.

If your business is covered by COBRA and has a group healthcare plan, the plan administrator—the person who handles the plan's paperwork— must give employees and their spouses a written explanation of their COBRA rights when they first become eligible to participate in the plan. A single notice can be sent to an employee and spouse if they live at the same address. Otherwise, the spouse is entitled to a separate notice.

Help Is Available

Small businesses usually find it convenient to let the insurance company serve as the plan administrator and coordinate COBRA notices. The insurance company can provide even more help and information, including a clear explanation of how the plan meets the requirements of COBRA and similar state laws. Any reputable company should be able to provide clear, concise explanatory materials that you can hand out to your employees and, if asked, may send representatives to conduct training seminars and answer employee questions.

When a qualifying event occurs that gives an employee or family member the right to continue coverage, you must notify the plan administrator within 30 days. The plan administrator then has 14 days to notify the beneficiaries of their rights under COBRA. These beneficiaries have 60 days following the notice to let you know if they want to continue their coverage.

If so, the employee or eligible family member sends you the premium each month and you send it on to the insurance company. If the beneficiaries don't send the payment when due—or within the grace period—you can cut off coverage.

Several states also have laws giving former employees the right to continue group healthcare insurance coverage after leaving a job. These state laws generally require continuation of healthcare plans that provide benefits through an insurance company such as Blue Cross/Blue Shield. They don't, however, require continuation of a self-insured plan—even one that's administered by a commercial insurance provider. Some of these laws cover smaller employers than COBRA does. (See the chart below.)

STATE HEALTH INSURANCE CONTINUATION LAWS

This is a synopsis of state laws that give you the right to continue group health insurance after leaving the employment of the company sponsoring the insurance.

Arkansas	Former employees and their dependents have the right to continue group insurance coverage for 120 days after the coverage would have ended because of a change in employment status. Ark. Stat. Ann. §23-86-114
California	Former employees and their dependents, including widows and widowers and divorced spouses, have the right to continue group insurance coverage for 90 days after termination. Cal. Health & Safety Code §§1373.62 and 1373.6
Colorado	Former employees who were terminated and had been covered for at least three months by group health insurance and their dependents have the right to continue that coverage 90 days or until re-employed, whichever comes first. Colo. Rev. Stat. §10-8-116
Connecticut	Former employees and their eligible dependents have the right to continue group health insurance for 78 weeks after the coverage would have ended, or until they are covered by another group plan, whichever comes first. Conn. Gen. Stat. §38-262d
Florida	Former employees who were terminated and had been covered by group health insurance for at least three months and their eligible dependents have the right to covert the coverage to an individual policy. Fla. Stat. §627.6675

Georgia	Former employees and their eligible dependents who have been covered by group health insurance have the right to continue coverage for three months after the end of employment. Ga. Code Ann. §33-24-21.1
Illinois	Former employees who were terminated and had been covered by group health insurance for at least three months have the right to continue group coverage unless they are covered by another group plan. Ill. Stat. Ann. ch. 73 §979e
Iowa	Former employees who were terminated have the right to continue group health insurance for nine months, but some types of coverage such as prescription drug benefits are excluded. Iowa Code Ann. §509B.3
Kansas	Former employees have the right to continue group health insurance for six months after the end of employment. Kan. Stat. Ann. §40-2209
Kentucky	Former employees who had been covered by group health insurance for at least three months have the right to continue that coverage for nine months. Ky. Rev. Stat. Ann. §304.18-110
Louisiana	A former employee's surviving spouse who is 50 years old or older can continue group health coverage. La. Civ. Code Ann. art. 22, §215.7
Maine	Former employees who have been covered by group health insurance for six months and have been terminated because of layoff or work-related injury or occupational disease can continue group coverage. Me. Rev. Stat. Ann. tit. 24-A, §2809-A
Maryland	Former employees who were involuntarily terminated and had been covered by group health insurance for at least three months have the right to continue that coverage. Md. Ann. Code Art. 48A, §§354FF, 477GG, 477K and 490G
Massachusetts	Former employees and their dependents may continue group health insurance for 31 days. If employment was terminated by plant closing, then insurance may be continued for 90 days. If employment ended by layoff or death, then insurance may be continued for 39 weeks. Mass. Gen. Laws Ann. ch. 175 §110G; ch. 176A, §8D; ch. 176B, §6A; ch. 176G, §4A
Minnesota	Former employees who quit or were terminated for reasons other than gross misconduct have the right to continue group health coverage for themselves and their families for 12 months after it would otherwise end or until they become covered by another group plan, whichever comes first. Minn. Stat. Ann. §62A.17

Missouri	Former employees who have been covered by a group health plan for at least three months have the right to continue that insurance for up to nine months after it would otherwise end. Mo. Ann. Stat. §376.428
Nebraska	Former employees are entitled to continue group health insurance for six months after employment ends unless termination was due to employee misconduct. Neb. Rev. Stat. §44-1633.
Nevada	Former employees who have been covered by a group health plan for at least three months are entitled to continue coverage for 18 months unless terminated for misconduct. Eligible dependents are entitled to continue coverage for 36 months. No coverage if employee voluntarily quits. Nev. Rev. Stat. Ann. §§689B.245 and 689B.246
New Hampshire	Former employees and eligible dependents are entitled to group health plan continuation if employee is terminated or dies, unless the termination is for misconduct or is for less than six months. Coverage continues for 29 months if termination is due to disability, 36 months for spouse upon separation or divorce or if employee dies, and 18 months in all other situations. N. H. Rev. Stat. Ann. §415.18
New Jersey	Former employees are entitled to continuation of group health coverage if termination is due to total disability and they have been covered for three months. N.J. Stat. Ann. §17B:27-51-12
New York	Former employees have the right to continue group health coverage for up to six months after date of termination. N.Y. Ins. Law §3221
New Mexico	Former employees have the right to continue group health insurance coverage for up to six months after it would otherwise end. Covered family members may convert to individual policies upon the former employee's death or divorce. N.M. Stat. Ann. §59-18-16(A)
North Carolina	Former employees and their eligible dependents are entitled to continue group health plan coverage for three months if they have been covered by the plan for at least three months. N. C. Gen. Stat. §58-53-35
North Dakota	Former employees who had been covered by group health insurance for at least three months have the right to continue that coverage. N.D. Cent. Code §26.1-36-23
Ohio	Former employees who were terminated involuntarily have the right to continue group health insurance coverage for six months after termination. Ohio Rev. Code. Ann. §1737.30

Oklahoma	Former employees are entitled to continue group health coverage for 30 days after termination. If the employee has been covered by the plan for at least six months and is suffering from a continuing medical condition, then basic medical coverage continues for three months and major medical coverage continues for six months. Okla. Stat. Ann. tit. 40, §§172 and 173
Oregon	Former employees and eligible dependents who have been covered by a group health insurance plan for at least three months are entitled to continuation of coverage for six months after the end of employment. Or. Rev. Stat. §742.850
Rhode Island	Former employees who were terminated due to an involuntary layoff or death have the right to continue group health insurance coverage for themselves and their dependents for up to 18 months after it would otherwise end. R.I. Gen. Laws §27-19.1-1
South Carolina	Former employees who have been covered by group health plan for at least three months are entitled to continue coverage after employment ends for one month. S.C. Code Ann. §38-45-946
South Dakota	Former employees and their dependents who have been covered by a group health insurance plan for at least six months have the right to continue that coverage for up to 18 months after it would otherwise end. S.D. Codified Laws Ann. §58-18-7.5
Tennessee	Former employees who had been covered by group health insurance for at least three months have the right to continue that coverage for up to three months after it would otherwise end. The employee is required to pay the premium in advance. Tenn. Code Ann. §56-7-1501
Texas	Former employees who have been covered by a group health insurance plan for at least three months and who are not terminated for cause are entitled to continue coverage for six months. Tex. Rev. Civ. Stat. Ann. art. 3.51-6
Utah	Former employees who have been covered by a group health insurance plan for at least six months are entitled to continue coverage for two months after end of employment. Utah Code Ann. § 31A-22-703
Vermont	Former employees who have been covered by a group health insurance plan for at least three months are entitled to continue such coverage unless terminated for misconduct. Vt. Stat. Ann. tit. 3, §§4090a through 4090g

Virginia	Former employees who have been covered by a group health insurance plan for at least three months may either continue coverage for 90 days after employment ends or convert to an individual policy at the employer's option. Va. Code Ann. §38.2-1541
Washington	Former employees are entitled to continue group health insurance benefits for a period of time and at a rate that employer and employee have agreed upon. Wash. Rev. Code Ann. §§48.21.250 through 48.21.270
West Virginia	Former employees who have been involuntarily laid off are entitled to continue group health benefits for 18 months. W.Va. Code §33-16-3
Wisconsin	Former employees who had been covered by group health insurance for at least three months have the right to continue coverage or convert it to an individual policy, unless they were fired for misconduct. If the former employee chooses group coverage, it will continue indefinitely and cannot be terminated unless the former employee moves out of state or becomes eligible for similar coverage. Wis. Stat. §632.897

Adapted from *Your Rights in the Workplace,* by Barbara Kate Repa (Nolo Press).

5. Reducing Costs

Small businesses often feel overwhelmed by the spiraling costs of providing healthcare benefits to employees. But there are some steps you can take that may hold down costs, mostly by eliminating unnecessary medical expenses.

Look for a healthcare plan that practices managed care—requiring participants to get a second opinion before they have surgery or requiring pre-approval by the insurance company for expensive diagnostic procedures.

Requiring employees to pay a part of the monthly coverage fee as well as a portion of each medical bill may encourage employees to be judicious in seeking treatment.

Look into offering coverage through a Health Maintenance Organization (HMO) or Preferred Provider Organization (PPO) instead of traditional insurance or reimbursement coverage. But be sure to shop around to see if the overall cost of a PPO or HMO plan is really lower than traditional coverage.

Money put into preventive care is well spent. You can, for example, call in experts to teach employees the benefits of a healthy diet, exercise and preventive care. Beyond that, you can set a good example by making low-fat food available in your lunchroom and installing exercise equipment in an unused area of the workplace. Also consider paying for seminars to help employees quit smoking and encourage periodic physical checkups—perhaps offering to pay part of the usual deductible payment.

6. Medical Savings Accounts

A new and intriguing addition to the line-up of tax-favored employee benefits is the medical savings account (MSA)—part of a pilot project lasting through the year 2000. You can offer this benefit only if your business is relatively small—meaning 50 or fewer employees at first, but increasing to as many as 200 as the program gets rolling.

The MSA program offers tax advantages for employees whose sole health coverage is a high-deductible catastrophic health plan; employees can't also be covered by basic health insurance with small deductibles and co-pay requirements.

To give employees the benefit of this program, you can pay the premium on a catastrophic health insurance policy that meets these guidelines:

• The deductible must range from $1,500 to $2,250 for individuals and from $3,000 to $4,500 for family coverage.
• Co-payments can't exceed $3,000 for individuals and $5,500 for family coverage.

These amounts will be indexed for inflation after 1998.

Once the catastrophic policy is in place, you can make a tax-free contribution each year to the employee's MSA of up to 65% of the deductible for an individual or 75% for a family. If you offer the MSA benefit, you must do so for all eligible employees.

The employee can use his or her MSA to pay for medical expenses not covered by the catastrophic insurance.

Example: Radiant Corporation, a company employing 45 people, buys a catastrophic health insurance policy for each of its employees. For Stan, who has a family, the deductible is $4,000. Radiant contributes $3,000 to Stan's MSA. Stan's wife is injured in a car accident and incurs $10,000 in medical expenses. Stan's MSA pays $3,000 of the deductible; Stan uses $1,000 from his bank account to pay the rest. The $3,000 that Radiant paid into Stan's MSA is a tax-deductible business expense for Radiant and is tax-free to Stan.

Unused money stays in the employee's MSA, earning tax-free income. For younger employees, there are penalties if money is removed for purposes other than medical care, but at age 65, an employee can remove the balance in his or her account for any reason, without penalty. During the test period, the program will be available only to the first 750,000 participants each year.

COVERAGE FOR PREGNANT WOMEN AND OLDER WORKERS

Federal law provides some special insurance requirements for pregnant women and older workers.

Women. You must treat women affected by pregnancy and related conditions the same as other employees based on their ability or inability to work. For example, if a woman can't work because she's pregnant, you must provide her with the same healthcare coverage as you generally provide to employees who become ill or have a disability. (See Chapter 8, Section D for more on the Pregnancy Discrimination Act.) The Family and Medical Leave Act allows workers to take up to 12 weeks a year of unpaid leave connected with childbirth, adoption and foster placement. (See Chapter 6.)

Older Workers. You must offer workers age 40 and older the same healthcare coverage you offer to younger workers—and, if your plan requires that all your workers be covered, you can't make older workers pay more to join. But if the insurance isn't mandatory, older workers can be charged more, so long as actuarial charts show their healthcare costs are higher.

B. Retirement Plans

Retirement plans provide income to older people when they're no longer part of the workforce. If the plans you offer meet certain IRS guidelines, your contribution to the benefits qualifies as a business expense and is deductible from your company's gross income.

1. Defined Benefit Plans

In a defined benefit plan, you promise to pay an employee a fixed amount of money, usually in monthly increments, after he or she retires. You may base the payments on a formula that combines the number of years the employee has worked and the amount of his or her earnings. You may also choose some other method of setting the timing and amount, such as a fixed monthly sum not tied to length of service or earnings.

To fund a defined benefit plan, you typically invest money in stocks, bonds and mutual funds that you expect will grow over the years. You must contribute enough to the plan to pay the promised benefit. Otherwise, you'll have to make up the difference if the plan's investments go bad.

2. Defined Contribution Plans

In a defined contribution plan, you set up an account for the employee and contribute to it. At retirement, the employee gets whatever is in the account. You don't promise that the employee will receive a specific amount of income after retirement.

You may structure the defined contribution plan as a money purchase pension plan, in which case you'll promise to contribute a specific amount per employee each year, such as five cents for each hour worked. Or you may structure it as a profit sharing plan in which you have the discretion to decide each year how much to contribute, with your contributions allocated to the employees' accounts in a specified way—usually in proportion to their pay. In either case, the size of the pension checks an employee receives each month after retirement will vary according to the interest rate paid on the employee's pension account and other economic factors.

KEEP IT SIMPLE

Retirement plans seem to thrive on paperwork and complexity—not a pleasant prospect if you're running a small business.

So take a close look at simplified employee pensions, or SEPs, which can eliminate much of the pain and drudgery. A SEP is basically an individual retirement account (IRA) that you fund for each employee. To make things easier, you can set up your SEP with a respected mutual fund group such as Fidelity or Vanguard. Employees can choose the particular mutual funds they want in their accounts, using the dollars you contribute annually. Each year, you can contribute an amount equal to up to 15% of an employee's pay—but you can't contribute more than $22,500 for any one employee.

Another option, if you employ 100 or fewer people, is the Savings Incentive Match Plan for Employees, or SIMPLE. An employee can put up to $6,000 a year of salary into a SIMPLE IRA account; taxes on the amount paid in are deferred. You must contribute, too. You can match the employee's contribution—dollar for dollar—up to 3% of the employee's compensation. Or if you prefer, you can match contributions for all eligible employees at a rate lower than 3% of each employee's compensation, but no lower than 1%. Employees who earn more than $5,000 a year must be allowed to participate in the SIMPLE plan. Additional rules apply. Whether SIMPLE is simple is a matter of opinion.

3. 401(k) Plans

A 401(k) plan consists of a retirement account for each employee who participates. An employer can choose whether or not to make contributions, and how extensive those contributions will be. You might, for example, choose to contribute only if company profits reach a certain level or to match contributions of only the lower paid employees. You can contribute an amount equal to up to 15% of an employee's salary to an employee's 401(k) account, but your contribution can't exceed $22,500 a year.

But whether or not you contribute to the 401(k) plan, it still constitutes a valuable benefit to employees because it helps them save for retirement with tax-deferred dollars. If you set up an employee funded 401(k) plan, employees can defer the income tax on the money they stash away, which allows their investments to grow faster.

A typical plan, administered by a major mutual fund company, calls for regular payroll deductions of from 1% to 15% of an employee's earnings, as specified by the employee. To comply with the tax laws in 1996, the employee's contribution can't exceed $9,500 a year. The limits are adjusted periodically for inflation. The employee gets to allocate his or her account among several different mutual funds—and to change the mix from time to time. The funds on the menu run the gamut from conservative to aggressive, so the employee can choose the level of risk with which he or she feels most comfortable. Be aware, however, that it may cost you a few thousand dollars to set up a 401(k) plan for your business—and there may be ongoing expenses for plan administration. (See Section 4b below.)

Special Protection for Older Employees

The federal Age Discrimination in Employment Act (29 U.S.C. §621) generally prohibits you from providing reduced benefits to older people in your retirement plan. But the Act does allow for some lesser coverage for certain benefits, such as health and disability insurance, if you can show there's a rational cost reason for doing it.

4. Meeting IRS and ERISA Requirements

For your contributions to a retirement plan to be tax deductible as a business expense, you must meet the requirements of the Internal Revenue Code. You must comply with the Employee Retirement Income Security Act or ERISA (29 U.S.C. §1001 and following), which is intended to protect the rights of employees.

a. Tax law requirements

While you don't have to include all workers in your retirement plan, you can't structure the plan to benefit only the top executives or to otherwise discriminate against lower paid workers. A retirement plan that passes muster with the IRS is called a qualified plan—meaning your contribution qualifies as a tax deductible business expense. Your contributions won't be taxed as income to employees until they actually receive the benefit. The IRS will review a proposed plan and let you know if it meets the tax law requirements.

For a helpful introduction to these requirements, see IRS Publication 535, *Business Expenses,* available at no charge from the nearest IRS office.

GETTING HELP WITH THE TECHNICALITIES

The usual and safest way to make sure your pension plan meets ERISA and tax law requirements is to seek assistance from a qualified expert—perhaps a lawyer or CPA experienced in pension plan matters. But that may be expensive, especially for a smaller business.

As an alternative, try contacting a few insurance companies and other groups that handle 401(k) and other benefit plans. They'll provide much information at no cost and will crunch numbers for you so you'll know the best way to structure the plan so that most employees can participate.

In addition to resolving technical problems, benefit providers may offer seminars to help your employees make sound investment choices.

b. Administration requirements

Under ERISA, you'll need to appoint a plan administrator—someone who is responsible for following through on the law's paperwork requirements. This can be a person in your business or an outsider who's associated with the retirement plan. If you have a relatively small business, it may be simpler and cheaper to have an outsider—such as a worker at a bank or mutual fund company—act as plan administrator. It's difficult to develop enough expertise within your business to meet all the legal requirements that affect retirement plans.

The ERISA requirements are heavy on paperwork. There are a number of documents your plan administrator must give to participating employees.

Summary plan description. This is a booklet that describes how your plan operates. Your plan administrator must give employees the summary plan description within 90 days after they begin participating in the plan. Employees are also entitled to plan updates. The description must include the formula for determining an employee's benefits or the contributions that you'll make to the plan. It must also explain any formula for vesting—the point at which the employee's right to retirement benefits becomes locked in and can't be taken away.

Summary annual report. This is a yearly accounting of the plan's financial condition and operations.

Survivor coverage data. This is a statement of how much the plan will pay to the surviving spouse of an employee if the employee dies.

In addition, each year the plan administrator must give participants a detailed, individual statement of the benefits they've earned. And you must annually file with the IRS a Form 5500, which includes a census of employees and participants and is accompanied by summary financial reports.

c. Plan termination requirements

If you decide to terminate a defined benefit plan—one which promises specific benefits—you must notify covered employees of the approaching termination at least 60 days before the plan ends.

If you decide to reduce the rate of benefit accruals or terminate either a defined benefit plan or a money purchase plan, you must notify covered employees after you amend the plan and at least 15 days before the amendment takes effect.

Former Spouses' Retirement Benefit Rights

In many divorces, an employee's retirement benefits are divided as part of the property settlement. The spouse of an employee may acquire rights under what ERISA calls a qualified domestic relations order (QDRO). When that happens, your company has ERISA obligations to the employee's spouse similar to your obligations to the employee. This includes reviewing the court order to see if it meets the requirements for a QDRO, paying out money to the spouse as required by the order and giving the spouse plan information if benefits aren't paid to the spouse immediately.

WHO'S IN—AND WHO'S OUT

You don't have a completely free hand in deciding who to include in a retirement plan. In general, ERISA requires you to include everyone who:

• is 21 years old or older, and
• has worked for your business for a year—1,000 or more hours in the last 12 months.

You can require employees to be with your company for two years before they will be eligible to participate in the plan. But if you do, you must also provide that an employee's rights become fully vested as soon as he or she begins participating in the plan.

C. Other Employee Benefits

Here's a rundown of several other benefit programs that the IRS recognizes as tax-deductible business expenses.

1. Life Insurance

One of the least expensive benefits you can offer to employees is group term life insurance. This is life insurance that pays off only if the employee dies during the policy term—usually 5, 10 or 20 years. You can deduct the premiums you pay for up to $50,000 of group term life insurance for each employee. And employees don't pay tax on the premiums you pay.

But to qualify for this tax treatment, the group insurance plan can't be discriminatory, meaning it can't be weighted in favor of highly paid employees.

Encourage Employees to Participate

Some employers pay for the first $10,000 or so of term life coverage, giving the employee the option of buying additional coverage under the same group plan. This allows employers to offer a growing benefit without having to put out a growing outlay of cash.

In selecting a group insurance policy, look for one that allows a terminated employee to switch to an individual policy without having to prove that he or she is still insurable. Of course, after such a conversion, a former employee becomes responsible for paying the premiums.

2. Disability Insurance

Consider offering disability insurance to help employees offset income lost if they suffer a serious injury or illness. You can probably find a group policy under which you pay part of the premium and the employee pays part. Some plans give employees the option of continuing their coverage after they leave your business. They then become responsible for the entire premium.

Your business can take a tax deduction for the premiums it pays, but if an employee receives payments under the insurance policy, the employee will owe income tax on those payments. If the employer and employee each pay part of the premium, the employee will owe income tax on part of the payments received.

3. Educational Assistance Programs

You may want to pay all or part of the cost of schooling that employees pursue outside working hours. You can set up a written plan with guidelines for the type of continuing education your business will finance, how much you're willing to spend and the point at which you'll reimburse an employee for tuition.

Under such a plan, you can deduct as a business expense up to $5,250 per year for the educational costs you pay for an employee—and these costs are not included in the employee's taxable income.

A few restrictions apply.

- The education assistance program can't favor high paid employees or their spouses or dependents.
- No more than 5% of the program's payments during a year can be used to benefit a business's shareholders or owners—or their spouses or dependents.
- You can't offer employees a choice between receiving the educational assistance or other payment that's includable in the employees' gross income.
- Assistance can't be used for courses involving sports, games or hobbies, or for graduate level education—courses, for example, leading to an advanced degree in law, business or medicine.

This tax break is scheduled to expire for tax years beginning May 31, 1997 and after. For tax years beginning in 1997, this employee benefit applies only to courses that start before July 1, 1997.

4. Dependent Care Assistance

The tax laws let your business deduct expenses you pay for assistance to employees who must care for their dependents—a major concern today with more workers having to take care of young children, aging parents, or both.

Your payments qualify for the tax deduction if they enable an employee to care for:

- a dependent age 12 or younger for whom the employee can claim a personal exemption
- a dependent who's physically or mentally incapable of taking care of himself or herself, or

- the employee's spouse if the spouse can't take care of himself or herself.

The amounts you deduct can be for bills you pay or money you reimburse to an employee for:

- at-home child care
- in-home care for elderly or disabled adults who live with the employee
- care at a licensed nursery school or kindergarten, or
- care at a dependent care center that provides day care for more than six people.

You can also provide dependent care assistance at your own on-site facility.

Dependent care payments up to $5,000 a year ($2,500 for a married employee filing a separate return) are tax-free to the employee; as noted, your business can deduct these payments as a business expense. For employees with lower household incomes, there's a dependent care tax credit that's more valuable to them than dependent care assistance provided by an employer even though the care the employer provides is not included in the employee's income for tax purposes. If you offer a dependent care plan, let employees know about tax credit alternatives so they can choose the best option.

5. Adoption Assistance Programs

You can assist employees with adoption expenses—up to $5,000 for the adoption of a single child. That limit rises to $6,000 if a state determines that the child has special needs. You'll need to write up an adoption assistance plan and make sure it meets requirements similar to the ones that apply to educational assistance programs. (See Section C3.)

With such a plan in place, you can deduct your payments for adoption expenses as a business expense. If an employee's tax return shows adjusted gross income of $75,000 or less, the employee can exclude the amounts you pay for adoption expenses. Above $75,000 the exclusion is phased out.

This tax break expires at the end of 2001.

CAFETERIA PLANS

Under a cafeteria plan, an employee gets to choose from a menu of
benefits such as:

- health insurance
- dental coverage
- vision care
- disability insurance
- group term life insurance
- group legal services
- additional contribution to a 401(k) plan
- additional paid vacation days, and
- cash.

Typically, the employer provides a monthly allowance to be allocated by the employee. If an employee selects benefits that exceed the
allowance, the additional amount is paid for through payroll deductions. If an employee doesn't use the full allowance, the leftover amount
is added to his or her paycheck.

These plans are attractive because they allow employees to tailor
their benefits to their particular needs, while giving the employer some
control over benefit costs.■

CHAPTER

5

TAXES

As an employer, one of your roles is that of tax collector. The government treats you as an unpaid revenue agent whose job it is to withhold income taxes and Social Security and Medicare taxes from employees' paychecks and to pay over those amounts to the IRS. In addition, Uncle Sam requires you to match employees' Social Security and Medicare taxes and to pay a federal unemployment tax based on your payroll. And Uncle's nieces and nephews in state government also look to you to help rake in their dough.

You must also account to every employee about the taxes you've withheld and the amounts being sent to the government.

Whether you personally handle employee tax matters or turn them over to someone else—a bookkeeper or an accountant—you must understand at least the fundamentals of the system. If you handle taxes incorrectly, you can be hit with interest and penalties. And you may even be held personally liable if your business fails to transmit employee withholdings to the government. The IRS doggedly pursues its targets, so you don't want to get caught in its clutches.

This chapter will help you acquire a good working knowledge of how the tax laws affect you as an employer and how the pieces of the tax system fit together.

Determine your own level of involvement in handling employee taxes and pinpoint whether there are tasks you want to delegate to others.

Fortunately, the IRS puts out some excellent publications to guide you through the process. Relevant IRS publications are noted throughout this chapter.

A parttime bookkeeper can help compile organized, detailed business records with a relatively small involvement of your time. An accountant can help you set up a plan for your bookkeeper to follow and periodically monitor it to ensure that you meet all tax obligations.

A word of caution about one other possible source of assistance: IRS employees. Most of them are hardworking and well-meaning, but their training and supervision are often inadequate. Unfortunately, it's common to receive bad advice in answer to your questions. And if the advice proves to be so inaccurate that it causes you to be assessed interest and penalties, the fact that you got it from an IRS employee won't get you off the hook. In short, it's often cheaper to rely on the advice of an experienced small business accountant than to rely on a free oral opinion from the IRS.

BEWARE OF THE STATE

In addition to being scrupulously mindful of federal payroll taxes, find out whether your state and municipality impose payroll taxes. For example, if your state or city has an income tax, you may be required to withhold taxes from employees' pay much like the federal system—but some states and cities follow different procedures. Contact your state and city treasurers for detailed information.

A. Employer Identification Numbers

When you start your business, get an Employer Identification Number (EIN) from the IRS. You must do this regardless of whether your business is a sole proprietorship, a partnership, an S corporation or a regular corporation—sometimes called a C corporation. Technically, if you're a sole proprietor and have no employees, you can use your personal Social Security number instead of an EIN. But even in that situation, it's a good business practice to get an EIN to differentiate cleanly between your personal and business finances.

1. How to Apply

To get an EIN, file Form SS-4, Application for Employer Identification Number. The instructions tell you where to send the completed form. A completed sample form is shown below.

The form isn't difficult to fill out if you follow the IRS instructions. However, here are a few pointers.

Space 1. Insert your official corporate name if you're a corporation. If you're a partnership, use the partnership name shown in your partnership agreement. If you're a sole proprietor, insert your full name.

Space 11. Here you're asked to state the closing month of your business accounting year. Your answer, however, isn't binding. You make your binding election of a fiscal year-end on the first federal income tax return that you file for the business.

Sole proprietors, partnerships, S corporations and personal service corporations are generally required to use a calendar year—that is, a year ending December 31—for tax purposes. Personal service corporations have two basic characteristics:

- the professional employees of the corporation own the stock, and
- the corporation performs its services in the fields of health, law, engineering, architecture, accounting, actuarial science, performing arts or consulting.

To use a tax year other than a calendar year, an S corporation must demonstrate to the IRS that there is a substantial business reason to do so, such as the seasonal nature of the business. Basically, the IRS wants to make sure that permitting you to claim a tax year other than the calendar year won't substantially distort your income.

See IRS Publication 589, *Tax Information on S Corporations* and IRS Publication 538, *Business Purpose Tax Year* for details.

A regular corporation that's not a personal service corporation is freer to choose a fiscal year. Most small businesses find that where there's a choice, the calendar year is the most convenient way to proceed. Sometimes, however, there are tax planning reasons for a business owner to choose a different tax year for the business.

An accountant or other experienced tax advisor can help you decide whether or not you and your corporation can realize a tax advantage by using a fiscal year instead of a calendar year.

Space 12. The IRS will send you computer-generated payroll tax forms based on your answer to this question.

Space 13. These numbers can be estimated.

Space 17a. This question refers to the business, not the owner. Normally, a partnership or corporation has only one Employer Identification Number (EIN). A sole proprietor may have several businesses, each with a separate number.

You'll need your EIN before you file a tax return or make a tax deposit. In some cases, a bank will require you to have an EIN before you open a business account.

There are three ways to obtain the number.

- **By mail.** If you have enough lead time, you can mail Form SS-4 to the IRS and wait for the number to be mailed to you, which will take about four weeks.
- **By telephone.** To get a Form SS-4 processed more quickly, use the TELE-TIN system operated by the IRS. Complete the form and, before you mail it, phone in the information to the IRS at the telephone number given for your region, as listed in the form's instruction sheet. An IRS employee will assign you an EIN, which you'll then write in the upper right corner of the form before sending it to the IRS.
- **By fax.** You can fax your IRS Form SS-4. To obtain the fax number, ask at the IRS office where you pick up your Form SS-4. You'll get your EIN

in a day or two. This is slower than the telephone method, but it avoids the frustration of repeated calling if the TELE-TIN voice line is tied up.

Use your EIN on all business tax returns, checks and other documents you send to the IRS. Your state tax authority may also require your EIN on state tax forms.

2. When to Get a New Number

If your S corporation chooses to change to a regular corporation—or your regular corporation chooses to change to an S corporation—it doesn't need a new EIN; the one you already have is still sufficient. However, you'll need to get a new EIN if any of these changes occur in your business:

- You incorporate your sole proprietorship or partnership.
- Your sole proprietorship takes in partners and begins operating as a partnership.
- Your partnership is taken over by one of the partners and begins operating as a sole proprietorship.
- Your corporation changes to a partnership or to a sole proprietorship.
- You purchase or inherit an existing business that you'll operate as a sole proprietorship.
- You represent an estate that operates a business after the owner's death.
- You terminate an old partnership and begin a new one.

SAMPLE APPLICATION FORM

Form **SS-4** (Rev. December 1993) Department of the Treasury Internal Revenue Service	**Application for Employer Identification Number** (For use by employers, corporations, partnerships, trusts, estates, churches, government agencies, certain individuals, and others. See instructions.)	EIN OMB No. 1545-0003 Expires 12-31-96

Please type or print clearly.

1 Name of applicant (Legal name) (See instructions.)
Ted Anderson

2 Trade name of business, if different from name in line 1
The Poster Warehouse

3 Executor, trustee, "care of" name

4a Mailing address (street address) (room, apt., or suite no.)
555 Main Street

5a Business address, if different from address in lines 4a and 4b

4b City, state, and ZIP code
Ann Arbor, MI 48104

5b City, state, and ZIP code

6 County and state where principal business is located
Washtenaw

7 Name of principal officer, general partner, grantor, owner, or trustor—SSN required (See instructions.) ▶   555-55-5555
Ted Anderson

8a Type of entity (Check only one box.) (See instructions.)
☒ Sole Proprietor (SSN) 555 55 5555
☐ REMIC
☐ State/local government
☐ Other nonprofit organization (specify) _____
☐ Other (specify) ▶
☐ Estate (SSN of decedent)_____
☐ Plan administrator-SSN _____
☐ Personal service corp.
☐ National guard
☐ Other corporation (specify) _____
☐ Federal government/military
(enter GEN if applicable) _____
☐ Trust
☐ Partnership
☐ Farmers' cooperative
☐ Church or church controlled organization

8b If a corporation, name the state or foreign country (if applicable) where incorporated ▶   State | Foreign country

9 Reason for applying (Check only one box.)
☒ Started new business (specify) ▶ retail
☐ Hired employees
☐ Created a pension plan (specify type) ▶
☐ Banking purpose (specify) ▶
☐ Changed type of organization (specify) ▶ _____
☐ Purchased going business
☐ Created a trust (specify) ▶ _____
☐ Other (specify) ▶

10 Date business started or acquired (Mo., day, year) (See instructions.)
August 1, 19xx

11 Enter closing month of accounting year. (See instructions.)
December

12 First date wages or annuities were paid or will be paid (Mo., day, year). Note: If applicant is a withholding agent, enter date income will first be paid to nonresident alien. (Mo., day, year) ▶   September 1, 19xx

13 Enter highest number of employees expected in the next 12 months. Note: If the applicant does not expect to have any employees during the period, enter "0." ▶

Nonagricultural	Agricultural	Household
1	0	0

14 Principal activity (See instructions.) ▶ Sale of posters

15 Is the principal business activity manufacturing? . . . . ☐ Yes ☒ No
If "Yes," principal product and raw material used ▶

16 To whom are most of the products or services sold? Please check the appropriate box.   ☐ Business (wholesale)
☒ Public (retail)   ☐ Other (specify) ▶   ☐ N/A

17a Has the applicant ever applied for an identification number for this or any other business? . . . . ☐ Yes ☒ No
Note: If "Yes," please complete lines 17b and 17c.

17b If you checked the "Yes" box in line 17a, give applicant's legal name and trade name, if different than name shown on prior application.

Legal name ▶ | Trade name ▶

17c Enter approximate date, city, and state where the application was filed and the previous employer identification number if known.
Approximate date when filed (Mo., day, year) | City and state where filed | Previous EIN

Under penalties of perjury, I declare that I have examined this application, and to the best of my knowledge and belief, it is true, correct, and complete. | Business telephone number (include area code)

Name and title (Please type or print clearly.) ▶ Ted Anderson, Owner | (313) 555-5555

Signature ▶ *Ted Anderson* | Date ▶ July 14, 19xx

Note: Do not write below this line.   For official use only.

Please leave blank ▶	Geo.	Ind.	Class	Size	Reason for applying

For Paperwork Reduction Act Notice, see attached instructions.   Cat. No. 16055N   Form **SS-4** (Rev. 12-93)

B. Federal Employment Taxes

There are several types of employment-related taxes the federal government exacts from businesses.

These taxes are all explained clearly and in great detail in *Circular E, Employer's Tax Guide,* published by the IRS. Updated whenever the tax rates change, *Circular E* is available at all IRS offices and is mailed automatically to all businesses with an EIN.

1. Federal Income Tax Withholding (FIT)

You must withhold income taxes from employees' paychecks based on:
- the filing status (single, married or married but withholding at the higher single rate)
- the number of dependents (withholding allowances) declared by the employee, and
- the size of the employee's salary.

Each employee should give you a signed Form W-4 stating the withholding allowance. Save these forms. You needn't send them to the IRS unless the employee:
- claims more than 10 allowances, or
- claims to be exempt from withholding and also normally earns more than $200 a week.

Use the tables in *Circular E* to figure out how much income tax to withhold.

IRS Publication 334, *Tax Guide for Small Business,* and if you're just getting started, IRS Publication 583, *Taxpayers Starting a Business* are well worth reading. These publications are free from your local IRS office or can be obtained by calling the main IRS number: 800/ 829-3676.

Small-Time Operator by Bernard Kamoroff (Bell Springs Publishing) is a modestly-priced—$16.95—and clearly-written book that covers not only taxes but also many other practical aspects of doing business, including bookkeeping.

U.S. Master Tax Guide (Commerce Clearing House) is updated annually and available in law libraries, business school libraries and the reference departments of major public libraries. It features in-depth explanations of tax complexities.

The Kiplinger Tax Letter, published by the Kiplinger Washington Editors, is a bi-weekly newsletter. It's pricy—$56 for one year—but does keep you up to date on what's happening in the tax field. The breezy—some would say breathless—style is fun to read.

Also, there is software that handles payroll, including tax computations. Look into *QuickPay, OneWrite* and *Peachtree.*

2. Social Security Taxes (FICA)

You must withhold the employee's share of the Social Security tax and Medicare tax from the employee's pay. And you must also pay the employer's share.

The amounts to be withheld are listed in the most current edition of *Circular E.* For 1997, for example, the employer and the employee are each required to pay 7.65% on the first $65,400 of the employee's annual wages; the 7.65% figure is the sum of the 6.2% Social Security tax and the 1.45%

Medicare tax. There is no Social Security tax on the portion of the employee's annual wages that exceed $65,400—only the Medicare tax; the employer and the employee each pay the 1.45% Medicare tax on the excess amount. The rates and the cut-off point for the Social Security tax change annually.

WITHHOLDING FROM AN OWNER'S PAYCHECK

If you own most or all of the stock of a regular corporation, chances are you pay yourself a salary—which means that you're an employee as well as an owner. Similarly, if you're an owner and officer of an S corporation and performing substantial services, you're considered an employee for tax purposes.

With either type of corporation, if you receive compensation for your services, you must complete and submit a Form W-4 to the corporation the same as any other employee, and the corporation must withhold income taxes and Social Security and Medicare taxes from your paychecks.

---

3. Federal Unemployment Taxes (FUTA)

Finally, you must report and pay the federal unemployment tax (FUTA). The employer is responsible for paying this tax; it's not withheld from the employee's pay. The FUTA rate for 1996 was 6.2% of the first $7,000 of the employee's wages for the year. Employers are given a credit for participating in state unemployment programs. In 1996, for example, the credit reduced the FUTA rate to 0.8% for most employers—which translated into $56 for an employee earning $7,000 or more per year. Use Form 940 or 940EZ to report federal unemployment tax. Sole proprietorships and partnerships don't pay the FUTA on the owners' compensation.

4. Periodic Deposits

You must periodically deposit the withheld income tax and the employer's and employee's shares of Social Security taxes at an authorized financial institution—usually a bank. The IRS sends you coupons to use in making these deposits. It also provides instructions on how often you're required to deposit these funds, which depends on the size of your payroll and amounts due; a typical small business makes monthly deposits.

Deposit Taxes on Time

Be sure to withhold taxes as required by the tax laws—and to deposit those taxes on time. There are substantial penalties if you don't. And if you're an owner of a small business and personally involved in its management, you can be held personally liable for these taxes and the additional penalties, even if the business has the funds to pay them. The IRS has discretion to go after whomever it chooses. If your business suddenly runs into financial trouble, put the withheld taxes at the top of the list for payment. If that means not paying suppliers and others, so be it. The debts of the other creditors can be wiped out in bankruptcy if the business continues to go downhill. Not so with the withheld taxes. You can remain personally liable for these amounts even if the business goes through bankruptcy.

Get a copy of IRS Publication 509, *Tax Calendars,* to see when to file returns and make tax payments. It's available from your local IRS office or can be obtained by calling the main IRS number: 800/ 829-3676. The publication is updated annually.

PAYROLL TAXES MADE EASY

If you're overwhelmed by the requirements for calculating payroll taxes and the fine points of when and where to pay them, you can pay a bank or payroll service to do the work for you. A reputable payroll tax service that offers a tax notification service will calculate the correct amount due, produce the checks to pay the employees and the taxes and notify you when the taxes are due.

One big advantage of a payroll service over a bank is that a bank will withhold the amount of the tax from your account when the payroll is done, even though the tax isn't due yet. That means the bank, not you, gets the use of the money for a while. If your payroll service offers tax notification, it will prepare the checks and tell you when they must be deposited. Depending on how often you must make payments, that can give you the use of the money an extra month or more.

At the end of each quarter, the payroll service will produce your quarterly payroll tax returns and instruct you about how to file them. At the end of the year, the service will also prepare W-2 forms and federal and state transmittal forms.

Payroll services can be cost-effective for even very small businesses. But when you look for one, it pays to shop around. Avoid services that charge set-up fees—basically, a fee for putting your information into its computer—or extra fees to prepare W-2 forms or quarterly and annual tax returns.

C. Self-Employment Taxes

The self-employment tax applies to income you receive from actively working in your business—but not as an employee of that business. Technically, it's not an employment tax, but a first cousin to that tax—so closely related that you should be aware of it to fully understand employment taxes.

If you're a sole proprietor or a partner, you must pay the federal self-employment tax in addition to regular income tax. The self-employment tax is equal to the employer's and employee's portion of the Social Security and Medicare taxes that you and your employer would pay on your compensation if you received it as an employee.

Compute this tax each year on Schedule SE, which you then attach to your personal Form 1040. Add the self-employment tax to the income tax that you owe. In 1996, for example, the self-employment tax is set at 15.3% on earnings up to $62,700 and 2.9% on earnings over $62,700.

If you have income from another job that's subject to withholding—common for people just getting started in business—the income from your other job will reduce the tax base for your self-employment tax.

Example: Morton works 3/4 time as a chemistry instructor at a local college, where he receives an annual salary of $45,000. He also does consulting, as a sole proprietor, for several chemical companies and earns an additional $30,000 a year after expenses. The $45,000 salary at the college—which is subject to withholding by the employer—is used to reduce the $62,700 cap on income that's subject to the 15.3% self-employment tax. So Morton computes the tax at the rate of 15.3% on $17,700 of his consulting business income ($62,700 less $45,000 = $17,700). On the remaining portion—$12,300 ($30,000 less $17,700 = $12,300)—he computes the tax at the rate of 2.9%.

COMPUTING YOUR ESTIMATED TAXES

Many taxpayers receive income from sources other than paychecks—for example, from investments and royalties. These taxpayers often owe surprising amounts in income taxes on April 15. Sometimes, that's because they had no employer to withhold income tax during the year. Other times, it's because even though there was an employer, the amounts withheld were insufficient to cover the taxpayer's non-employment income.

As you may know, the IRS doesn't want you to wait until April 15 to pay. Instead, the IRS requires you to pay your taxes in advance in quarterly installments if not enough is being withheld from your salary. This system is known as estimated taxes. If you don't pay sufficient taxes in advance, you face the burden of paying interest and penalties.

In figuring out what your tax bill will be and whether you need to pay any quarterly installments of estimated taxes, don't overlook the self-employment tax which is added to your regular income tax on your Form 1040 as part of your tax obligation. Make sure your quarterly installments are large enough to cover your self-employment tax as well as your usual income tax.

For more on this subject, see IRS Publication 505, *Tax Withholding and Estimated Tax,* available at the nearest IRS office.

D. Tax Deductions for Salaries and Other Expenses

A number of employee-related expenses can be deducted from business income in computing your federal income tax.

1. Salaries

You can deduct from gross income the salaries, wages and other forms of compensation that you give to employees for their services, as long as the payments are reasonable. Fortunately, you have broad discretion to decide what's reasonable. Short of a scam—such as paying a huge salary to a spouse or relative who does little or no work—the IRS will almost always accept your notion of what pay is reasonable.

If your business is on the cash method of accounting, you deduct the payments that were actually made during the tax year. For employers using an accrual method of accounting, the rule is different and more complicated. The salaries are deductible for the tax year in which you established your obligation to make the payments, even though you deferred payment to a later time.

2. Vacation Pay

You can also deduct vacation pay from business income in determining the base for your federal income tax.

If you're on a cash basis accounting method, you deduct vacation pay as wages when you pay the employee.

If you use an accrual method, you can deduct vacation pay in the year it's earned only if you pay it by the close of your tax year or within two and a half months after the close. If you pay later than this, you deduct it in the year you actually pay it.

CASH AND ACCRUAL METHODS: DEFINED

Most small businesses and many mid-sized business use the cash method of accounting. With the cash method, you include in your gross income all the cash, checks and other payments you receive during the tax year. Usually, you deduct expenses in the tax year in which you pay them.

There are, however, a few exceptions. Some business costs, such as the purchase of a building, must be spread over a number of years; this is known as capitalization. And if you prepay expenses, you can only deduct them for the year to which they apply. If, for example, you pay a two-year premium on a liability insurance policy, you can only deduct half one year and must wait until the next year to deduct the other half.

With the accrual method, income is included in gross income when you earn it even though you don't get paid until the next tax year. Suppose you're in the business of selling television sets and you do your taxes on a calendar year basis. On December 28, you sell a TV set. In January, you bill the customer and in February, you receive payment. The income was earned on December 28, so it's included with the gross income for that year rather than the next. Similarly, you deduct or capitalize expenses when you become liable for them, whether or not you pay them in the same year.

The accrual method is more complicated than the cash method and can lead to more mistakes. Before choosing the accrual method, get professional advice to make sure it's best for your business and that it meets IRS guidelines.

3. Bonuses and Gifts

Many businesses give bonuses to employees to reward them for a job well done, or because the company has had a profitable year. You can take a tax deduction for bonuses you pay to employees if they're intended as additional payment for services and not as gifts; most bonuses qualify for deduction. The bonuses are subject to payroll tax withholding.

If your business distributes cash or gift certificates that can be converted to cash, the value of these gifts is considered additional wages or salary regardless of the amount—and is subject to employment taxes and withholding rules.

Noncash gifts are also generally treated as income to the employee, but not those that are clearly of an advertising nature, such as pens embossed with your company name that cost $4 or less. Other noncash gifts to employees may also be excluded from the employee's income is they are of nominal value.

Example: To promote employee goodwill, Pebblestone Partnership distributes turkeys, hams and other merchandise of nominal value at holidays. The partnership also gives each employee a check for $200. The value of the turkeys, hams and other merchandise isn't salaries or wages, but the partnership can deduct the cost of these items as a business expense. The checks can also be deducted, but must be treated as income to the employees subject to withholding.

4. Meals and Lodging

You can deduct at least some of the cost of meals and lodging you provide to employees if these expenses are a reasonable part of doing business. In some cases, the value of the meals or lodging you furnish must be reported as part of the employees' income for tax purposes.

a. Meals

Normally, you can deduct as a business expense only 50% of the cost of providing meals to employees. You can, however, deduct the full cost if:

- you operate a restaurant or catering service and furnish the meals to employees at the worksite
- you furnish the meals as part of a recreational or social activity, such as a company picnic, or
- the value of the meals is included in employees' income. Meals must be included in an employee's income unless the meals are furnished on your premises and for your convenience, or consist of food that qualifies as a minimal fringe benefit—coffee, doughnuts or soft drinks, for example, or the occasional meal you provide to enable an employee to work overtime.

  Example: Carol is a waitress at Sunshine Cafe. The restaurant provides two meals at no charge during her 7 a.m. to 4 p.m. workday. Sunshine Cafe encourages—but doesn't require—Carol to eat breakfast there before starting work. She must eat lunch there. Since Carol works during the normal breakfast and lunch periods, the value of her breakfast and lunch are not treated as income to her. If Sunshine Cafe allows Carol to have free meals there on her days off, the value of those meals would be included as income to Carol.

  Example: Frank is a clerk at Omni Department Store, working 9 a.m. to 5 p.m. Omni gives Frank his lunch without charge at a lunch buffet it maintains at the store. This helps Omni limit Frank's lunch break to 30 minutes—a benefit to Omni since its busiest time is during the normal lunch period. If Frank left the store to have lunch, he'd be away much longer than 30 minutes. The value of these meals is not income to Frank.

b. Lodging

You can deduct as a business expense the cost of furnishing lodging to employees if it's a reasonable part of doing business. Generally, you must include the value of lodging as part of the employees' income. The value can be excluded, however, if you furnish the lodging on your business premises for your convenience and require the employee to live there to perform the job.

Example: Felice is a swimming pool attendant at The Highlands, a resort complex that's 15 miles from town. The Highlands gives Felice the choice of living at the resort free of charge. If Felice chooses to live at The Highlands, the resort must include the value of the lodging in her income. It is not necessary for Felice to live at the resort to properly perform her job duties. It's merely a matter of convenience.

5. Fringe Benefits

Your business may be able to deduct as a business expense a number of employee fringe benefits, including:
- health and dental insurance
- medical reimbursement plans for items not covered by health insurance
- group term life insurance—limits apply, based on the policy value
- educational assistance programs
- adoption asssistance programs
- moving expenses
- qualified employee benefit plans, including profit-sharing plans, stock bonus plans and money purchase pension plans, and
- cafeteria plans that allow employees to choose among two or more benefits consisting of cash and qualified benefits.
 (See Chapter 4 for a detailed discussion of employee benefits.)
 Be aware that there are restrictions—some of them complex—on deducting these benefits and that deductions may be available to some forms of business and not others. Not only are employee benefits tax deductible by your business, they are not taxed to the employee.

But while these benefits sound attractive, there are two serious draw-backs. First, many small businesses—particularly those just starting out—won't have the funds to finance them. Second, the IRS has stringent rules to discourage top-heavy plans—those designed to benefit primarily the owners of a business and highly paid employees. If your plan doesn't meet strict IRS guidelines, your business won't be able to deduct the cost.

E. Independent Contractors

Some people you hire will be independent contractors rather than employees. (The differences between these two categories are explained in detail in Chapter 11.) If you do hire someone who meets the IRS tests for an independent contractor, you don't have to withhold income taxes or Social Security taxes from that person's pay, nor are you required to make an employer's contribution to the worker's Social Security fund.

If, however, you pay an independent contractor $600 or more during a calendar year, you must report this to the IRS on Form 1099-MISC.

Example: Marilyn, a computer consultant, works out of her home. She's listed in the Yellow Pages of the telephone book and offers her services to many different businesses during the course of a year. In January, Flowers Unlimited hires Marilyn to install a new computer it has purchased, and pays her $350 for this work. Two months later, Flowers Unlimited has Marilyn add a second computer and install a local area network, paying her $500. Toward the end of the year, Flowers Unlimited asks Marilyn to design special software to track inventory and sales; she's paid $2,000 for this assignment. Flowers Unlimited doesn't withhold income taxes or make Social Security payments. Because Marilyn is an independent contractor, the business sends the IRS and Marilyn a Form 1099-MISC showing it paid Marilyn $2,850 during the year.

Ask all independent contractors you hire to complete Form W-9 giving their Social Security numbers or their Employer Identification Numbers. You'll need this information when you report the payments you made. Because some independent contractors have tried to foil the IRS's attempts to track income, the government has enacted regulations to protect the integrity of the system. If an independent contractor doesn't give you an identification number—Social Security or Employer Identification Number—or if the IRS says you were given a wrong number, you may have to withhold 31% of the independent contractor's pay to assure that taxes aren't evaded.

Be Sure Workers Are Properly Classified

The IRS believes it has lost large amounts of tax revenues because many employers and workers have improperly agreed to classify the workers as independent contractors rather than employees. In many of these cases, the employer hasn't withheld taxes—and the worker has neglected to report the income and pay tax on it.

Given that background, the IRS feels its tax collection record is better when workers are classified as employees rather than as independent contractors. For that reason, it enforces strict tests for determining who is and who isn't an independent contractor—and if you misclassify someone who should have been called an employee, you may be heavily penalized. In recent years, the IRS has mounted a vigorous campaign to crack down on alleged abuses. Small and mid-sized businesses are being targeted. (To avoid costly problems, see Chapter 11 for a fuller explanation of the IRS criteria.)

F. Statutory Employees

Statutory employees are a kind of legal hybrid. They tend to be people you might not ordinarily think of as employees, but as independent contractors. For statutory employees, your responsibilities for withholding taxes are less extensive than your responsibilities for common law employees. You don't withhold income taxes from their pay, but you must withhold Social Security and Medicare taxes and you must make the matching employer's contribution as well.

The following are statutory employees:

Deliverypeople. A driver who distributes meat products, vegetable or fruit products, bakery products, or beverages other than milk, or who picks up or delivers laundry or dry cleaning, if the driver is your agent or is paid on commission.

Insurance salespeople. A fulltime life insurance salesperson.

Home workers. A person who works at home on materials that you supply and that must be returned to you or someone you name, if you also furnish specifications for the work to be done.

Traveling salespeople. A fulltime traveling salesperson, who's not an agent or commission driver, who works on your behalf and turns in orders to you from wholesalers, retailers, contractors, hotels, restaurants, or other similar businesses. The goods sold must be merchandise for resale or supplies used in the buyer's business operation.

There's another twist in the statutory employee story: not every person who falls into one of the above four categories is treated as a statutory employee. A statutory employee must meet three additional conditions.

- There must be a service contract stating or implying that the person must personally perform the services.
- Someone other than the worker must have invested substantially in the facilities used to perform the services—except for a car or truck.
- The worker must perform the services on a continuing basis.

If these conditions all apply, then you become responsible for withholding the worker's share of Social Security and Medicare taxes and paying the employer's share.

One more wrinkle: You need only pay federal unemployment tax (FUTA) on statutory employees who are deliverypeople or traveling salespeople.

Reality check. Statutory employees are rare birds. Your chances of having a statutory employee are only a bit better than your chances of winning the lottery—but at least you'll know one if you see one. ■

CHAPTER

6

FAMILY
AND
MEDICAL
LEAVE

It's often been difficult for a working individual to deal with family obligations such as caring for a seriously ill child or parent, or attending to the special needs of a newborn infant or newly adopted child. And some employees who have taken time off work to recover from their own serious illnesses have worried about being demoted or fired.

To help employees balance the demands of the workplace with personal and family needs, Congress enacted the Family and Medical Leave Act or FMLA (29 U.S.C. §2601 and following). Under the FMLA, if your business has 50 or more employees, it may be required to give an employee up to 12 weeks of unpaid leave for certain family and medical reasons. And the law requires that the employee be allowed to return to the same or a similar position after taking the leave—except when it would be prohibitively expensive for a business to take back a highly paid employee.

A. Who Is Covered

The FMLA covers your business if you have 50 or more employees who work within a 75-mile radius. The count, for FMLA purposes, includes all employees on your payroll—parttime, fulltime and those already on leave.

An employee in a covered business is eligible for FMLA leave only if he or she has worked for you:

• for at least one year, and
• for at least 1,250 hours during the 12 months before the leave.

INFORMING EMPLOYEES

If your business is subject to the FMLA, you must display in the workplace a poster titled "Your Rights Under the Family and Medical Leave Act of 1993." It's available at the nearest office of the U.S. Department of Labor's Wage and Hour Division. Your state labor department may also be able to provide this poster, as well as posters describing workplace rights and responsibilities under state law. (See the Appendix for contact details.)

You must also inform employees about their rights to FMLA leave in your employee handbook, if your have one. Otherwise, you must give employees written guidance when they request FMLA leave. The easiest way to do this is to give them a copy of the booklet, *Compliance Guide to the Family and Medical Leave Act*. It's free at the nearest office of the U.S. Department of Labor's Wage and Hour Division, or you can order copies by calling (202) 219-8743.

B. Reasons for Taking a Leave

If your business is covered, you must grant unpaid leave to an eligible employee to attend to a child, to care for a parent or spouse or to recover from a serious illness. Generally, the employee is entitled to a total of 12 workweeks of leave during any 12-month period.

1. Birth, Adoption or Foster Care

An eligible employee may take a total of 12 workweeks of unpaid leave because of the birth of a child, or because a child has been placed with the employee for adoption or foster care. Under the FMLA, foster care is defined as 24-hour care for a child away from his or her parents or guardians—and it must be based on a court order or an agreement approved by a state agency.

The period for taking a leave based on birth, adoption or child care expires one year after the child is born or placed. Men as well as women are eligible for this leave. An expectant mother may begin FMLA leave before the birth of the child for prenatal care, or if her condition makes her unable to work. You can require medical documentation of the need for prenatal care or inability to work before you grant a pre-birth leave.

Similarly, FMLA leave can begin before actual placement or adoption of a child if an absence from work is necessary. Such an absence may be necessary, for example, if an employee must attend counseling sessions, appear in court, consult with a lawyer or the doctor representing the birth parent, or submit to a physical exam.

Special Rules for Spouses

If a husband and wife both work for your company, the total number of workweeks taken by both spouses may be limited to 12 during any 12-month period. Interestingly, if the child's parents are not married to one another, each parent is entitled to the full allotment of 12 workweeks of leave.

2. Family Health Problems

An eligible employee may take a total of 12 workweeks of unpaid leave during any 12-month period to care for a spouse, son, daughter or parent who has a serious health condition.

The FMLA rules for determining who has a serious health condition are complicated. Generally, however, an injury or illness may qualify as a serious health condition if it involves inpatient care—an overnight stay in a hospital or other medical care facility. The person who has been hospitalized is considered to have a serious health condition for as long as he or she can't work, attend school or perform other normal life activities.

In addition, an injury or illness may qualify as a serious health condition if the patient requires continuing treatment and perform normal activities for more than three consecutive days. A person who needs continuing treatment for pregnancy or prenatal care, a chronic health condition or a long-term or permanent health condition may also be deemed to have a serious health condition.

FAMILY TIES

The FMLA defines family relationships in both expected and unexpected ways.

A spouse is an employee's husband or wife as recognized under state law, which may include common law spouses in the minority of states that recognize common law marriage. Same-sex partners don't qualify as spouses.

An employee's parent can be a biological parent or a person who took the place of a parent when the employee was a child—someone, for example, who took care of and financially supported the child.

An employee's son or daughter can be a biological, adopted or foster child, a stepchild or a legal ward. It can also be a child who the employee cares for and financially supports. The child must be under age 18—or, if age 18 or older, he or she must be incapable of caring for himself or herself because of a mental or physical disability.

3. Employee's Health Problems

An eligible employee may take a total of 12 workweeks of unpaid leave during any 12-month period for a serious health condition that makes the employee unable to perform his or her job. (For more on serious health conditions, see Section B2 above.)

C. Scheduling Leave

You and an employee can agree to flexible work scheduling for the leave time to which employees are entitled under the FLMA.

The leave may be intermittent rather than consecutive if you agree to make it so.

Example: Bill, an employee of Rendex Corporation, normally works Monday through Friday. Bill's wife has given birth to a son. Rendex and Bill agree that he'll use his leave rights in two-day segments by working Monday through Wednesday and staying home on Thursday and Friday.

You and an employee may also agree that the leave will be taken through reducing the weekly workhours.

Example: Carla, an employee of Cormark Company, has adopted a daughter. Cormark and Carla agree that she'll exercise her leave rights by temporarily working from 1:00 to 5:00 p.m. rather than her normal 8 a.m. to 5 p.m. schedule.

Example: Tim works for Enterprise Associates. His father has a serious health condition requiring radiation treatments each week at a university medical center 100 miles away. Tim needs to drive his dad to treatment every Friday. Enterprise Associates must allow Tim to use unpaid leave time to take Fridays off work.

CREATIVE SOLUTIONS FOR HARD PROBLEMS

Family and medical leave laws address only a small part of the issues facing employers and employees in balancing the competing demands of the family and the workplace. To assure a happy and productive workforce, you may need to work with employees to come up with creative solutions. Consider this list of possibilities from Renee Magid, founder and president of the consulting firm Initiatives Inc.:

- flexible career paths
- flexible work times for fulltime employees
- permanent parttime employment, with benefits
- job sharing
- work-at-home options
- cafeteria-style benefit plans
- education and support programs
- financial assistance with child care, and
- direct childcare.

For more information, contact Initiatives Inc., 550 Pinetown Road, Suite 224, Ft. Washington, PA 19034; 215-628-8438.

D. Temporary Transfer to Another Job

If it is disruptive to your business to allow a particular employee to have a flexible or reduced work schedule, check to see whether there's another job open that will accommodate the employee's request with less disruption. If so, you can transfer the employee temporarily to the other job. But be sure the alternative job has equivalent pay and benefits. The duties, however, needn't be equivalent.

Example: Hilda works for Project Systems Inc. as a manager of ten employees. She is suffering from a major depressive episode which will require psychotherapy three times a week for six months. Project Systems must grant Hilda's request for a reduced leave schedule to permit her to get the necessary treatment. The company also transfers Hilda temporarily to a research position in which her absences will be less disruptive to the company.

WORKPLACE POLITICS: A DELICATE BUSINESS

When you temporarily transfer an employee, other employees—especially those who have been eyeing the open job—may feel resentful. This is a delicate situation and you may be inclined to reduce tensions by informing the other employees about the medical reasons behind the transfer. Restrain yourself. Unless you have the transferred employee's permission to disclose the reasons for the transfer, you must respect that person's privacy.

E. Substituting Paid Leave

You're not required to pay for FMLA leave, but if you offer paid time off—vacation, personal, family or sick leave—as a job benefit, you or the employee can substitute paid leave for unpaid FMLA leave in most situations.

Accrued paid vacation or personal leave. You or the employee can substitute accrued paid vacation or personal leave for unpaid FMLA leave whether based on birth, childcare, foster placement, caring for a ill family member or attending to the employee's own medical needs.

Accrued paid family leave. You can substitute accrued paid leave for unpaid FMLA leave based on birth, adoption, foster placement or caring for an ill family member. An employee can require such a substitution only for reasons permitted by your company's leave plan.

Example: Lou works for Star Baking Company. Star's leave plan allows paid family leave for an employee to care for a child, but not a parent. Lou needs to care for his mother. He can't require Star to substitute paid family leave for unpaid FMLA leave.

Accrued paid medical or sick leave. You can substitute paid medical or sick leave for unpaid FMLA leave based on the employee caring for an ill family member or the employee's own serious health condition. An employee can only require a substitution if the reasons for the leave are normally covered by your company's leave plan. For example, an employee can't require you to substitute paid leave to care for a seriously ill family unless your plan specifies that leave can be used for this purpose. And an employee doesn't have the right to substitute paid medical or sick leave for a serious health condition that's not covered by your leave plan. In such a case, the employee is restricted to the leave available under the FMLA.

How Much Time Off Is Owed

If an employee uses paid leave under circumstances which don't qualify as FMLA leave, the leave won't count against the 12 weeks of FMLA leave to which the employee is entitled. For example, if an employee uses paid sick leave for a condition which isn't a serious health condition as defined in the FMLA, the time off doesn't count against the 12 weeks of unpaid FMLA leave to which he or she may later be entitled.

F. Advance Notice of Leave

Often, an employee can foresee the need for an unpaid leave. For example, most employees know well in advance when a baby will be born, and usually have ample knowledge of when a placement will occur for adoption or foster care. Similarly, an employee often is aware early on of planned medical treatment for a serious health condition of the employee or of a family member. You can require, in these situations, that an employee notify you at least 30 days before the unpaid leave is to begin.

But such advance notice isn't always possible—and the FMLA takes this into account. For example, if a child is born prematurely or an adoption or placement goes through unexpectedly, the employee can give you a shorter notice; the test is what is practical. Typically, the employee should at least notify you orally within one or two business days of learning of the need for leave.

Similarly, where there's a medical emergency involving the employee or a member of the employee's family, it usually won't be practical for the employee to give you any advance notice of the need for unpaid leave. In such cases, advance notice isn't required. Where the need for FMLA leave isn't foreseeable, the employee or a family member can notify you either in person or by phone, fax or e-mail of the circumstances requiring the leave.

If an employee's leave is based on a serious health condition that requires planned medical treatment, you can require the employee to make a reasonable effort to schedule the treatment so that it won't unduly disrupt your business.

G. Certification

Theoretically, an employee could abuse the system by falsely claiming that he, she or a family member has a serious health condition. The FMLA recognizes this and allows you to require proof—a certificate from the patient's doctor stating:

- the date when the serious health condition started
- the length of time the condition is likely to last
- diagnosis of the condition
- treatment prescribed, and
- whether inpatient treatment is required.

You're free to decide when to ask for a certificate and when not to—but it's best to follow a uniform policy, rather than being selective. Otherwise, someone who's required to provide a certificate may claim you're discriminating against them. You may have trouble justifying why a particular employee was singled out.

Since most people are honest, the simplest and legally safest policy is an honor system in which you accept employees' statements at face value.

1. Requesting Clarification

Depending on the reason for FMLA leave, you can require that additional information be included on the certificate.

a. Employee's own condition

If the employee seeks medical leave because of his or her own serious health condition, you can require that the certificate state that the employee can't perform work of any kind, or that the employee can't perform the essential functions of the job. Give the employee or the doctor a list of the essential functions.

b. Family member's condition

If the employee seeks leave to care for a family member, you can require that the certificate state that the patient needs help in meeting basic medical, hygiene, nutritional, safety or transportation needs—or that the employee's presence would be beneficial or desirable. The employee must indicate on the certificate what care he or she will provide and how long that care is likely to be required.

c. Intermittent leave or reduced leave schedule

If the employee seeks to take intermittent leave or asks for a shortened work schedule, you can require that the certificate state the medical need for or desirability of such leave and how long the situation requiring leave is expected to last.

CERTIFICATION MADE EASY

The U.S. Department of Labor has developed Form WH-380, Certification of Physician or Practitioner, for doctors to use in certifying medical conditions under the FMLA. While this form is optional, using it is probably the best way to assure that you and the doctor comply with FMLA regulations.

Most doctors will have copies of the form, but to make sure the process goes smoothly, have a supply on hand for employees to take to their doctors. The forms are available at the nearest office of the U.S. Department of Labor's Wage and Hour Division. (See the Appendix for contact details.)

---

2. Second and Third Opinions

If an employee submits a complete certificate signed by the doctor, you can't ask the doctor for more information to verify it. You can, however, require the employee to get an opinion from a second doctor. This can be someone you designate or approve—but it can't be someone you regularly employ, such as a company doctor. And you, rather than the employee, must pay for the second opinion.

Weigh the Odds of Asking for More

Just because the FMLA allows you to get a second opinion doesn't mean it's a smart thing to do. Often it's not. Think long and hard before getting adversarial with employees over health determinations. If you make an employee jump through hoops to qualify for an unpaid absence, you'll probably wind up with a resentful employee who will never again give you his or her full effort and loyalty. And the fallout from being unnecessarily suspicious about one employee can easily infect the entire workplace.

If you wind up with conflicting opinions, you can require a third opinion from another doctor—one approved by both you and the employee. This third opinion is binding on both of you.

HEALTHCARE PROVIDERS: WHAT'S IN A NAME?

Generally, a doctor of medicine or osteopathy will sign the employee's medical certificate or render the second or third opinion. But technically, under the FMLA and its regulations, such certificates can be signed by a healthcare provider—a term that includes not only MDs and DOs, but others such as podiatrists, dentists, clinical psychologists, optometrists and chiropractors.

In addition, nurse practitioners and nurse-midwives who diagnose and treat certain conditions, especially at health maintenance organizations and in rural areas where other healthcare providers may not be available, are included as healthcare providers, as are Christian Science practitioners.

3. Recertification

You can ask an employee to give you a recertification of a medical condition to support a leave request. You can request a recertification at reasonable intervals—generally not more often than every 30 days. The intervals can be shorter, however, if:

- the employee requests an extension of leave
- circumstances have changed significantly—for example, the duration or nature of the illness becomes different than anticipated, or
- you receive information casting doubt on the continuing validity of the certification.

H. Health Benefits

If you have a group health plan for employees, you must maintain coverage for employees who are on FMLA leave. You must keep the coverage at the same level the employees would have if they worked continuously.

In some cases, however, you can require an employee to repay the premiums you paid for this continuing coverage. Generally, you can demand reimbursement if the employee doesn't come back to work after the leave period expires. But you can't demand reimbursement if the employee doesn't return to work because:

- the employee or a family member has suffered continuation, recurrence or onset of a serious health condition—the kind of thing that would have justified taking the unpaid leave in the first place, or
- there are other circumstances beyond the control of the employee. Examples of this include: an employee's spouse is unexpectedly transferred to a job location more than 75 miles from the employee's worksite, a person other than an immediate family member has a serious health condition and the employee is needed to provide care, or the employee is laid off while on leave.

The FMLA regulations give two examples of situations within the employee's control: an employee desires to remain with a parent in a distant city even though the parent no longer requires the employee's care; a mother decides not to return to work to stay home with a newborn child. In such cases, the employee must repay the health insurance premiums you paid for coverage during his or her leave.

⚠

The High Cost of Retaliation

The FMLA prohibits you from discharging or otherwise retaliating against an employee who has asked for or taken leave under the statute.

I. Returning to Work

The FMLA normally gives employees the right to return to their jobs when their leave has been completed.

1. Job Protection

When an eligible employee returns from taking a leave, your company must restore the employee to the job that he or she held when the leave began or to a similar job—one with equivalent pay, benefits and other terms of employment. However, an employee has no greater right to reinstatement or other benefits than if he or she had been continuously employed during the FMLA leave period.

Example: Anton takes 10 weeks of unpaid family leave from his job as a production worker at Smokestack Industries, Inc. While he's away, Smokestack eliminates the night shift on which Anton was working and lays off all employees working on that shift. Smokestack would have laid off Anton had he been working instead of taking leave. Smokestack doesn't have to re-employ Anton.

2. Exemption for Highly Paid Employees

Recognizing that it's difficult for many businesses to carry on in the absence of the customary executives and decisionmakers, the FMLA let's you decline to take back some highly paid employees after their leave. The exemption applies only if:

- the employee is among the highest paid 10% of the salaried people you employ within 75 miles of the place where the employee works, and
- taking back the employee will cause "substantial and grievous economic injury" to your business.

Unfortunately, the FMLA regulations don't precisely set the level of economic hardship or injury that excuses you from taking back an employee. It's likely that future regulations will provide more guidance. For now, though, it's clear that minor inconveniences and costs are not enough to justify cutting off a key employee who's taken a leave. On the other hand, you don't have to show that taking back the employee would threaten the existence of your business.

One test is whether it's feasible to temporarily replace or do without the employee on FMLA leave—or whether you must hire a permanent replacement. If the employee on leave is your company's $75,000 a year sales manager, you may find that no competent people are willing to take over the job on a short-term basis. And since you need a sales manager, you have no real choice but to hire a permanent replacement. Reinstating the employee on leave to an equivalent job may be much too costly for your business—particularly if you must create a new job to do this. In such a situation, you'd likely be excused from taking back the employee after the leave.

As soon as you determine that substantial economic harm will result if you take back a key employee who has sought a leave under the FMLA, notify him or her in writing. In a letter, explain that your decision is based on your wish to prevent major injury to the business. If the employee then starts or continues the leave, you'll be protected by the FMLA.

Note that if an employee doesn't return to work after you notify him or her that you intend not to hire him or her back, you must still maintain the employee's health benefits for the full leave period and you can't recover the cost of health insurance premiums. (See Section G.)

3. Fitness to Work

If an employee has taken a leave because of a serious health condition, the FMLA lets you require a medical certification that he or she is able to resume work. You can only impose this requirement if it's part of a policy you uniformly apply to employees returning from medical leave.

There may be a state law, local ordinance or union contract that governs the terms under which employees who have taken medical leave can return to work. The FMLA doesn't supersede these other legal controls. You must also comply with the Americans With Disabilities Act (ADA) rule that any physical required of an employee returning to work must be job-related. (For more on the ADA, see Chapter 9 and Section 2 below.)

J. Related Laws

You must comply with other laws that affect an employee's right to take a leave.

1. State Laws

Nearly half of the states have laws guaranteeing some form of family or medical leave. (See the chart below.) The FMLA doesn't cancel out state law provisions that provide greater family or medical leave rights than the FMLA does. You must comply with both laws. Leaves granted under a state leave law and the FMLA usually run simultaneously and are not added together.

Example: State law where Tess works entitles her to 16 weeks of leave over two years. Tess takes her 16 weeks of state permitted leave in one year. This also exhausts her 12 weeks of FMLA leave for that year—she can't take 16 weeks plus 12 weeks. The following year, however, she's entitled to her full 12 week allotment of FMLA leave.

Your obligation under the FMLA to maintain an employee's health benefits while he or she is on FMLA leave applies only to the first 12 weeks of leave each year.

STATE FAMILY AND MEDICAL LEAVE LAWS

Nearly half the states guarantee private sector employees the right to take work leaves because of pregnancy, childbirth or the adoption of a child. A few also have laws that give employees the right to take time off from work to care for a family member who is ill. Here is a synopsis.

Alaska	If you employ 21 or more people, you must grant any employee who has worked fulltime for six months or halftime for one year 18 weeks of unpaid leave per 12-month period for pregnancy, childbirth or adoption, or 24 months for care of a family member during a serious illness. Employees who take such leave must be restored to their same or comparable position. Alaska Stat. §23.10.500
California	You must grant a leave of up to four months for a female employee who is disabled as a result of pregnancy, childbirth or related medical conditions. Cal. Gov't Code §12945
	Employees who have worked for at least one year and have 1,250 hours of work during the previous year may take up to 12 working weeks in any 12 month period for family care and medical leave, with re-employment guaranteed. This applies only if you to employ 50 people or more; it does not apply if you employ fewer than 50 people within 75 miles of the employee's worksite. Cal. Gov't Code §1245.2.
	If you employ 25 or more people at the same location, you must grant parents, guardians or custodial grandparents up to 40 hours per school year of unpaid time off (but not more than eight hours per calendar month) to participate in school activities of a child in grades kindergarten through 12, as long as the employee gives reasonable advance notice. You may require verification from the school. Cal. Labor Code §230.8
	You may not discharge or discriminate against an employee who is called to attend a child's school following a suspension. The employee must give reasonable advance notice. Cal. Labor Code §230.7

Colorado	Your policies applying to leaves for biological parents must also extend to adoptive parents. Colo. Rev. Stat. §19-5-211
Connecticut	If you employ at least 75 people, you must give 16 weeks of unpaid leave within any two-year period. Leave may be for birth or adoption of child or for care of a child, spouse, or parent during serious illness. Employees who take such leave must be allowed to return to either their original or equivalent jobs. Conn. Gen. Stat. §§31-51cc, 31-51dd, 31-51ff
District of Columbia	If you employ at least 20 people, an employee who has worked with your company for at least one year, and who has worked at least 1,000 hours during the previous 12-month period, must be granted up to 16 weeks of unpaid leave during any 24-month period in connection with the birth or adoption of a child or serious illness of a family member. D.C. Code Ann. §36-1302
	Family member includes a child who lives with the employee and for whom the employee resumes parental responsibility. It also includes a person with whom the employee shares and maintains a residence. Employees who take such leaves must be restored to either their original or equivalent jobs.
Hawaii	If you employ at least 100 people, you must grant them an unpaid leave of up to four weeks per calendar year for the birth or adoption of a child or for care of a child, spouse or parent during a serious illness. Employees who take such leave must be restored to their same or comparable positions. Haw. Rev. Stat. §§398-1 to 11
Illinois	You must give employees up to eight hours during each school year to attend a child's classroom activities and conferences that cannot be scheduled during non-work hours. The employee must first exhaust all vacation and compensatory time and must give you seven days of notice except in an emergency. 820 Ill. Comp. Stat. 147/15
Iowa	If you employ at least four people, you must grant employees who are disabled by pregnancy, childbirth or related medical conditions an unpaid leave for the duration of their disabilities, up to a maximum of eight weeks. Iowa Code Ann. §216.6
Kentucky	You must grant up to six weeks unpaid leave to an employee who has adopted a child under seven years old. Ky. Rev. Stat. Ann. §337.015
Louisiana	You must give an employee up to six weeks of leave, and must grant an additional leave for a "reasonable period of time" not to exceed four months. La. Rev. Stat. Ann. §22:215.7

You may grant up to 16 unpaid hours per year for an employee to attend or participate in school conferences and activities of a child for whom the employee is the legal guardian, if those activities can't be scheduled during non-work hours. The employee must give reasonable notice and schedule the time off so that it does not unduly disrupt your operations. La. Rev. Stat. Ann. §23:1015

Maine

If you employ at least 25 people at the worksite, an employee who has worked at least 12 consecutive months at your company must be granted up to ten consecutive weeks of unpaid leave in any two-year period for the birth or adoption of a child under 16 years old or to care for a family member during illness. Employees who take such leaves must be restored to either their original or equivalent jobs. Me. Rev. Stat. Ann. tit. 26 §844

Massachusetts

If you employ at least six people, you must grant employees who have completed their probationary periods or have worked fulltime for at least three months up to eight weeks of unpaid leave for the birth or adoption of a child under 18 or the adoption of a child under 23 if the child is mentally or physically disabled. Mass. Gen. Laws Ann. ch. 149, §105D

Minnesota

If you employ 21 or more people, you must grant employees up to six weeks of unpaid leave for the birth or adoption of a child. However, only employees who have worked for your company an average of at least 20 hours per week for at least 12 months before the request for leave is made are covered.

During the leave, you must offer the employee the option of continuing group healthcare insurance coverage. Employees who take such leaves must be returned to either their original or equivalent jobs, unless they would have been laid off. Minn. Stat. Ann. §181.941

An employee may use paid sick leave to care for a sick child. Minn. Stat. Ann. §181.943

You must grant up to 40 hours with pay to enable an employee to donate bone marrow. Minn. Stat. Ann. §181.945

An employee is entitled to 16 hours of paid leave per year to attend school conferences or classroom activities that can't be scheduled during non-work hours. Minn. Stat. Ann. §181.9412

Montana

You may not dismiss an employee who becomes pregnant, or refuse to allow a reasonable unpaid leave for pregnancy, or refuse to allow accrued disability or other leave benefits for a pregnancy leave. Employees also cannot be required to take pregnancy leave for an unreasonable period of time. Employees who take pregnancy-related leaves must be returned to their original jobs or equivalents unless your business's circumstances have changed to make it unreasonable or impossible to do so. Mont. Code Ann §49-2-310 and §49-2-311

Nevada

The same leave policies that apply to other medical conditions must be extended to female employees before and after childbirth, or after a miscarriage. Nev. Rev. Stat. §613.335

New Jersey

If you employ at least 50 people, you must grant to those who have worked for at least 12 months, and who have worked at least 1,000 hours in the preceding 12 months, up to 12 weeks of unpaid leave in any 24-month period for the birth, adoption or care during the serious illness of a child under 18 years old, or one older than 18 who is incapable of self-care or a parent or a spouse.

Employees who take such leaves must be restored to either their original or equivalent jobs. You may deny leave if the employee is among the seven highest paid employees, or is in the highest 5%, whichever is greater, and if substantial and grievous economic injury to the business would result. You must notify the employee of your intent to deny leave when you determine that denial is necessary. If leave has commenced, the employee must return within ten days. Family Leave Act, N.J. Stat. Ann. §§34:11B-1 to B16

New York

If you permit leave for the birth of a child, you must grant leave for adoption. N.Y. Labor Law §201-c

You must grant an employee up to 24 hours leave to donate bone marrow, and may not retaliate against an employee who requests a leave for this purpose. N.Y. Labor Law §202-a

North Carolina

An employee who is a parent, guardian or acting as a parent may take up to four hours per year without pay to be involved in the child's school—including a public or private school or daycare. The hours taken must be at a mutually agreed-upon time; you may require 48 hours notice for the request and may require verification that the employee actually attended or was involved. You may not retaliate against an employee who exercises rights under this law. N.C. Gen. Stat. §95-28.3

Oregon

If you employ at least 25 people, employees who have worked with your company for at least 90 days must be granted up to 12 weeks of unpaid leave for childbirth or the adoption of a child less than six years old. You may require employees to give 30 days of notice of intent to take such a leave, and employees returning from such a leave must be returned to either their original or equivalent jobs. Pregnant employees must also be given the right to transfer to less strenuous jobs. Or. Rev. Stat. §659.360

If you employ 50 or more employees, you must grant to employees who have worked an average of at least 25 hours per week for 180 days or more a leave of absence to care for a seriously ill family member of up to 12 weeks in a two-year period. Or. Rev. Stat. §659.570

Rhode Island

If you employ 50 or more people, you must grant those who have worked with you for at least 12 consecutive months up to 13 weeks of unpaid leave in any two calendar years for the birth or adoption of a child or for the care of a family member during illness. Employees who take such leaves must be restored to either their original or equivalent jobs. R.I. Gen. Laws §§28-48-2 and 28-48-3

Tennessee

If you employ 100 or more people, you must grant up to four months of unpaid leave to any fulltime female employee (who has worked at least 12 consecutive months) for pregnancy or childbirth. If the employee gives you at least three months of advance notice of her intent to take such a leave, or, if a medical emergency makes the leave necessary, she must be restored to her original job or its equivalent upon returning to work.

You must allow an employee who takes such a leave to continue benefits such as healthcare insurance, but you're not required to pay for the benefits during the leave period. If the employee's job is "so unique" that the you can't, with reasonable efforts, fill the position temporarily, then you needn't reinstate the employee. Reinstatement rights don't apply if the employee uses the time to actively pursue other employment opportunities or has worked fulltime or parttime for another employer. Tenn. Code Ann. §4-21-408

Vermont

If you employee 15 or more people, you must allow those who have worked an average of at least 30 hours per week, for at least one year, to take up to 12 weeks of unpaid leave per year for pregnancy, childbirth, the adoption of a child under the age of 16 or the serious illness of the employee or a family member. The employee must provide you with written notice of the intent to take such a leave and of its anticipated duration.

The employee must be allowed to use accrued vacation or sickness leave for up to six weeks of leave. The employee must also be given the option of continuing benefit programs at his or her own expense. After returning from such a leave, the employee must be restored to the original job or its equivalent, unless you can demonstrate that the employee performed unique services and hiring a permanent replacement worker, after giving notice to the employee, was the only alternative to preventing substantial and grievous economic injury to your business.

An employee who doesn't return to the job after taking such a leave for reasons other than his or her serious illness must refund to you any compensation paid during the leave, except payments for accrued vacation or sickness leave. Vt. Stat. Ann. tit. 21 §472

Washington

If you employ 100 or more people, you must grant up to 12 weeks of unpaid leave during any two-year period in connection with the birth or adoption of a child or to care for a child under the age of 18 who is terminally ill. The employee must give you at least 30 days of advance notice in most situations.

Employees who take such leaves must be restored to their original or equivalent jobs. If circumstances have changed to the point that no equivalent job is available, the employee must be given any vacant job for which he or she is qualified. You may limit or deny family leave to either the highest paid 10% of the employees or 10% designated as "key" personnel. Wash. Rev. Code §49.12.270

Wisconsin

If you employ 50 or more people, you must grant employees who have been with your company one year and worked 1,000 hours up to six weeks of unpaid leave for the birth or adoption of a child and up to two weeks for the care of a parent, child or spouse with a serious health condition. This leave, when combined with any other family-related leave, may not exceed a total of eight weeks within a 12-month period. Wis. Stat. Ann. §103.10

Adapted from Your Rights in the Workplace, by Barbara Kate Repa (Nolo Press).

2. Americans With Disabilities Act

An employee who becomes disabled has rights under the Americans With Disabilities Act (ADA) as well as the FMLA. (See Chapter 9.) It requires special attention to coordinate your responsibilities under these two laws.

The FMLA entitles an employee to a reduced work schedule until 12 weeks of leave are used, with health benefits maintained during this period. At the end of the FMLA leave, you must reinstate the employee to the same or an equivalent position.

If the employee can't perform the equivalent job because of a disability and he or she has used up his or her FMLA leave, the ADA may permit or require you to place the employee in a parttime job, with only the benefits provided to parttime employees.

Here are two other variations:

- The ADA may require you to offer an employee a job with a reasonable accommodation. If the FMLA entitles an employee to unpaid leave, you can't avoid granting the leave by requiring the employee to take such a job.
- If you require certification that an employee is fit to return to work as permitted by the FMLA under a uniform policy imposed by your business, you must also comply with the ADA requirement that the certification be related to the job.

K. Enforcement

An employee who believes his or her rights have been violated may file a complaint against your business with the U.S. Secretary of Labor or file a private lawsuit. If a violation is proven, you may have to pay the employee wages, employment benefits or other compensation, depending on the nature of the violation. If no such loss has occurred—for example, you unlawfully denied FMLA leave—you may have to reimburse the employee for the cost of providing care for a child or ill family member, up to a sum equal to 12 weeks of wages. You may also have to pay penalties and interest, and you may be ordered to reinstate or promote the employee, and to pay reasonable fees for the employee's lawyer and expert witnesses.

A number of government publications offer guidance on the emerging legal requirements for family and medical leave.

Compliance Guide to the Family and Medical Leave Act is free at the nearest office of the U.S. Department of Labor's Wage and Hour Division. See the Appendix for contact details. Or call (202) 219-8743.

For more depth, get *Federal Regulations Part 825, The Family and Medical Leave Act of 1993,* also free from the Department of Labor. ■

CHAPTER

7

HEALTH
AND
SAFETY

A s an employer, there are many good reasons—in addition to your humane instincts—for creating a safe and healthy workplace. Obviously, healthy workers will be happier and more productive. There will be fewer disruptions of work schedules due to absenteeism. And health insurance costs may be reduced. An incidental benefit may be an improvement in worker efficiency; workers generally are more efficient in a safer workplace. Then there are the more obvious obligations. Federal and state laws and an increasing number of local ordinances require you to take steps to make the workplace safe and healthy.

Workers today are well-informed about the link between workplace conditions and health problems. Most know, for example, that second-hand smoke can cause or aggravate respiratory and heart problems, and that repetitive motions can lead to Carpal Tunnel Syndrome. And an increasing number of workers will not hesitate to press legal claims against employers who fail to rectify unsafe or unhealthy conditions.

In addition to health and safety statutes, state law requires your business to provide workers' compensation coverage to pay for medical bills and partial wage loss when an employee is injured in the workplace. By reducing on-the-job injuries and eliminating the workplace causes of disease, you can lower the cost of workers' compensation coverage. (See Section E.)

Get Employees Involved

In meeting your legal responsibilities for keeping the workplace safe and healthy, don't overlook an obvious resource: the workers. Involve them in identifying safety and health problems and suggesting ways to solve such problems. Organizing a safety committee made up of equal numbers of employees and managers is a good starting point. If workers can voice their safety concerns to you and to other workers who are able to initiate changes, there's less chance that they'll jump the gun and go straight to government authorities to report a complaint. Having such a safety committee can also earn you a break on workers' compensation insurance premiums. To further involve workers, consider holding company safety seminars at which you encourage employee suggestions.

A. The Occupational Safety and Health Act

In 1970, Congress passed the Occupational Safety and Health Act or OSHA (29 U.S.C. §§651 to 678)—a comprehensive law designed to reduce workplace hazards and to improve health and safety programs for workers. It broadly requires employers to provide a workplace free of physical dangers and to meet specific health and safety standards. Employers must also provide safety training to employees, inform them about hazardous chemicals, notify government administrators about serious workplace accidents and keep detailed safety records.

Although there can be heavy penalties for not complying with OSHA, such penalties are usually reserved for extreme cases in which workplace conditions are highly dangerous and the employer has ignored warnings about them. If your workplace is inspected—an unlikely event for a typical small business—OSHA will work with you to eliminate hazards.

1. Who Is Covered

Generally, you must comply with the Act if your business affects interstate commerce. The legal definition of interstate commerce is so broad that almost all businesses are covered. But Congress did make some very limited exceptions. OSHA won't apply to your workplace if:

- you're self-employed and have no employees
- your business is a farm that employs only your immediate family members, or

- you're in a business such as mining, which is already regulated by other federal safety laws.

2. Safety Standards

OSHA sets a general standard for all covered businesses. As an employer, you must provide a place of employment that's "free from recognized hazards that are causing or are likely to cause death or serious physical harm to employees." Recognized hazards are not clearly defined, which can make it difficult for you to know how to comply with the law. The broad language covers an almost impossibly large range of potential harm—from sharp objects that might cause cuts to radiation exposure.

But there's more. In the Act, Congress created the Occupational Safety and Health Administration—also called OSHA—as a unit of the U.S. Department of Labor. And Congress authorized this agency to set additional workplace standards, which it has done in great profusion. The specific standards cover a wide range of workplace concerns, including:

- exposure to hazardous chemicals
- first aid and medical treatment
- noise levels
- protective gear—goggles, respirators, gloves, work shoes, ear protectors
- fire protection
- worker training, and
- workplace temperatures and ventilation.

3. Posting, Reporting and Recordkeeping

You must post a notice called "Job Safety and Health Protection," which is available from the nearest OSHA office. If your business is located in a state that has its own approved OSHA program, there may be a state form for you to post instead of the national version. Check with your state OSHA office to find out. (See the listing in Section C for contact details.)

You must notify OSHA within eight hours after learning that an employee has died from a job-related accident or that three or more employees have been hospitalized because of a workplace accident. Call or visit an OSHA office to report the location and time of the incident, the number of fatalities or hospitalized employees, the name and phone number of a contact person and a brief description of the incident. Expect a follow-up investigation.

Unless your business is exempt from OSHA recordkeeping requirements (see below), you must maintain several types of records.

Injury and Illness Log. You must keep a log (OSHA Form 200) of all workplace injuries and illnesses, except minor injuries requiring only first aid. Throughout February, you must post the log for the previous year.

Medical Records. You must keep up-to-date medical records and records of employee exposure to hazardous substances or harmful physical agents.

Training Records. You must keep records of your safety training records and make them available for review by employees.

Retention. You must maintain required records for specified periods of time—sometimes as long as 30 years.

EXEMPTION FROM RECORDKEEPING

The OSHA requirements for recordkeeping apply only to businesses with 10 or more employees—although state OSHA regulations may apply the recordkeeping requirements to smaller businesses. In addition, the following businesses are exempt from recordkeeping:

- retail trade—except for businesses selling general merchandise, building materials and garden supplies
- real estate, insurance and financial businesses, and
- service businesses—except for hotels and other lodging places, repair facilities, amusement and recreation facilities and health services.

4. Training

Under OSHA, you're responsible for safety training. Make sure that all employees know about the materials and equipment with which they'll be working, the known hazards in your business and how you're controlling those hazards. Pay special attention to the use of chemicals, being sure to train employees in:

- methods of detecting the release of a hazardous chemical in the work area—for example, monitoring devices or appearance or odor of chemicals when being released
- physical and health hazards of the chemicals
- measures employees can take to protect themselves from the hazards—safe work practices, emergency procedures and protective equipment, and
- details of your labeling system and where employees can look at chemical safety data. (See Section D.)

Don't let an employee start a job until he or she has received instructions in how to do it safely. The exact training you offer will, of course, vary according to the nature of the business. It may be helpful to call in an OSHA consultant to recommend specific training for your workplace.

Don't overlook the need to train existing employees who are moving into new jobs or are starting to use new equipment. And all employees need refresher instruction from time to time, since it's human nature to become complacent and forget the safety rules.

You must maintain records of your safety training efforts and be prepared to show these records to OSHA inspectors.

5. Inspections

OSHA inspectors can inspect your workplace at any time without advance notice or authorization by a court and—based on what they find there— issue citations and impose penalties. However, it's unlikely inspectors will make random inspections unless you're in a particularly hazardous business such as construction. That's because there aren't enough inspectors to go around; OSHA must use its resources prudently.

If you have a workplace with 10 or fewer employees and you're in an industry that has a low injury rate, you're exempt from random inspections by federal OSHA officials. State safety and health laws, however, may empower local inspectors to randomly inspect smaller businesses. But if yours is a small insurance agency, retail store, computer repair shop or similar low injury business, your chances of receiving a random inspection are remote.

Most small businesses are inspected only if:
- an employee has complained to OSHA
- a worker has died from a job-related injury, or
- three or more employees have been hospitalized because of a workplace condition. Of course, you're required to report such fatalities and hospitalizations to OSHA. (See Section A3.)

Even though you may be at low risk of inspection, you're not free to ignore safety and health concerns. You're legally required to take the initiative in identifying and eliminating safety and health problems that can affect employees.

Inspectors Can Obtain Search Warrants

OSHA officials can't inspect your place without your consent. If you refuse an inspector entry, he or she must obtain a search warrant from a judge before coming into your workplace. But by insisting on a search warrant, you practically assure that when the inspector returns, he or she will go through your place with a fine-tooth comb. Cooperation rather than resistance is usually the wiser course of action. However, if you're nervous about what an inspection may disclose, ask the inspector for an extension of time and seek advice immediately from a lawyer.

A typical inspection follows a set pattern.

The opening conference. The inspector meets with you and a representative selected by your employees. All of you discuss procedures for the inspection. The inspector reviews your records on health and safety problems as well as any monitoring you're performing in such areas as noise, ventilation and hazardous chemicals.

The walkaround. The inspector observes the working conditions, looking for signs of health and safety hazards. Are all required signs and notices posted? Are there strong odors in the air? Eye irritants? Dust or fumes? How about noise and temperature levels? Are there signs of spilled or leaking chemicals? These and other problems are noted. The inspector may make measurements of noise levels and take samples of dust and air to be analyzed.

Review of safety and health programs. The inspector checks on whether you have qualified people and the right equipment to monitor levels of hazardous materials—and also looks at whether your employees are taking part in training programs on workplace hazards and emergency procedures.

The closing conference. The inspector discusses the safety hazards that have been found and ways to correct the problems. You're given a specific deadline by which you must make the corrections. The inspector documents all violations of OSHA standards and, if a violation is more than a minor one, issues a citation. If you receive an OSHA citation, you must post it near where the violations occurred. This allows employees to get involved in any further enforcement actions by OSHA.

6. Penalties for Violations

Penalties ordered by OSHA depend on the seriousness of the violation. For willful or repeated violations, your company may have to pay thousands of dollars in penalties. And if a worker has died because you violated OSHA

standards, you could even be sent to prison. For less serious violations—
problems that are unlikely to cause serious harm or death—the penalty may
be up to $1,000. In assessing penalties, OSHA looks at several factors,
including:

- the seriousness of the hazard
- your history of violations
- whether you've made a good faith effort to comply with OSHA standards, and
- the size of your business.

    There's an appeal process through which you can challenge an OSHA
citation against your business. If the citation is issued by the federal OSHA,
you have 15 days to file a notice of contest with the agency. If a state OSHA
issues citations in your state, check with that agency to confirm the filing
deadline. It makes sense to consult a lawyer before embarking on an appeal.

    After the notice of contest is filed, an administrative law judge will
conduct a hearing, giving you and others concerned a chance to present
evidence. If you disagree with the decision of the administrative law judge,
there's an additional appeal process within OSHA. Ultimately, you can
appeal to a court if you can't reach an acceptable resolution within OSHA.
Fortunately, most OSHA disputes are resolved through a voluntary settlement.

7. Workers' Rights

Keep in mind that workers have two basic rights under OSHA—rights that
make good common sense.

    First, workers have a right to complain to OSHA about safety or health
conditions without being penalized for doing so. Firing or discriminating
against employees who have made such complaints is a violation of OSHA
provisions.

    Second, in some situations, workers have a right to refuse to work if
they think the workplace is unsafe. The legal test is this: Does the worker
have a reasonable and good faith belief that there's an immediate risk of
serious injury or death? If so, the worker can walk off the job and refuse to

work until you've corrected the problem or you've determined, after an investigation, there's no imminent danger. While you investigate or correct the problem, you can place the worker temporarily in another job at equal pay. It's usually unwise to react by demoting or firing the complaining employee—which can be another violation of OSHA if the complaint is determined to be well-founded.

Example: Mildred runs a local delivery service. One afternoon, Arlene, one of the drivers, hears that the brakes locked that morning on one of the business vans. She refuses to drive that van until the brakes are checked out by a qualified mechanic. Mildred, believing that the brake problem was caused by careless driving, orders Arlene to use the van. When Arlene says no, Mildred fires her. Arlene sues. Even though the brakes are later found to be adequate, Arlene wins because the court determines that, based on the information she had, Arlene had a reasonable and good faith belief that she'd be exposed to an immediate risk of serious injury or death if she used the truck. Mildred is ordered to reinstate Arlene and to pay her for the time she missed since being fired.

B. Getting Help

Your eyes will probably become glazed at the thought of poring over pages of federal regulations on health and safety in the workplace. Fortunately, there are easier ways to learn what you must do to comply with OSHA requirements—and the learning will cost you little or nothing.

1. Worksite Consultations

In each state, there's an agency funded mostly by the federal office of OSHA that offers free, on-site consultations. (See the listing below.)

As in a formal OSHA inspection, you and the consultant will tour the workplace together. The consultant will point out safety and health risks and then, at a closing conference, give you practical advice on how to eliminate hazards. He or she won't issue citations or propose penalties. Nor will the consultant provide information about your workplace to the OSHA inspection staff, except in extreme circumstances.

Although OSHA encourages employees to participate in the consultant's walk-through, you're free to exclude employees from the consultation process—unless a union contract gives employee representatives the right to take part.

Opening the Door to Enforcement Action

If the consultant finds a "serious condition"—one from which it's reasonably predictable that death or serious harm could result—he or she will work with you to control or eliminate the hazard within a time period that you jointly determine. If the consultant isn't satisfied with your progress, he or she may report you to an OSHA official. According to OSHA, consultants rarely find conditions which require them to report a business.

SOURCES FOR OSHA CONSULTATIONS

Alabama	7(c)(1) Onsite Consultation Program Martha Parham West P.O. Box 70388 Tuscaloosa, AL 35487 (205) 348-3033
Alaska	Division of Consultation and Training ADOL/OSHA 3301 Eagle Street P.O. Box 10702 Anchorage, AK 99510 (907) 269-4957
Arizona	Consultation and Training Division of Occupational Safety and Health Industrial Commission of Arizona 800 West Washington Phoenix, AZ 85007-9070 (602) 542-5795
Arkansas	OSHA Consultation Arkansas Department of Labor 10421 West Markham Little Rock, AK 72205 (501) 682-4522
California	CAL/OSHA Consultation Service Department of Industrial Relations Room 5246 45 Fremont Street San Francisco, CA 94105 (415) 972-8515
Colorado	Occupational Safety & Health Section Colorado State University 115 Environmental Health Building Fort Collins, CO 80523 (970) 491-6151
Connecticut	Division of Occupational Safety & Health Connecticut Department of Labor 38 Wolcott Hill Road Wethersfield, CT 06109 (203) 566-4550

Delaware	Occupational Safety and Health Division of Industrial Affairs Delaware Department of Labor 4425 Market Street Wilmington, DE 19802 (302) 761-8219
District of Columbia	Office of Occupational Safety and Health District of Columbia Department of Employment Services 950 Upshhur Street, NW Washington, DC 20011 (202) 576-6339
Florida	7(c)(1) Onsite Consultation Program Bureau of Industrial Safetyand Health Department of Labor and Employment Security 2002 St. Augustine Road Building E., Suite 45 Tallahassee, FL 32399-0633 (904) 488-3044
Georgia	7(c)(1) Onsite Consultation Program Georgia Institute of Technology O'Keefe Building - Room 22 Atlanta, GA 30332 (404) 894-2643
Guam	OSHA Onsite Consultation Department of Labor, Government of Guam Post Office Box 9970 Tamuning, Guam 96931 (671) 475-0136
Hawaii	Consultation and Training Branch Department of Labor and Industrial Relations 830 Punchbowl Street Honolulu, HI 96813 (808) 586-9100
Idaho	Safety & Health Consultation Program Boise State University Department of Health Studies 1910 University Drive, ET-338A Boise, ID 83725 (208) 385-3283

Illinois	Illinois Onsite Consultation Industrial Services Divislon Department of Commerce and Community Affairs State of Illinois Center 100 West Randolph Street Suite 3-400 Chicago, IL 60601 (312) 814-2337
Indiana	Division of Labor Bureau of Safety, Education and Training 402 West Washington Room W195 Indianapolis, IN 46204-2287 (317) 232-2688
Iowa	7(c)(1) Consultation Program Iowa Bureau of Labor 1000 East Grand Avenue Des Moines, IA 50319 (515) 281-5352
Kansas	Kansas 7(c)(1) Consultation Program Kansas Department of Human Resources 512 South West 6th Street Topeka, KS 66603-3150 (913) 296-7476
Kansas	Kansas 7(c)(1) Consultation Program Kansas Department of Human Resources 512 South West 6th Street Topeka, KS 66603-3150 (913) 296-7476
Kentucky	Division of Education & Training Kentucky Labor Cabinet 1047 U.S. Highway 127, South Frankfort, KY 40601 (502) 564-6895
Louisiana	7(c)(1) Consultation Program Louisiana Department of Labor P.O. Box 94094 Baton Rouge, La 70804-9094 (504) 342-9601

Maine	Division of Industrial Safety Maine Bureau of Labor Standards Division of Industrial Safety State House Station #82 Augusta, ME 04333 (207) 624-6460
Maryland	Division of Labor and Industry 501 Saint Paul Place 10th Floor Baltimore, MD 21202 (410) 333-4210
Massachusetts	The Commonwealth of Massachusetts Department of Labor & Industries 1001 Watertown Street New Newton, MA 02165 (617) 727-3982
Michigan	Michigan Department of Public Health Division of Occupational Health 3423 N. Logan Street P.O. Box 30195 Lansing, MI 48909 (517) 335-8250
	Bureau of Safety and Regulation Michigan Department of Labor 7150 Harris Drive P.O. Box 30015 Lansing, Ml 48909 (517) 322-1809
Minnesota	Consultation Division Department of Labor and Industry 443 Lafayette Road St. Paul, MN 55155 (612) 297-2393
Mississippi	Mississippi State University Center for Safety and Health 2906 North State Street, Suite 201 Jackson, MS 39216 (601) 987-3981
Missouri	Onsite Consultation Program Division of Labor Standards Department of Labor and Industrial Relations 3315 West Truman Boulevard

	Jefferson City, MO 65109
	(314) 751-3403
Montana	Department of Labor & Industry
	Bureau of Safety
	P.O. Box 1728
	Helena, MT 59624-1728
	(406) 444-6418
Nebraska	Division of Safety, Labor and Safety Standards
	Nebraska Department of Labor
	State Office Building
	301 Centennial Mall, South
	Lincoln, NE 68509-5024
	(402) 471-4717
Nevada	Division of Preventive Safety
	Department of Industrial Relations
	2500 West Washington, Suite 106
	Las Vega, NV 89106
	(702) 486-5016
New Hampshire	New Hampshire Department of Health
	Division of Public Health Services
	6 Hazen Drive
	Concord, NH 03301-6527
	(603) 271-2024
New Jersey	Division of Workplace Standards
	New Jersey Department of Labor
	Station Plaza 4, CN953
	22 South Clinton Avenue
	Trenton, NJ 08625-0953
	(609) 292-3923
New Mexico	New Mexico Environmental Department
	Occupational Health & Safety Bureau
	525 Camino de los Marquez, Suite 3
	P.O. Box 26110
	Sante Fe, NM 87502
	(505) 827-4230
New York	Division of Safety and Health
	State Office Campus
	Building 12, Room 457
	Albany, NY 12240
	(518) 457 2481

North Carolina	Bureau of Consultative Services North Carolina Department of Labor—OSHA Division 319 Chapanoke Road, Suite 105 Raleigh, NC 27603-3432 (919) 662-4644
North Dakota	Division of Environmental Engineering 1200 Missouri Avenue, Room 304 Bismarck, ND 58506-5520 (701) 328-5188
Ohio	Division of Onsite Consultation Bureau of Employment Services 145 South Front Street Columbus, OH 43216 (614) 644-2246
Oklahoma	OSHA Division Oklahoma Department of Labor 4001 North Lincoln Boulevard Oklahoma City, OK 73105-5212 (405) 528-1500
Oregon	7(c)(1) Consultation Program Department of Insurance and Finance Labor and Industries Building, Room 430 350 Winter Street, N.E. Salem, OR 97310 (503) 378-3272
Pennsylvania	Indiana University of Pennsylvania Safety Sciences Department 205 Uhler Hall Indiana, PA 15705 (412) 357-2561/2396 Toll free in state (800) 382-1241
Rhode Island	Division of Occupational Health Rhode Island Department of Health 3 Capitol Hill Providence, Rl 02908 (401) 277-2438
South Carolina	7(c)(1) Onsite Consultation Program Consultation and Monitoring, SC DOL 3600 Forest Drive P.O. Box 11329 Columbia, SC 29211 (803) 734-9614

South Dakota	Engineering Extension Onsite Technical Division South Dakota State University P.O. Box 510 210 Rugsley Circle Brookings, SD 57007 (605) 688-4101
Tennessee	OSHA Consultative Services Tennessee Department of Labor 710 James Robertson Parkway, 3rd Floor Nashville, TN 37219 (615) 741-7036
Texas	Workers' Compensation Commission Health & Safety Division Southfield Building 4000 South I H 35 Austin, TX 76704 (512) 440-3834
Utah	Utah Industrial Commission Consultation Services 160 East 300 South, 3rd Floor Salt Lake City, UT 84114-6650 (801) 530-6868
Vermont	Division of Occupational Safety & Health Vermont Department of Labor & Industry National Life Building, Drawer #20 Montpelier, VT 05602-3401 (802) 828-2765
Virginia	Virginia Department of Labor & Industry Occupational Safety and Health Training and Consultation 13 South 13th Street Richmond, VA 23219 (804) 786-6359
Virgin Islands	Division of Occupational Safety & Health Virgin Islands Department of Labor 3021 Golden Rock Christiansted St. Croix, VI 00840 (809) 722-1315

Washington	Washington Department of Labor & Industries Division of Industrial Safety & Health P.O. Box 44643 Olympia, WA (360) 902-5638
West Virginia	West Virginia Department of Labor State Capitol, Building 3, Room 319 1800 E. Washington Street Charleston, WV 25305 (304) 558-7890
Wisconsin	Section of Occupational Health Wisconsin Department of Health and Human Services 1414 E. Washington Avenue Room 112 Madison, Wl 53703 (608) 266-8579
	Wisconsin Department of Industry Labor and Human Relations Bureau of Safety Inspection 401 Pilot Court, Suite C Waukesha, Wl 53188 (414) 521-5063
Wyoming	Occupational Health and Safety State of Wyoming 122 West 25th, Herschler Bldg. Cheyenne, WY 82002 (307) 777-7786

2. Safety Codes

Written safety codes are a good way to let employees know that you take safety seriously. Since each workplace is different, make sure your safety code is tailored to the specific needs of your business.

OSHA has suggested a safety code that you may find useful as a starting point—but you'll undoubtedly need to make changes to make it fit.

SAFETY CODE OF ABC, INC.

1. All employees of this company must follow these safe practice rules and report all unsafe conditions or practices to a supervisor.

2. Supervisors will require employees to comply with all safety rules.

3. All employees periodically will be given instruction on workplace safety and health.

4. Anyone under the influence of alcohol or drugs will not be allowed on the job while in that condition.

5. No one will be permitted or required to work while his or her ability or alertness is impaired by fatigue or illness.

6. Employees must make sure that all guards and other protective devices are in place, and must wear protective equipment and clothing in specified work areas.

7. Horseplay, scuffling and other acts which may endanger employees are prohibited.

8. Work should be planned to prevent injuries when working with equipment and handling heavy materials. Back injuries are the most frequent and often the most persistent and painful type of workplace injury.

9. Workers must not handle or tamper with electrical equipment, machinery or air or water lines unless they have received instructions from their supervisors.

10. Report injuries promptly to a supervisor. A first aid kit is located at

   _____ .

   Emergency phone numbers are located at _____ .

Source: OSHA Handbook for Small Business

For additional help with OSHA rules and regulations, see the *OSHA Handbook for Small Business*—OSHA Publication 2209—available for $4 from the U.S. Government Printing Office, Washington, DC 20402, (202) 783-3238. It contains self-inspection checklists covering such topics as fire protection, personal protective equipment and clothing, walkways, floor and wall openings, stairs and stairways, elevated surfaces, exit doors, hand tools and equipment. These checklists can help you and employees identify potential problems.

If you want to order the full text of the OSHA regulations, these materials are available from the U.S. Government Printing Office at a small cost, or can be found in the Code of Federal Regulations at most law libraries. There are four separate sets of standards:

General Industry—29 Code of Federal Regulations 1910
Construction—29 Code of Federal Regulations 1926
Maritime Employment—29 Code of Federal Regulations 1915 - 1919
Agriculture—29 Code of Federal Regulations 1904

Also very useful is Primer on Occupational Safety and Health, by Fred Blosser (BNA Books). Call 800/372-1033 for current price and ordering information.

C. State OSHA Laws

If a state has a health and safety law that meets or exceeds federal OSHA standards, the state can take over enforcement of the standards from federal administrators. This means that all inspections and enforcement actions will be handled by your state OSHA rather than its federal counterpart.

So far, 23 states have been approved for such enforcement regarding private employers. They include: Alaska, Arizona, California, Hawaii, Indiana, Iowa, Kentucky, Maryland, Michigan, Minnesota, Nevada, New

Mexico, North Carolina, Oregon, South Carolina, Tennessee, Utah, Vermont, Virginia, Washington and Wyoming. (See the contact details below.)

New York and Connecticut also have OSHA-type laws, but they only apply to government employees. Other states are considering passing OSHA laws—and some of the above states are considering amending coverage and content of existing laws.

If your business is located in a state that has an OSHA law, contact your state agency for a copy of the safety and health standards that are relevant to your business. State standards may be more strict than federal standards, and the requirements for posting notices may be different.

STATE OSHA OFFICES

Alaska Department of Labor
1111 West 8th Street, Room 306
Juneau, AK 99802
(907) 465-2700

Industrial Comm. of Arizona
800 West Washington
Phoenix, AZ 85007
(602) 542-5795

California Department of Industrial Relations
455 Golden Gate Avenue, 4th Floor
San Francisco, CA 94102
(415) 703-4590

Hawaii Department of Labor and Industrial Relations
830 Punchbowl Street
Honolulu, Hl 96813
(808) 586-8844

Indiana Department of Labor
State Office Building, Room W-195
402 West Washington Street
Indianapolis, IN 46204
(317) 232-2378

Iowa Div. of Labor Services
1000 East Grand Avenue
Des Moines, IA 50319
(515) 281-3447

Kentucky Labor Cabinet
1049 US Highway 127 South
Frankfort, KY 40601
(502) 564-3070

Maryland Div. of Labor and Industry
Dept of Licensing and Regs.
501 Street Paul Place, 2nd Floor
Baltimore, MD 21202
(301) 333-4179

Michigan Department of Labor
P.O. Box 30015
Victor Office Center
201 North Washington Square
Lansing, MI 48933
(517) 373-9600

Michigan Department of Public Health
P.O. Box 30195
3423 North Logan Street
Lansing, MI 48909
(517) 335-8022

Minnesota Department of Labor and Industry
443 Lafayette Road
Street Paul, MN 55155
(612) 296-2342

Nevada Department of Industrial Relations
Division of Occupational Safety and Health
Capitol Complex
1370 S. Curry Street
Carson City, NV 89710
(702) 687-3032

New Mexico Environment Department
Occupational Health and Safety Bureau
P.O. Box 26110
1190 St. Francis Drive
Santa Fe, NM 87502
(505) 827-2850

North Carolina Department of Labor
4 West Edenton Street
Raleigh, NC 27601
(919) 733-0360

Oregon Occupational Safety and Health Div.
Department of Insurance and Finance, Room 160
21 Labor and Industry Building
Summer and Chemekita Streets, N.E.
Salem, OR 97310
(503) 378-3272

South Carolina Department of Labor
P.O. Box 11329
3600 Forest Drive
Columbia, SC 29211
(803) 734-9594

Tennessee Department of Labor
501 Union Bldg, 2nd Floor, S. "A"
Nashville, TN 37243
(615) 741-2582

Utah Occupational Safety and Health
160 E. 300 South
P.O. Box 5800
Salt Lake City, UT 84110
(801) 530-6900

Vermont Department of Labor and Industry
120 State Street
Montpelier, VT 05620
(802) 828-2288

Virgin Islands Department of Labor
2131 Hospital Street
Christiansted, St Croix VI 00840
(809) 773-1994

Virginia Department of Labor and Industry
Powers-Taylor Building
13 South 13th Street
Richmond, VA 23219
(804) 786-2376

Washington Department of Labor and Industries
P.O. Box 44001
Olympia, WA 98504
(206) 956-4200

Wyoming Department of Employment
Occupational Health and Safety Administration
Herschler Bldg, 2nd Floor East
122 West 25th Street
Cheyenne, WY 82002
(307) 777-7672

D. Hazardous Chemicals

The OSHA rules include a section called the Hazard Communication
Standard. Many people call this the right to know law. Basically, the
standard requires you to give information to your employees about the
hazardous chemicals they handle.

Many states also have right to know laws, including:

Alabama (Ala. Code §22-33-1)
Alaska (Alaska Stat. 18.60.067(a))
California (Cal. Lab. Code (Deering's) §§6360 to 6399.9)
Connecticut (Conn. Gen. Stat. §31-401(a))
Delaware (16 Del. Code Ann. §§2406(c), 2415(a))

Florida (Fla. Stat. §442.115(1)(4))

Illinois (Ill. Rev. Stat. ch. 48 §1402)

Iowa (Iowa Code §89B.8(1))

Maine (26 Me. Rev. Stat. Ann. §1709)

Maryland (Md. Ann. Code Art. 89 §32E(a))

Massachusetts (Mass. Ann. Laws ch. 111 F §15)

Michigan (Mich. Comp. Laws Ann. §408.1027(8))

Minnesota (Minn. Stat. Ann. §182.653)

Montana (Mont. Code Ann. §50-78-202(2))

New Hampshire (N.H. Rev. Stat. Ann. §277-A:5)

New Jersey (N.J. Rev. Stat. 34:5A-13(a))

New York (N.Y. Labor Law §876 sub. 1)

North Carolina (N.C. Gen. Stat. §95-191)

Oklahoma (Okla. Hazard Comm. Standard)

Oregon (Or. Rev. Stat. §437-144-010)

Pennsylvania (97 Pa. Cons. Stat. §7305(e))

Rhode Island (R.I. Gen. Laws §28-21-1)

Tennessee (L. 1985, House Bill No. 731)

Vermont (18 Vt. Stat. Ann. §1725(a))

Washington (Wash. Rev. Stat. §49.70.100)

West Virginia (W. Va. Code §21-3-18(c))

Wisconsin (Wis. Stat. Ann.§111.581(1))

The requirements of informing employees vary somewhat from state to state. If your business handles any chemicals, be sure to get a copy of your state's rules. Because most of the state laws are similar to the federal right to know rules, this discussion will focus on the federal law. If your state has standards that are more stringent than the federal ones, there are still some unresolved questions about whether you need only comply with the federal standards. Until this legal issue is clearly resolved, it's wisest to follow the stricter standards.

To understand the right to know laws—state or federal—you must first become familiar with the Material Safety Data Sheets (MSDS) supplied by manufacturers of all hazardous chemicals. They contain a wealth of information, including:

- the physical hazards of the chemical such as flammability and explosiveness
- health hazards—the symptoms of exposure and the medical conditions that can be made worse by exposure
- how the chemical enters the body and the limits of safe exposure
- whether the chemical is known to cause cancer
- how to safely handle the chemical
- recommended protection methods including protective clothing and equipment, and
- first aid and emergency procedures should a chemical be mishandled.

Obviously, if an employee is working with hazardous chemicals, this is essential information. That's why the law requires you to keep the MSDS for each hazardous chemical and make it accessible to employees. You must also keep a list of all the hazardous chemicals used in your business and label all containers. And you're required to train employees in the safe use of hazardous chemicals.

Example: Ace Water Treatment Corporation sells water treatment systems to rural homeowners whose water comes from underground wells. Ace issues demonstration kits to its sales staff so they can demonstrate to potential customers the extent of impurities in the homeowner's water supply. In one test, the salesperson adds a few drops of potassium hydroxide to a sample of the customer's water so that certain impurities will collect at the bottom of the test tube. Potassium hydroxide is a hazardous chemical sometimes known as lye.

The chemical comes from the manufacturer with an MSDS explaining its dangers and how it should be handled—for example, goggles should be used to protect the user's eyes. To comply with the right to know law, Ace keeps the MSDS and makes it available to employees. Ace makes sure that all containers are properly labeled, and that all employees are thoroughly trained in how to use and handle the chemical. To further protect its employees, Ace issues protective goggles to those who perform water tests using the chemical.

E. Workers' Compensation

The workers' compensation system provides replacement income and medical expenses to employees who suffer work-related injuries or illnesses. Benefits may also extend to the survivors of workers who are killed on the job.

Workers' compensation is a no-fault system. The employee is entitled to receive stated benefits whether or not the employer provided a safe workplace and whether or not the worker's own carelessness contributed to the injury or illness. But the employer, too, receives some protection because the employee is limited to fixed types of compensation—basically, partial wage replacement and payment of medical bills. The employee can't get paid for pain and suffering or mental anguish.

To cover the cost of workers' compensation benefits for employees, you'll usually need to pay for insurance—either through a state fund or a private insurance company. While self-insurance is a possibility in some states, the technical requirements usually make this an impractical alternative for a small business.

1. Coverage Requirements

Each state has its own workers' compensation statute. While the details differ from state to state, one thing is clear: if you have employees, you generally need to obtain workers' compensation coverage. Your state workers' compensation bureau can tell you about any legal requirements for informing employees of their rights—generally by displaying a poster.

State laws vary as to whether sole proprietors, partners and executive officers can or must be covered by workers' compensation. In some states, these owners and managers have the option of being covered or not. If you're in one of these states and you want this coverage—which will give you the same benefits as other workers who are injured—mention this when you apply for coverage through a state fund or a private insurance carrier. (For more on arranging for coverage, see Section E2.)

Similarly, in some states, sole proprietors, partners and executive officers are automatically covered but you have the option of excluding them. Ask a representative of the state fund or private insurance carrier how to do this when you apply for coverage.

A few states require workers' compensation coverage only if you have three or more employees.

YOU'RE STILL LIABLE FOR INTENTIONAL TORTS

While workers' compensation is the employee's exclusive remedy for most work-related injuries or illnesses, there's a major exception: injuries or illnesses caused by the intentional actions of the employer. An employee who can prove that your intentional actions caused an injury or illness can take you to court, seeking a full range of damages—including, for example, damages for pain and suffering as well as economic losses.

Obviously, if you or a supervisor were to physically assault an employee, that would qualify as an intentional action. But courts sometimes treat other workplace events as intentional, too. Suppose, for example, that to speed up production, you remove the safety devices from a dangerous machine. An employee is injured using the machine, but you continue to require workers to use the machine in its unsafe condition. You've probably set yourself up for an intentional injury claim because you know with "substantial certainty" that additional workers will be injured by that machine.

In that situation, injured employees would not be limited to their remedies under your state's workers' compensation law. They would be able to sue you and your business under traditional tort theories.

Rejecting Coverage Can Be a Mistake

In three states—New Jersey, South Carolina and Texas—workers' compensation coverage isn't mandatory for an employer. You can choose whether or not you want to secure workers' compensation insurance for your workplace. But if you opt not to and you're sued by an employee who claims to have been injured on the job by your negligence, you won't be able to use the employee's own carelessness as a defense. Therefore, most wise employers obtain workers' compensation, no matter where their businesses are located.

2. Arranging for Coverage

Some states allow an employer to self-insure—a process that typically requires the business to maintain a hefty cash reserve earmarked for workers' compensation claims. Usually, this isn't practical for small businesses. Most small businesses buy insurance through a state fund or from a private insurance carrier. If private insurance is an option in your state, discuss it with the insurance agent or broker who handles the basic insurance policy for your business. Often you save money on premiums by coordinating workers' compensation coverage with property damage and public liability insurance. A good agent or broker may also be able to explain the mechanics of a state fund where that's an available option or is required.

In the following states, you must purchase coverage from the state fund: Nevada, North Dakota, Ohio, Washington and West Virginia.

In the following states that have state-run workers' compensation funds, you have a choice of buying coverage from the state or a private insurer: Arizona, California, Colorado, Hawaii, Idaho, Maryland, Michigan, Minnesota, Montana, New York, Oklahoma, Oregon, Pennsylvania and Utah.

Rhode Island may soon be added to this list. In Wyoming, an employer must buy coverage from the state for hazardous occupations. Otherwise, the employer can choose between the state fund and a private insurer.

Insurance rates are based on the industry and occupation involved, as well as the size of the payroll. Your safety record can also influence the rate; if you have more accidents than is usually anticipated, your rate is likely to be increased.

3. Controlling Costs

Premiums are based on two factors: industry classification and payroll. If your premium is above a certain amount—$5,000 in many states—your actual experience with workers' compensation claims will affect your premiums. Your rate can go up or down, depending on how your claims compare with other businesses in your industry. The number of claims filed by your employees affects your premium more than the dollar value of the claims. That's because if you have a lot of accidents, it's assumed that you have an unsafe workplace and the insurance company eventually will have to pay out some large claims.

Here are some steps you can take to try to keep your workers' compensation costs down.

a. Preventing accidents

Emphasize safety in the workplace. Provide proper equipment, safety devices and protective clothing. Train and re-train your employees in safe procedures and in how to deal with emergencies. Set up a safety committee comprised of both managers and workers. Promote employee health by offering wellness and fitness programs.

b. Buying coverage wisely

Seek out a participating plan in which the insurance company pays dividends to its insured employers. It helps to find a solid company with a long history of paying dividends—but dividends are never guaranteed.

Consider being put on a retrospective rating plan which, unfortunately, isn't usually available to many small businesses. In such plans, the insurance company agrees to adjust your premium at the end of the year based on your actual claims experience. If you have a strong safety program, this program can be better for you than a dividend-type program—which generally looks at the insurance company's claims experience and not just the history of your business.

Make sure your business and your employees are properly classified. Don't let the insurance company mistakenly place your business in a class that pays a higher premium because of job hazards. And, since workers are also classified based on the nature of their work, check to see that the insurance company has classified them correctly.

Remove overtime pay from the payroll figures on which the insurance company calculates your premium.

c. Following Up

Use light duty or modified work assignments to help workers who have been injured on the job but are allowed back to work on a trial basis.

Monitor claims. If you learn that an employee seems to have recovered but is still accepting workers' compensation benefits, ask him or her for an explanation. If something still seems amiss, notify the insurance company or state fund.

For more information on workers' compensation insurance—as well as business insurance in general—see *Insuring Your Business*, by Sean Mooney (Insurance Information Institute Press). The book costs $22.50 and can save you hundreds of dollars on insurance premiums. For ordering information, call 800/331-9146. The publisher also offers a free brochure containing a sampling of the money-saving advice found in the book.

Also see *Workers' Comp for Employers—Taking Control: How to Cut Claims, Reduce Premiums and Stay Out of Trouble*, by James Walsh (Merritt Publishing); the cost is $29.95.

4. Injuries and Illnesses Covered

As an employer, you needn't dig very deeply into the fine points of workers' compensation law. The state fund or private insurance company that covers your workplace will have its own lawyers resolve legal questions about whether a worker is entitled to compensation for a particular disability and, if so, how much the worker is entitled to receive. When a worker seeks to receive benefits that are questionable, these lawyers will challenge the employee in your behalf.

Still, as a well-informed employer, you may want to learn a bit more about how the system works. While workers' compensation law varies somewhat from state to state, there's enough similarity among the states to justify some general statements.

To be covered by workers' compensation, an employee's injury needn't be caused by a sudden accident such as a fall. Basically, any injury that occurs in connection with work is covered. Many workers, for example, receive compensation for repetitive motion injuries such as Carpal Tunnel Syndrome, which primarily afflicts the wrists, hands and forearms. (See Section I.)

In theory, if a worker's injury was intentionally self-inflicted or was caused by substance abuse or by some other non-work cause such as a hobby, the injury won't be covered. But in a disputed case, the worker is still likely to get the benefits by showing that his or her behavior wasn't the only thing that caused the injury.

Workers may also be compensated for some illnesses and diseases. An illness is likely to be covered by workers' compensation when the nature of the job increases the workers' chances of suffering from that disease. Illnesses that are the gradual result of work conditions—for example, emotional illness, heart conditions, lung disease and stress-related digestive problems—increasingly are being covered by workers' compensation.

Finally, there are death benefits. Dependents of workers killed on the job can usually collect workers' compensation benefits.

Don't Penalize Workers Who File Claims

In most states, it's a violation of the workers' compensation statute or public policy to discriminate against an employee for filing a workers' compensation claim.

5. Benefits Paid

Workers' compensation covers the employee's medical and rehabilitation expenses. It also provides income to the employee to offset a big part of lost wages. Typically, a worker receives two-thirds of his or her average wages up to a fixed ceiling. But since these payments are tax free, a worker who receives average wages fares reasonably well.

In most states, workers become eligible for wage loss replacement benefits as soon as they've lost a few days of work because of an injury covered by workers' compensation. The number of days required to qualify varies by state. Some states allow the payments to be paid retroactively to the first day of wage loss if the injury keeps the employee out of work for an extended period.

Workers may receive lump sum benefits if they have a total disability or a permanent partial disability. In some states, there are specific amounts provided for permanent partial disability such as the loss of an eye or a foot.

6. Independent Contractors

Workers' compensation insurance is required only for employees—not for independent contractors who work for you. (Independent contractors are covered in greater detail in Chapter 11.) Small businesses sometimes buy services from independent contractors to save money on workers' compensation insurance, as well as taxes and other expenses normally associated with employees. That's fine as long as you correctly label people as independent contractors rather than employees. But if you make a mistake, and a person improperly labeled as an independent contractor is injured while doing work for your business, you may have to pay large sums to cover medical bills and lost wages which should have been covered by workers' compensation insurance.

In addition, you can sometimes have a problem with a properly classified independent contractor who hires employees to perform some work for you. The trouble can come if the independent contractor doesn't carry workers' compensation insurance.

Require Proof of Insurance

When hiring an independent contractor, ask to see an insurance certificate establishing that the independent contractor's employee's are covered by workers' compensation insurance. For good measure, make sure too that the independent contractor has general liability insurance.

F. Disease Prevention

Under OSHA, your business may need to take precautions to protect employees from infection in the workplace. The OSHA rules apply to employees who may be exposed to blood or other potentially infectious material—and so primarily affect employees who work in hospitals, clinics, medical offices and nursing homes.

If it's reasonably likely that your employees will come into contact with blood and other infectious materials, check with OSHA to learn the requirements for protective practices and equipment.

EMPLOYEES WITH HIV OR AIDS

Under the Americans With Disabilities Act (ADA) and similar state laws, a person who is HIV positive or has AIDS is considered to have a disability. You can't discriminate against that person—or use the disability as a reason for rejecting a person if he or she is otherwise qualified for a particular job. You may also need to reasonably accommodate that person so that he or she can perform the work required. Normally, your duty to reasonably accommodate a person with a disability—including AIDS—is triggered by that person requesting an accommodation. In the case of someone who has AIDS, the accommodation may consist of a flexible work schedule, reduced hours, work at home arrangements or a reduction in travel.

You don't have to permit an HIV-infected person to continue in a position if the infection poses a health threat to others. Almost all such positions are in the healthcare field.

The ADA also prohibits discrimination against people who associate with those who have AIDS. So it's unlawful, for example, to reject a job applicant because he or she lives with someone who has AIDS.

If you learn that an employee has AIDS or is HIV positive, keep the information confidential. Use it only to accommodate the person in performing his or her job.

G. Tobacco Smoke

A state law or municipal ordinance may limit or prohibit smoking on your business premises. Some laws and ordinances are designed primarily to protect nonsmoking employees from second-hand tobacco smoke. Others seek to protect nonsmoking customers and other visitors as well.

Here are a few examples of state laws.

- In Alaska, if your business has a designated smoking area, you must ventilate it to ensure that nonsmokers aren't subjected to tobacco smoke.

- In California, you can't permit smoking in an enclosed place of employment—although there are some exceptions such as employee break rooms; if you do allow smoking in permitted areas, you must separately ventilate these areas.

- In Florida, you must create smoking and nonsmoking areas, based on the proportion of workers who smoke and those who don't.

- In Minnesota, you can't allow smoking in an enclosed workplace, except for private enclosed offices occupied exclusively by smokers.

- In Vermont, you must adopt a smoking policy that either prohibits smoking throughout the workplace or restricts it to enclosed designated areas—although in certain circumstances, with employee approval, you can allow smoking in designated areas even if they are not enclosed.

For up-to-date information on your responsibilities and options concerning smoking in the workplace, check with your state and local health departments.

In addition to meeting the requirements of laws and ordinances that limit or prohibit smoking in the workplace, be aware that you may be liable to nonsmoking employees if you don't take appropriate action on their complaints. For example, an employee who develops bronchial asthma from exposure to tobacco smoke may be entitled to workers' compensation benefits. And an employee who has a severe respiratory ailment that's aggravated by tobacco smoke may be entitled under the ADA to a smoke-free workplace.

While you can prohibit smoking on the job, avoid a policy that prohibits an employee from smoking off the job as well. Such a broad prohibition can invade a worker's privacy and is specifically barred by some state laws.

Smokers Can Use Some Help

Recognize that giving up smoking on the job can be difficult. Some experts equate nicotine addiction with a cocaine or heroin habit. To demonstrate your concern, you might offer to pay the cost of an employee's tuition in a stop smoking program if the smoker successfully kicks the habit.

H. Drug and Alcohol Abuse

There is no law that prevents you from combating the use of the drugs and alcohol in the workplace. There are, however, some limits on your ability to test employees for drug usage.

Legally, you're free to:

* prohibit the use of drugs and alcohol in the workplace
* require that employees not come to work or return from meals or breaks under the influence of alcohol or drugs, and

• require that employees who use alcohol or illegally use drugs meet the same performance standards you impose on other employees.

You needn't tolerate absenteeism, tardiness, poor job performance or accidents caused by alcohol or illegal drug use.

Helping Those in Need

One enlightened approach—especially if an employee with a drug or alcohol problem has valuable skills—is to offer an assistance program to help the employee deal with the problem. Or you might consider a modified work schedule to permit the person to attend a self-help program.

1. Illegal Drug Use

There's nothing wrong with firing an employee or rejecting an applicant who uses, possesses or distributes drugs illegally. This includes the use of illegal drugs and the illegal use of prescription drugs that are deemed controlled substances under federal drug laws.

Example: Starbright Corporation fires Lucy after determining that she takes amphetamines without a doctor's prescription. Amphetamines can be legally prescribed, but are classified as "controlled substances" because of their potential for abuse. If a doctor didn't prescribe amphetamines for Lucy, Starbright would be justified in firing her for illegal use of drugs.

The most reliable way to establish that an employee is using drugs illegally is through a drug test. Testing is left to your discretion. If you choose to test, however, you must observe legal guidelines.

a. Federal laws

There are a few situations in which a private employer is required to test employees for drug usage. The U.S. Department of Transportation, for example, requires drug testing of airline pilots and other transportation employees who hold jobs in which drug abuse can affect public safety. And the U.S. Department of Defense requires similar testing by companies that contract with it.

The Drug-Free Workplace Act of 1988 (41 U.S.C. §701) requires all contractors with the federal government to certify that they will provide a drug-free workplace. To comply, you must:

- inform workers that illegal drug use is prohibited in the workplace
- create and maintain a drug awareness program
- require employees to notify you of any conviction for drug usage in the workplace—in which case you must notify the government, and
- impose remedial measures on employees convicted for using drugs in the workplace.

Note, however, that the Drug-Free Workplace Act doesn't require you to test employees.

b. Discretionary testing

Pre-employment testing is the legally safest type of testing. (Drug testing of job applicants is covered in Chapter 1, Section F.) After an employee is hired, testing is controlled by federal and state laws, as well as court decisions. Because these laws are rapidly changing, be sure to doublecheck your state law at a nearby library. (See Chapter 13, Section D for guidance on how to do legal research.)

If you do decide to test, your primary motive should be to ensure the safety of workers, customers and members of the general public. You're most likely to withstand a legal challenge if you limit testing of employees to three situations.

Safety and security. You can require periodic testing of employees whose jobs carry a high risk of injury to people and property—for example, heavy equipment operators and workers who handle explosives. Similarly, periodic testing is generally permitted for security workers—for example, those who transport large sums of cash or guards who carry guns.

Accidents. You can require testing of an employee who's been involved in an accident—for example, a food server who's dumped a carafe of scalding coffee on a customer or a maintenance worker who's drilled through a water pipe.

Retesting. You can require periodic retesting of an employee who is currently in or has completed a drug rehabilitation program, or an employee to whom you've given a second chance—for example, one who tested positive for drugs after a personal injury accident, but was kept on the job anyway.

Even though you have a right in these situations to require a drug test as a condition of continued employment, you can't force an employee to submit to a test against his or her will. You can, however, fire an employee who refuses to be tested.

In general, avoid a policy of testing all employees since not all of them will be in a position to cause harm through drug usage. Similarly, avoid a program of random drug testing. If you test all employees, test them randomly or test without a good reason, you may get sued for invasion of privacy or infliction of emotional harm.

To keep your drug testing program on a solid legal footing:

• use a test lab that's certified by the U.S. Department of Health and Human Services or accredited by the College of American Pathologists

• keep the results of drug tests confidential, and

• be consistent in dealing with those who test positive.

Documentation Is Essential

Because drug testing is always subject to a legal challenge, it's important to keep good records documenting why and how tests are administered. Request a receipt from each employee acknowledging that he or she has been given a copy of your drug and alcohol policy—or include the policy in your employee handbook and get a receipt for the handbook. (See Chapter 2, Section B.) Don't give a drug test without having the employee sign a consent form. Keep a record of what tests were performed, what drugs were found and in what amounts. Finally, document the chain of custody of the tested sample so you can show who handled it at all pertinent times.

For more information on how to set up a drug testing program, read *Workplace Drug Testing: An Employer's Development & Implementation Guide,* by Mark A. de Bernardo (Institute for a Drug-Free Workplace) available for $35. For ordering information, call (202) 842-7400.

2. Alcoholism

The law treats alcoholism differently than drug abuse. A person disabled by alcoholism is entitled to the same protection from job discrimination as any other person with a disability.

On the other hand, you're not required to overlook the effects that this disability has on job performance. Under the Americans With Disabilities Act (ADA), you can discipline, discharge or deny employment to an alcoholic if the person's job performance or conduct is so badly affected by alcohol usage that he or she isn't qualified to do the job.

Example: Don, an alcoholic, often is late for work and sometimes is unable to perform his job. His employer disciplines him because of his tardiness and poor performance. The company holds Don to the same standards as its other employees—and disciplines him in a like way. This doesn't violate the ADA.

Neither the ADA nor its regulations define alcoholic or alcoholism. The lack of definitions may have little practical effect, however, since the ADA allows you to judge the employee by his or her ability to do the job. People who have an alcohol problem aren't legally entitled to any special consideration. (For more on the ADA, see Chapter 9.)

I. Repetitive Stress Disorder

The number of workers suffering from repetitive stress disorder (RSD) is rapidly growing—due in large part to the increased use of computers in workplaces. A familiar form of RSD is Carpal Tunnel Syndrome in which there's swelling inside the tunnel created by bone and ligament in the wrist. This swelling can put pressure on nerves passing through the tunnel—leading, in turn to pain, tingling and numbness. Other types of RSD include:

* tendonitis—tears in tissue connecting bones to muscles
* myofascial damage—tenderness and swelling from overworking muscles
* tenosynovitis—irritation of the boundary between the tendon and surrounding sheath, and
* cervical radiculopathy—compression of disks in the neck.

The last disorder often develops in workers who hold a phone on their shoulders while using computers. All of these disorders are painful and can be disabling.

In an attempt to stem the rising tide of RSD cases, OSHA is working on regulations that will set ergonomic standards in the workplace. Employers would be required to accommodate work conditions to workers rather than making workers adapt to their environment. But even without a specific ergonomics rule in place, OSHA can take action.

In proceeding against one employer, for example, OSHA cited the company for positioning employee workstations in a way that required typists to reach extreme distances, twist their wrists and keep their hands suspended for prolonged periods. OSHA also said that the employer required workers to remain in static, seated positions for long periods without breaks—thus exposing them to muscular or skeletal injury and Carpal Tunnel Syndrome.

To reduce the risk of Carpal Tunnel Syndrome and other repetitive strain disorders, you may change the equipment employees use, train them in improving work techniques and modify the layout of workstations. Larger employers might opt to hire consultants to advise them. Smaller employers may need to rely on videos designed to give tips on sound workplace practices.

WHAT THE FUTURE MAY BRING

Several states are considering regulations for businesses that use video display terminals—better known as computer workstations. This area of law is just developing, but rules adopted in New Mexico for state employees who use computers can serve as a model for your business.

- Maintain room lighting at a level that reduces eyestrain and glare.
- Control glare by indirect lighting and nonreflecting furnishings.
- Use acoustic pads to control noise levels.
- Locate workstations at a reasonable distance from heating and cooling vents.
- Provide chairs that are flexible and easily adjusted.
- Allow frequent work breaks. ■

CHAPTER

8

ILLEGAL DISCRIMINATION

T o give workers a fair opportunity to get and keep jobs, Congress and
state legislatures have passed laws prohibiting discrimination in the workplace. It's illegal to discriminate against workers because of race, color,
religion, gender, national origin—or age if an employee is at least 40 years
old. In some situations, it's also illegal to discriminate against workers based
on other factors such as testing positive for HIV, or being pregnant, divorced, extremely overweight, gay or lesbian.

The main law prohibiting discrimination in the workplace is Title VII of
the federal Civil Rights Act of 1964. It outlaws discrimination based on
race, color, religion, gender and national origin. (See Section A2.) Sexual
harassment in the workplace is also prohibited as a variety of illegal gender
discrimination. (See Section B.)

Federal laws also bars several other kinds of workplace discrimination.

- *Age*. The Age Discrimination in Employment Act prohibits discrimination against older workers. The Older Workers Benefit Protection Act
  outlaws discrimination in employee benefit programs based on an
  employee's age. The protections in both laws apply to workers who are
  40 years old and older. (See Section C.)
- *Pregnancy*. The Pregnancy Discrimination Act makes it illegal to discriminate against a woman in any aspect of employment because of
  pregnancy, childbirth or related medical conditions. (See Section D.)
- *Citizenship*. The Immigration Reform and Control Act prohibits discrimination based on whether a person is or is not a U.S. citizen. (See Section
  E.)
- *Gender*. The Equal Pay Act outlaws discrimination in wages on the basis
  of gender. (See Chapter 3, Section B.)
- *Disability*. The Americans With Disabilities Act makes it illegal to
  discriminate against people because of a disability. (See Chapter 9.)
- *Union Membership*. The National Labor Relations Act prohibits discriminating against workers because they do or do not belong to a labor
  union. (See Chapter 12.)

For more information on laws prohibiting discrimination in the workplace, see *Primer on Equal Employment Opportunity*, by Nancy J. Sedmak and Michael D. Levin-Epstein (The Bureau of National Affairs, Inc.).

JOBS THAT REQUIRE DISCRIMINATION

Under Title VII and other anti-discrimination laws, you have a very limited right to hire on the basis of gender, religion or national origin if a job has special requirements that make such discrimination necessary. Such a special circumstance is called a bona fide occupational qualification (BFOQ).

Example: A religious organization employs counselors who answer telephone inquiries from those interested in becoming members of that religion. The organization can require that the counselors it hires are people who believe in that religion. Being a member of that denomination is a BFOQ.

Example: A department store hires young women to model clothing for teenage girls. Being a woman under the age of 20 is a BFOQ for this job.

(For more on BFOQs, see Chapter 1, Section B2.)

A. Title VII of the Civil Rights Act

Title VII (42 U.S.C. §2000 and following) enforced by the U.S. Equal Employment Opportunities Commission (EEOC), addresses many types of workplace discrimination.

1. Businesses Covered

Title VII applies to your business if you employ 15 or more people—either fulltime or parttime. State laws, with similar prohibitions against discrimination, generally cover employers with fewer employees. (See Section G.)

2. Discrimination Prohibited

Under Title VII, you can't use race, color, religion, gender or national origin as the basis for decisions on hirings, promotions, dismissals, pay raises, benefits, work assignments, leaves of absence—or just about any other aspect of the employment relationship. Title VII applies to everything from Help Wanted ads, to working conditions, to performance reviews, to post-employment references.

Obviously, a business that flatly refused to hire women or black or Hispanic applicants would be ripe for legal action under Title VII or its state equivalents. Of course, few businesses today would attempt such a flagrant violation of the law. But the mere absence of a discriminatory policy isn't enough to avoid enforcement action.

A business violates the law if it treats people differently because of their race or gender or religion. If a 20-year-old company with 50 employees always passes over its black employees for managerial positions, there's a good chance the company is discriminating—even though the company hasn't explicitly stated a policy of no blacks in management. Call it corporate culture. Call it coincidence. But if the end result is that blacks don't get management jobs, it looks like discrimination in the workplace.

If challenged by an employee or the EEOC, the business should be prepared to show that its promotion decisions have been based on objective criteria and that the more qualified applicant has always gotten the promotion. Without a convincing business reason for the failure to have any black managers, the company will likely be found to have violated Title VII.

Title VII also prohibits employer practices that seem neutral, but may have a disproportionate impact on a group of people. A policy is legal only if there's a valid business reason for its existence. For example, refusing to hire people who don't meet a minimum height and weight is permissible if it's clearly related to the physical demands of the particular job—felling and hauling huge trees, for instance. But applying such a requirement to exclude applicants for a job as a cook or receptionist wouldn't pass legal muster. The height and weight standard seems neutral on its face, but would have a disproportionate impact on women and people of Asian descent, for example. There is no legitimate business reason to require a cook or receptionist to meet this requirement, so it would violate Title VII. (For more about indirect discrimination, see Chapter 1, Section A1.)

Stay Alert for Indirect Discrimination

To head off allegations of indirect discrimination, review your employment practices at least once a year to make sure you have a solid business reason for everything you do. And don't brush aside complaints you get about practices that seem neutral to you, but may unfairly affect some employees. Take such complaints seriously. The workers who complain may be doing you a big favor by alerting you to a potential discrimination problem.

3. EEOC Enforcement of Title VII

If an employee files a complaint with the EEOC, a staff lawyer or investigator will interview the employee. The interviewer will probably then interview you and possibly some other employees.

The EEOC will likely try to work out a settlement of the complaint through conciliation—an informal process that resolves any legal violation for the employee who filed the complaint—and any employees who are in a similar situation. Terms of the agreement will be set out in a written statement. In it, the complaining employee must give up the right to sue your business.

If the agreement requires you to take some action—such as restoring a demoted employee to an earlier job or holding training sessions to make managers more sensitive to subtle discrimination in the workplace—the EEOC will follow up periodically to make sure you're complying.

If you and the employee who filed the complaint can't reach an agreement, the EEOC will likely give the employee a right to sue letter, allowing him or her to sue your business in federal court for violating Title VII. In rare cases that it finds may be especially compelling, the EEOC may file a lawsuit against your business on behalf of the employee.

If an employee files a complaint with a state fair employment agency, the investigation procedure will be much the same.

Confidentiality is the Best Policy

Never pass up the chance to resolve a complaint through conciliation. You have everything to gain and nothing to lose. A key advantage is that conciliation is confidential. Information in EEOC files concerning settlement attempts generally isn't available to the public. Neither the EEOC nor the complaining employee is allowed to make public anything that occurs during conciliation, and they can't use information disclosed there as evidence in a later proceeding without your consent.

Since the stakes can be high in a confrontation over alleged job discrimination, it may be prudent to consult a lawyer. If, however, you choose to attend the conciliation conference without legal counsel, you should at least ask a lawyer to review any written agreement before signing it. And because the anti-discrimination laws are unusually technical, you'll undoubtedly need assistance from a lawyer in defending a lawsuit in which your business has been accused of employment discrimination.

CONSIDER ARBITRATING DISCRIMINATION CLAIMS

The Civil Rights Act of 1991 encourages employers to resolve job discrimination disputes through settlement negotiations, mediation and arbitration. In mediation, a neutral expert—the mediator—helps the employer and employee reach a voluntary resolution of the dispute. In arbitration, a neutral expert, the arbitrator, makes a binding decision that can be enforced in court.

Arbitration is often an excellent way to bring a dispute to a swift conclusion because it's quicker and cheaper than judicial proceedings and is conducted in private.

If the arbitration isn't voluntary, however, it may not be legally binding. Increasingly, judges are rejecting contracts that force employees to arbitrate discrimination disputes, since such contracts may allow employers to avoid the full impact of civil rights laws.

SAMPLE ARBITRATION CLAUSE FOR EXISTING DISPUTE:

Employer and employee agree that the employee's claim of illegal discrimination, which has been filed with the U.S. Equal Employment Opportunities Commission, will be submitted to arbitration by the American Arbitration Association. A judgment of a court having jurisdiction may be entered upon the arbitrator's award

There are a number of remedies that a court can order if it finds workplace discrimination. You may be ordered to:

- rehire, promote or reassign the employee to whatever job he or she lost because of the discrimination.
- compensate the employee for salary and benefits lost because of the discrimination. This can include wages, pension contributions, medical benefits, overtime pay, bonuses, vacation pay and participation in your profit-sharing plan.
- pay damages to compensate the employee for emotional suffering, inconvenience and mental anguish—and punitive damages to punish your business if you've acted maliciously or recklessly. The total amount of these damages is limited to between $50,000 and $300,000— depending on the number of people you employ.
- change your policies so that similar discrimination won't take place in the future, and
- pay the employee's legal fees.

An Employee May Have Additional Recourse

If the EEOC doesn't issue a right to sue letter or file a lawsuit on the employee's behalf, the employee may take other legal action against your business, such as suing in state court for breach of contract or wrongful discharge. (See Chapter 10.)

4. Retaliation

It's illegal for you to retaliate against an employee for opposing illegal discrimination, for filing a complaint under Title VII or for cooperating in the investigation of such a complaint. This means you can't use these activities as a basis for firing, disciplining or refusing to promote an employee.

The best antidote to a claim that you've retaliated is to show that you had valid reasons for your actions, completely unrelated to the employee's assertions that you discriminated. Those reasons should be supported, if possible, by prior warnings to the employee which are documented and preserved in your files.

Example: George works for Cool Sweats—a company that sells sportswear by mail order. He files a complaint with the EEOC, complaining that he was passed over for a supervisor's position because he is black. A month later, Cool Sweats suspends George without pay for three days for a violation of company rules. George asserts that the suspension was in retaliation for filing the Title VII complaint.

Cool Sweats is able to refute this allegation by showing that George violated the company rules against charging personal expenses on the company's credit card and using the company van for personal business—rules stated in Cool Sweats' employee handbook. Cool Sweats is also able to show that six weeks earlier it warned George about similar infractions, and that a three-day suspension is consistent with the discipline meted out to other employees for such rule violations.

(For more on documenting worker misconduct, see Chapter 2, Section C.)

A NEW DEFENSE IN DISCRIMINATION CASES

Some employers are fighting back in cases of alleged discrimination by arguing that the employee shouldn't have been hired in the first place. Employers often win these cases.

Example: Local Transit, Inc. hires Lorna to drive a delivery van. In the first few months, Local Transit cites Lorna for the same infractions male drivers committed, but which went unpunished. Then the firm fires Lorna. She sues, claiming sex discrimination. In defending the lawsuit, Local Transit argues that Lorna lied on her job application by claiming she had a perfect driving record and failing to reveal two drunk driving convictions. Local Transit claims that had Lorna disclosed the truth about her driving record, the company never would have hired her. Since she isn't entitled to the job, says the company, she can't complain about discrimination. The court rules that Local Transit had a valid reason to fire Lorna.

But employers don't always win based on this defense. One skeptical judge wrote: "A false statement on an employment application is not an insurance policy covering bigotry."

To set the stage for this type of defense in a discrimination or wrongful discharge case, consider adding the following language to your job application forms in prominent type above the applicant's signature:

"I acknowledge that any misrepresentations or omissions in this application will be grounds for termination."

B. Sexual Harassment

Title VII of the Civil Rights Act of 1964 doesn't specifically mention sexual harassment. But in 1980, the U.S. Equal Employment Opportunity Commission (EEOC) issued guidelines stating that sexual harassment in the workplace is a form of sex discrimination prohibited by Title VII.

In 1986, the U.S. Supreme Court agreed that sexual harassment on the job is, indeed, a form of sex discrimination—and illegal (*Meritor Savings Bank v. Vinson,* 477 U.S. 57). The Court held that illegal sexual harassment occurs when unwelcome sexual advances, requests for sexual favors and other verbal or physical conduct of a sexual nature creates a hostile or abusive work environment. In 1993, the Supreme Court made it clear that a harassed employee is entitled to legal relief even without proof that the offending behavior has injured the employee psychologically (*Harris v. Forklift Systems Inc.,* 114 S.Ct. 367).

All states except Alabama have additional laws prohibiting sexual harassment in the workplace. The specifics often differ from federal law.

1. Prohibited Conduct

It's sexual harassment for an employer or manager to make unwelcome sexual advances or to demand sexual favors in return for job benefits, promotions or continued employment. But sexual harassment in the workplace can consist, as well, of many other activities, including:

• posting sexually explicit photos that offend employees
• telling sex-related jokes or jokes that demean people because of their gender
• commenting inappropriately on an employee's appearance
• requiring employees to dress in scanty attire
• repeatedly requesting dates from a person who clearly isn't interested
• having strippers perform at a company gathering, and

- stating that people of one gender are inferior to people of the other gender or can't perform their jobs as well.

In short, any hostile or offensive behavior in the workplace that has a sexual component can constitute sexual harassment—and is illegal.

Although sexual harassment is most often behavior engaged in by men against women, there are instances in which men sexually harass men. Laws prohibiting sexual harassment protect both genders from being sexually harassed on the job. The courts, however, are sharply divided on whether these laws protect employees who have been harassed by a supervisor of the same gender.

For an excellent in-depth explanation, see *Sexual Harassment on the Job: What It Is and How to Stop It,* by William Petrocelli and Barbara Kate Repa (Nolo Press).

2. Complying With the Law

Your business can be held responsible for sexual harassment if executives or supervisors knew, or should have known, that it was being committed. You're also under a legal duty to take all necessary steps to prevent sexual harassment. Promptly investigate every complaint. If you determine that there's merit to a complaint, discipline any employee who sexually harassed another on the job. Depending on the seriousness of the offense, consider reprimanding or suspending the offending employee, or placing him or her on probation. Where the harassment is especially serious, the only reasonable solution may be to fire the offending employee.

If you learn of workplace conditions that might create an uncomfortable work environment for some workers—such as the presence of pornographic magazines—take decisive steps to eliminate the offending conditions. An employee may challenge you by asking: "Who's offended by this?" The simple answer: "Me."

You're also required to take corrective action if an employee is being sexually harassed by other people who come into the workplace—clients, patients, customers, suppliers—who are not employees of your business.

Example: Stella waits on tables at the lounge at Take Ten Bowling Lanes. One night after winning the league championship, a boisterous team of male bowlers comes into the lounge and begins to harass Stella. The lounge manager quickly sizes up the situation, switches Stella to another table and compensates her for the tip she missed from the boisterous bowlers. The manager also threatens to expel the rowdies if they continue their behavior. Through this prompt action, Take Ten met its legal duty to Stella.

Look Beyond Legal Liability

Avoiding legal liability is just one reason for a business to crack down on sexual harassment. Sexual harassment has a negative impact on employees, causing anxiety and unhappiness. You can't expect high morale and productivity in a workplace in which sexual harassment is tolerated.

3. Preventing Sexual Harassment

Your attitude toward sexual harassment—and the steps you take to prevent it—can help assure that you won't become the object of a formal complaint. Most potential charges can be handled effectively within the workplace.

Start by adopting a formal policy stating clearly that sexual harassment won't be tolerated. Let employees know who within your business they can complain to if they've been sexually harassed. And provide for a back-up person to handle the complaint just in case the main person handling complaints is the accused harasser. Distribute a copy of the policy to each employee or put the policy statement in your company's employee handbook. (See Chapter 2, Section B.)

When you receive complaints, promptly investigate them and take action. Since employees may not always recognize the difference between permitted and unpermitted behavior, consider hiring outside experts to provide training workshops. These experts can be remarkably effective in making employees and managers aware of their rights and responsibilities—and they send a signal that your business is taking strong steps to squelch sexual harassment.

Here is a good start for a sexual harassment policy that can be modified to fit the needs of most workplaces.

SAMPLE SEXUAL HARASSMENT POLICY

[Employer name] is committed to providing a work environment where women and men can work together comfortably and productively, free from sexual harassment. Such behavior is illegal under both state and federal law—and will not be tolerated here.

This policy applies to all phases of employment—including recruiting, testing, hiring, upgrading, promotion or demotion, transfer, layoff, termination, rates of pay, benefits and selection for training, travel or company social events.

Prohibited Behavior

Prohibited sexual harassment includes unsolicited and unwelcome contact that has sexual overtones. This includes:

- written contact, such as sexually suggestive or obscene letters, notes, invitations

- verbal contact, such as sexually suggestive or obscene comments, threats, slurs, epithets, jokes about gender-specific traits, sexual propositions

- physical contact, such as intentional touching, pinching, brushing against another's body, impeding or blocking movement, assault, coercing sexual intercourse, and

- visual contact, such as leering or staring at another's body, gesturing, displaying sexually suggestive objects or pictures, cartoons, posters or magazines.

Sexual harassment also includes continuing to express sexual or social interest after being informed directly that the interest is unwelcome—and using sexual behavior to control, influence or affect the career, salary or work environment of another employee.

It is impermissible to suggest, threaten or imply that failure to accept a request for a date or sexual intimacy will affect an employee's job prospects. For example, it is forbidden either to imply or actually withhold support for an appointment, promotion, or change of assignment, or suggest that a poor performance report will be given because an employee has declined a personal proposition.

Also, offering benefits, such as promotions, favorable performance evaluations, favorable assigned duties or shifts, recommendations or reclassifications in exchange for sexual favors is forbidden.

Harassment by Nonemployees
In addition, [Employer name] will take all reasonable steps to prevent or eliminate sexual harassment by non-employees including customers, clients and suppliers, who are likely to have workplace contact with our employees.

Monitoring
[Employer name] shall take all reasonable steps to see that this policy prohibiting sexual harassment is followed by all employees, supervisors and others who have contact with our employees. This prevention plan will include training sessions, ongoing monitoring of the worksite and a confidential employee survey to be conducted and evaluated every six months.

Discipline
Any employee found to have violated this policy shall be subject to appropriate disciplinary action, including warnings, reprimand, suspension or discharge, according to the findings of the complaint investigation.

If an investigation reveals that sexual harassment has occurred, the harasser may also be held legally liable for his or her actions under state or federal anti-discrimination laws or in separate legal actions.

Retaliation

Any employee bringing a sexual harassment complaint or assisting in investigating such a complaint will not be adversely affected in terms and conditions of employment, or discriminated against or discharged because of the complaint. Complaints of such retaliation will be promptly investigated and punished.

Complaint Procedure and Investigation

[Title of person appointed] is designated as the Sexual Harassment Counselor. All complaints of sexual harassment and retaliation for reporting or participating in an investigation shall be directed to the Sexual Harassment Counselor or to a supervisor of your choice, either in writing, by filling out the attached Complaint Form, or by requesting an individual interview. All complaints shall be handled as confidentially as possible. The Sexual Harassment Counselor will promptly investigate and resolve complaints involving violations of this policy and recommend to management the appropriate sanctions to be imposed against violators.

Training

[Employer name] will establish yearly training sessions for all employees concerning their rights to be free from sexual harassment and the legal options available if they are harassed. In addition, training sessions will be held for supervisors and managers, educating them in how to keep the workplace as free from harassment as possible and in how to handle sexual harassment complaints.

A copy of the policy will be distributed to all employees and posted in areas where all employees will have the opportunity to freely review it. [Employer name] welcomes your suggestions for improvements to this policy.

Source: Sexual Harassment on the Job: What It Is and How to Stop It, *by William Petrocelli and Barbara Kate Repa (Nolo Press).*

C. Age

There are increasing numbers of older people in the workforce today—and there are laws protecting them from being discriminated against on the job.

1. The Age Discrimination in Employment Act

The Age Discrimination in Employment Act (ADEA) is an amendment to Title VII that prohibits discrimination against those 40 years old or older. It applies to businesses with 20 or more employees. As with the rest of Title VII, the ADEA prohibits discrimination in all aspects of employment—hiring, firing, compensation and all other terms of employment.

The ADEA not only prohibits you from discriminating against older workers in favor of those under 40 years old. You must also avoid discriminating among older workers themselves.

Example: Mary is 53 years old and Wilbur is 43 years old. Both apply for the same job. The employer can't choose Wilbur simply because he's younger. But the employer is on safe ground if Wilbur is chosen because of his superior skills.

Some employers believe that it costs more to hire older workers than younger workers. They overlook the possibility that younger workers may be less competent and need more training, making them more expensive. At any rate, a desire to save costs isn't a legitimate reason to discriminate against older workers.

AVOIDING AGE DISCRIMINATION CLAIMS

A few sensible precautions can help you avoid discrimination claims by older workers.

Become aware of remarks that betray a subtle—or not-so-subtle—age bias. A thoughtless comment such as "You can't teach an old dog new tricks" may be used against you if an older employee sues your company. Emphasize to supervisors that your business won't tolerate such dangerous and unfair comments.

Apply your performance standards evenhandedly to all employees, regardless of their age. Since juries often contain a strong representation of older people, you want to be able to show that your business deals equally with all employees.

Offer equal training opportunities for employees of all ages. If you're inclined to put more money into training younger workers on the assumption that they'll be with your company longer, forget it. That kind of strategy is a great way to invite an age discrimination lawsuit.

2. Older Workers Benefit Protection Act

Another law, the Older Workers Benefit Protection Act (29 U.S.C. §623 and following) makes it illegal for your business to use an employee's age as the basis for discrimination in benefits. Like the ADEA, this Act covers employees who are at least 40 years old. Under this law, you cannot, for example, reduce health or life insurance benefits for older employees, nor can you stop their pensions from accruing if they work past their normal retirement ages. The Act also discourages your business from targeting older workers when you cut staff. Most of the provisions of this law are very difficult for anyone but an experienced benefits administrator to understand. You'll probably have to consult with such an expert if you plan to take action involving a cutback of older workers' benefits.

One provision of the law that's relatively clear regulates the legal waivers that some employers ask employees to sign in connection with early retirement programs. You might, for example, offer a handsome retirement package to induce an older employee to leave your company voluntarily. As part of the process, you'd ask the employee to sign a waiver—often called a release or covenant not to sue—in which the employee would agree not to take any legal action against your business.

The law sets limits on your use of such waivers.

- You must write the waiver in plain English.
- The waiver can't cover rights or claims that may arise after the worker signs the waiver.
- The waiver must specifically state that the worker is waiving any rights or claims he or she may have under the federal Age Discrimination in Employment Act.
- You must offer the worker something of value—something substantially over and above what you already owe to the worker—in exchange for the waiver.
- You must advise the worker, in writing, to consult with a lawyer before signing the waiver. Of course, you can't require the worker to hire a lawyer.
- You must give the employee a fixed period of time in which to decide whether to sign the waiver. That period must be at least 21 days if the waiver has been presented to the employee alone. If you've presented the waiver to a group or class of employees, you must give each worker at least 45 days to decide whether or not to sign. In either case, a worker has seven days after agreeing to such a waiver to revoke his or her decision.

(See Chapter 10, Section F2 for a sample release contained in a severance agreement.)

In addition, if you're making the offer to a group or class of employees as part of an incentive program to encourage early retirement, you must tell each employee in writing and in plain English what class or group of employees is covered by the program; what it takes to be eligible for the program; any time limits for acceptance; and the job titles and ages of all the individuals to whom the offer is being made—and the ages of all the employees in the same job classification or unit who are not eligible for the program.

Because the statute doesn't specify how many employees it takes to constitute a class or group, it's prudent to provide the information any time you seek a waiver from an employee who's at least 40 years old if you're also offering a retirement incentive package to one or more other employees.

D. Pregnancy

The Pregnancy Discrimination Act or PDA (92 U.S.C. §2076) is an amendment to Title VII. Under the PDA, it's a form of gender discrimination to treat an employee differently because of pregnancy, childbirth or related medical conditions. If a woman is affected by such a condition, you must treat her the same as you treat other people in the workforce who are either able or unable to work. You violate the PDA, for example, if you fire a woman whose pregnancy keeps her from working, but you don't fire other workers who are temporarily unable to do the job because of other physical problems. Similarly, if a pregnant worker is able to do the job, you can't lay her off because you think it's in her best interests to stay home.

On the other hand, you don't violate the PDA if you apply medically based job restrictions on a pregnant woman—as long as you apply those same policies to employees who not pregnant but who are under medical restrictions.

Note also that a new law, the Family and Medical Leave Act, allows unpaid leave for childbirth, adoptions and foster care placements. (See Chapter 6.)

ENGLISH ONLY RULES

The law remains unclear on whether and when you can require employees to speak only English on the job. The EEOC views English only rules as a form of national origin discrimination—and takes a very dim view of such rules. The EEOC says you can require that workers speak only in English at certain times, provided you can show there's a business necessity for the rule.

The courts, however, may take a more lenient position toward employers than the EEOC does. In a leading case, Spun Steak Company received complaints that two employees were making derogatory, racist comments in Spanish about two co-workers—one of whom was African-American and the other Chinese-American. For this and other reasons, Spun Steak adopted this rule:

"It is hereafter the policy of this Company that only English will be spoken in connection with work. During lunch, breaks and employees' own time, they are obviously free to speak Spanish if they wish. However, we urge all of you not to use your fluency in Spanish in a fashion which may lead other workers to suffer humiliation."

Spanish-speaking workers sued. The court of appeals held that to show that the English-only rule was discriminatory, the workers would have to show that the rule had a significant, adverse impact on them. Nearly all of the workers were bilingual; as to those workers, the court held that the rule didn't have a significant, adverse legal and, therefore, wasn't discriminatory. As to workers who weren't bilingual, the court sent the case back to the trial judge to determine whether there was an adverse impact. (*Garcia v. Spun Steak Co.*, 998 F.2d 1480 (1993). .

Even though that employer won, if you're thinking of implementing an English-only rule, it's best to proceed cautiously and to be quite sure you can show there's a business necessity for the rule. If language is a problem in your workplace, one alternative is to offer instruction in English as a second language so that workers can become more proficient in its use and not feel under attack because they're more comfortable speaking in another language.

E. National Origin

The Immigration Reform and Control Act of 1986 (IRCA) makes it illegal to discriminate against a person because he or she isn't a U.S. citizen or national. The law forbids you from discriminating against aliens who have been lawfully admitted to the U.S. for permanent or temporary residence—and aliens who have applied for temporary residence status.

This can be tricky because, as an employer, you must meet specific legal requirements to avoid hiring illegal aliens, including asking new employees to show you documents verifying their citizenship and their legal ability to be employed in the United States. (See Chapter 1, Section A.) In meeting these verification duties, you can't ask to see more or different documents than those required for completion of INS Form I-9—and it's illegal to refuse to honor documents offered by the employee that appear to be genuine.

AFFIRMATIVE ACTION PLANS MAY CORRECT PAST ABUSES

An affirmative action plan is one means of erasing the effects of past illegal discrimination. Under such a plan, an employer makes employment decisions based on race or sex—factors that ordinarily can't be considered.

When a court finds that a business has discriminated and there are no other effective means to remedy the discrimination, the court may require the business to take affirmative action. For example, a court may order a company to hire one black employee for every two new white employees hired—until the company's workforce resembles the racial mix of the community.

A business may also have to set up an affirmative action plan as part of voluntarily settling a court case or EEOC proceeding. Any voluntary program must meet the EEOC's Guidelines on Affirmative Action Plans.

F. Gay and Lesbian Workers

Federal law doesn't specifically prohibit workplace discrimination based on sexual orientation, but several states have such laws—including California, Connecticut, the District of Columbia, Hawaii, Massachusetts, Minnesota, New Jersey and Wisconsin.

Over 100 cities prohibit discrimination based on sexual orientation. They include: Tucson, Arizona; Sacramento, California; Aspen, Colorado; Hartford, Connecticut; Atlanta, Georgia; Chicago, Illinois; Iowa City, Iowa; Boston, Massachusetts; Detroit, Michigan; Minneapolis, Minnesota; Buffalo, New York; Raleigh, North Carolina; Columbus, Ohio; Portland, Oregon; Philadelphia, Pennsylvania; Austin, Texas; Seattle, Washington and Milwaukee, Wisconsin.

Taking action based on an employee's sexual orientation can sometimes lead to a lawsuit for invasion of privacy.

Example: On behalf of a lesbian group, Janine testifies before the state legislature in support of legislation that would require employers to provide the same job benefits to the same-sex partners of employees as are provided to spouses. After her testimony is shown on the 11 o'clock news, Janine's employer fires her. Janine wins a lawsuit against the employer based on invasion of privacy, because the employer has unfairly intruded into Janine's private life.

RELIGION IN THE WORKPLACE

An increasing number of employees are claiming religious discrimination. In the past, the typical complaint would have been that a person was fired or disciplined or denied a promotion because he or she practiced a certain faith. But today, claims of religious discrimination tend to be much more subtle—and challenging. An employee might claim, for example, that a supervisor is seeking to impose his or her own religious beliefs on the employee by pressuring the employee to attend prayer sessions or Bible study meetings at work. Or an employee may claim that he or she is being unfairly deprived of the right to pray at work or to use a company meeting room to discuss the Koran with other employees. Still another employee may claim that wearing a "Stop Abortion" badge with a color photo of a fetus is an exercise of religious rights—while other employees may find the badge disturbing and offensive and a violation of their own rights.

Unfortunately, the law in this delicate area is unclear. Often, tolerance and common sense are your best guides. It also helps to be blessed with the wisdom of Solomon, so to speak.

The law protects your right to discuss your own religious beliefs with an employee, if you're so inclined, but you can't persist to the point that the employee feels you're being hostile, intimidating or offensive. So if an employee objects to your discussion of religious subjects or you even get an inkling that your religious advances are unwelcome, back off. Otherwise, you may find yourself embroiled in a lawsuit or administrative proceeding.

If employees complain to you that a co-worker is badgering them with religious hectoring, you have a right—if not a duty—to intervene, although you must, of course, use the utmost tact and sensitivity.

While you may feel that the best way to resolve these knotty problems is to simply banish religion from the workplace, that's generally not a viable alternative. You're legally required to make a reasonable accommodation to the religious needs of employees. You don't, however, need to do anything that would cost more than a minimum amount or that would cause more than minimal inconvenience. Allowing workers to use an empty office for voluntary group prayer at lunchtime might be a reasonable accommodation. Letting workers take a limited amount of time off of work to attend religious observances might also be a reasonable accommodation—although it might be better to simply give all employees a few days of personal leave time each year so that religious workers aren't viewed as receiving special privileges.

G. State and Local Laws

Nearly all state and local laws prohibiting discrimination in employment are echoes of federal anti-discrimination law in that they outlaw discrimination based on race, color, religion, gender, age and national origin. But the state and local laws also tend to go into more detail and may create categories of protection against discrimination—such as discrimination based on marital status—that aren't covered by federal law.

State laws prohibiting discrimination in employment are listed in the chart below. You can usually find out about additional local anti-discrimination laws at the headquarters of your community's government, such as your local city hall or county courthouse.

STATE LAWS PROHIBITING DISCRIMINATION IN EMPLOYMENT

This is a synopsis of factors that private employers may not use as a basis for employment discrimination. Keep in mind that it is only a synopsis, and that each state has its own way of determining such factors as what qualifies as a physical disability. Also, many state laws apply only to employers with a minimum number of employees, such as five or more.

In states where no special agency has been designated to enforce anti-discrimination laws, your state's labor department or attorney general's office should be able to direct you to the proper enforcement agency.

Alabama

No true anti-discrimination law, but you're encouraged to employ people who are blind or otherwise physically disabled. (Ala. Code §21-71-1)
If you have an affirmative action program, the term minority, in addition to an ethnic group or other classification, includes American Indians or Alaskan Natives, as identified by birth certificates or tribal records. Ala. Code § 25-1-10.
Enforcing agency: None

Alaska

Race, religion, color, national origin, age, physical disability, gender, marital status, changes in marital status. Alaska Human Rights Law (Alaska Stat. §18.80.110)
Pregnancy or parenthood. (Alaska Stat. §18.80.220)

Mental illness. (Alaska Stat. §47.30.865)
Enforcing agency:
Human Rights Commission
800 A Street, Suite 204
Anchorage, AL 99501
907-274-4692

Arizona

Race, color, religion, gender, age, physical disability (excluding current alcohol or drug
use), AIDS, national origin. Arizona Civil Rights Act (Ariz. Rev. Stat. Ann. §41-1401)
Enforcing agency:
Civil Rights Division
1275 West Washington Street
Phoenix, AZ 85007
602-542-5263

Arkansas

No general discrimination law.
Discrimination in wages on the basis of gender is prohibited. (Ark. Code Ann. §11-4-601)
Enforcing agency: None

California

Race, religious creed, religion, color, national origin, ancestry, physical disability, mental
disability, medical condition, marital status, gender, age (40 or older), pregnancy,
childbirth or related medical conditions. (Cal. Gov't. Code §§12940, 12941, 12945)
AIDS or HIV: If an employee's participation in a research study regarding AIDS-HIV is
disclosed, you can't use that information to determine the employability or insurability of
that person. Cal. Health & Safety Code §121115
Political activities or affiliations, including sexual orientation. (Cal. Lab. Code §§1101,
1102 and 1102.1)
Enforcing agency:
Department of Fair Employment and Housing
2014 T Street, Suite 210
Sacramento, CA 95814
916-445-9918

Colorado

Race, religion, color, age, gender, national origin, ancestry. Fair Employment Practices
Act (Colo. Rev. Stat. §24-34-401)
Physical or mental disability. (Colo. Rev. Stat. §27-10-115)
Enforcing agency:
Civil Rights Commission
1560 Broadway, Suite 1050
Denver, CO 80202-5143
303-894-2997

Connecticut

Race, color, religion, age, gender, pregnancy, marital status, sexual orientation, national origin, ancestry, present or previous mental or physical disability. Fair Employment Practices Act (Conn. Gen. Stat. Ann. §46a-60)
Enforcing agency:
Commission on Human Rights and Opportunities
1229 Albany Avenue
Hartford, CT 06112
203-566-7710

Delaware

Race, color, religion, gender, national origin, marital status, refusal to grant sexual favors, age (if between ages 40 and 70), or physical disability as long as the cost to you of accommodating the employee's physical disability doesn't exceed 5% of that employee's annual compensation. Fair Employment Practices Act (Del. Code Ann. tit. 19 §710)
Enforcing agency:
Department of Labor
Labor Law Enforcement Section
State Office Building, 6th Floor
820 North French Street
Wilmington, DE 19801
302-577-2900

District of Columbia

Race, color, religion, national origin, age (if between ages 18 and 65), gender, personal appearance, marital status or family responsibilities, sexual orientation, political affiliation, matriculation or physical disability. Human Rights Act (D.C. Code Ann. §1-2512)
Enforcing agency:
Human Rights Commission
441 4th Street, NW
Washington, DC 20001
202-724-1385

Florida

Race, color, religion, gender, national origin, age, marital status, physical disability, political activity. Human Rights Act (Fla. Stat. Ann. §760.01)
AIDS-HIV condition. (Fla. Stat. Ann. §760.50)
Enforcing agency:
Commission on Human Relations
325 John Knox Road, Bldg. F, Suite 240
Tallahassee, FL 32303-4149
904-488-7082

Georgia

Mental or physical disability (excluding the use of alcohol or any illegal or federally controlled drug). (Ga. Code Ann. §66-501)
Age, if between 40 and 70 years old. (Ga. Code Ann. §§54-1102 and 54-9927)
Enforcing agency: None

Hawaii

Race, religion, color, ancestry, gender, sexual orientation, age, marital status, mental or physical disability, pregnancy, childbirth or related medical conditions. Fair Employment Practices Law (Haw. Rev. Stat. §378-1 and following)
Enforcing agency:
Hawaii Civil Rights Commission
888 Mililani Street, 2nd Floor
Honolulu, HI 96813
808-586-8640

Idaho

Race, color, religion, national origin, gender, age (if age 40 or older), or physical or mental disability. Fair Employment Practices Act (Idaho Code §67-5901)
Enforcing agency:
Commission on Human Rights
450 West State Street
Boise, ID 83720
208-334-2873

Illinois

Race, color, gender, national origin, ancestry, age, marital status, physical or mental disability. Human Rights Act (Ill. Ann. Stat. ch. 68, §1-101)
Enforcing agency:
Department of Human Rights
James R. Thompson Center
100 West Randolph Street, 10th Floor
Chicago, IL 60601
312-814-6245

Indiana

Race, color, gender, national origin, ancestry, religion, age if between 40 and 70 years old or physical disability. Civil Rights Law (Ind. Code Ann. §22-9-1-1)
Enforcing agency:
Civil Rights Commission
100 North Senate Avenue, Room N-103
Indianapolis, IN 46204
317-232-2600

Iowa

Race, color, religion, age, gender, national origin or physical disability. Civil Rights Act (Iowa Code Ann. §216.1)
Enforcing agency:
Civil Rights Commission
211 East Maple Street, 2nd Floor
Des Moines, IA 50319
515-281-4121

Kansas

Race, color, religion, gender, age (if over age 18), national origin or ancestry, or physical disability. Act Against Discrimination (Kan. Stat. Ann. §44-1001)
Enforcing agency:
Civil Rights Commission
Landon State Office Building
900 SW Jackson, Suite 851 South
Topeka, KS 66612-1258
913-296-3206

Kentucky

Race, color, religion, national origin, gender, age (if between ages 40 and 70). Civil Rights Act (Ky. Rev. Stat. §344.040)
Physical disability. (Ky. Rev. Stat. §207.130)
Enforcing agency:
Human Rights Commission
332 West Broadway, 7th Floor
Louisville, KY 40202
502-595-4024

Louisiana

Race, color, religion, gender, national origin, pregnancy, sickle cell traits. Discrimination in Employment Act (La. Rev. Stat. Ann. §23:1001)
Physical or mental disability. (La. Rev. Stat. Ann. §46:2251)
Age (40 to 70 years old). (La. Rev. Stat. Ann. §23:972)
Participation in investigations relating to state's employment laws. (La. Rev. Stat. Ann. §23:964)
Enforcing agency: none

Maine

Race, color, gender, religion, national origin, ancestry, age, or physical or mental disability. Human Rights Act (Me. Rev. Stat. Ann. tit. 5 §4572)
Enforcing agency:
Human Rights Commission
Statehouse, Station 51
Augusta, ME 04333
207-624-6050

Maryland

Race, color, religion, gender, national origin, age, marital status, past or current physical or mental illness or disability as long as the disability does not prevent the worker from performing the job. Human Relations Commission Act (Md. Code Ann. art. 49B, §16)
Enforcing agency:
Commission on Human Relations
20 East Franklin Street
Baltimore, MD 21202
301-333-1700

Massachusetts

Race, color, religion, gender, sexual orientation, national origin, ancestry, age or physical or mental disability. Fair Employment Practices Act (Mass. Gen. Laws Ann. ch. 151B, §1)
Enforcing agency:
Commission Against Discrimination
One Ashburton Place
Boston, MA 02108
617-727-3990

Michigan

Race, color, religion, gender, national origin, height, weight, marital status, or age. Elliot Larsen Civil Rights Act (Mich. Stat. Ann. §§3.548(101) and following)
Physical disability and mental disability. (Mich. Stat. Ann. §§3.550(103) and following)
Enforcing agency:
Department of Civil Rights
1200 6th Street, 7th Floor
Detroit, MI 48226
313-256-2615

Minnesota

Race, color, religion, creed, gender, marital status, sexual orientation, national origin, age, physical disability or receipt of public assistance. (Minn. Stat. Ann. §363.03)
Enforcing agency:
Department of Human Rights
Bremer Tower
7th Place and Minnesota Streets
St. Paul, MN 55101
612-296-5663

Mississippi

No statute for private employers.

Missouri

Race, color, religion, gender, national origin, ancestry, age (between ages 40 and 70) or physical or mental disability. Human Rights Act (Mo. Ann. Stat. §213.055)
AIDS condition, except individuals currently contagious and who pose a direct threat to the health and safety of others or who, because of current contagious disease, are unable to perform the duties of their employment. (Mo. Ann. Stat. §191.655)
Enforcing agency:
Commission on Human Rights
3315 West Truman Boulevard
Jefferson City, MO 65102-1129
314-751-3325

Montana

Race, color, religion, creed, gender, age, national origin, marital status, or physical or mental disability. Human Rights Statute (Mont. Code Ann. §49-2-303)
Enforcing agency:
Human Rights Commission
1236 Sixth Avenue
Helena, MT 59624
406-444-2884

Nebraska

Race, color, religion, gender, national origin, age (between ages 40 and 70), marital status or disability (excluding addiction to alcohol, other drugs or gambling). Fair Employment Act (Neb. Rev. Stat. Ann. §48-1104)
Enforcing agency:
Equal Opportunity Commission
301 Centennial Mall South
Lincoln, NE 68509-4934
402-471-2024

Nevada

Race, color, religion, gender, age (if over 40 years old), national origin, physical disability. Fair Employment Practices Act (Nev. Rev. Stat. Ann. §613.330)
Enforcing agency:
Equal Rights Commission
2450 Wrondel Way, Suite C
Reno, NV 89502
702-688-1288

New Hampshire

Race, color, religion, gender, age, national origin, marital status, or physical or mental disability. Law Against Discrimination (N.H. Rev. Stat. Ann. §354-A:1)
Enforcing agency:
Human Rights Commission
163 Loudon Road
Concord, NH 03301
603-271-2767

New Jersey

Race, color, religion, gender, national origin, ancestry, age (between ages 18 and 70), marital status, sexual or affectional orientation, atypical hereditary cellular or blood trait, past or present physical or mental disability or draft liability for the armed forces. Law Against Discrimination (N.J. Stat. Ann. §10:5-12)
Enforcing agency:
Division of Civil Rights
31 Clinton Street, 3rd Floor
Newark, NJ 07102
201-648-2700

New Mexico

Race, color, religion, gender, age, national origin, ancestry, medical condition, or physical or mental disability. Human Rights Act (N.M. Stat. Ann. §28-1-7)
Enforcing agency:
Human Rights Commission
1596 Pacheco Street
Aspen Plaza
Santa Fe, NM 87505
505-827-6838

New York

Race, color, religion, creed, gender, age (if age 18 or older), national origin, marital status, physical or mental disability. Human Rights Law (N.Y. Exec. Law §296)
Enforcing agency:
Division of Human Rights
55 West 125th Street
New York, NY 10027
212-961-8400

North Carolina

Race, color, religion, gender, age, national origin. Applies only if you regularly employ more than 15 employees. Equal Employment Practices Act (N.C. Gen. Stat. §143-422.2)
Sickle cell or hemoglobin C traits. (N.C. Gen. Stat. §95-28.1)
Physical or mental disability. (N.C. Gen. Stat. §§168A-1 to A-5)
AIDS or HIV condition. Applies to discrimination against existing employees. Statute specifically allows you to request applicants to take an AIDS test and to deny employment based solely on a positive test result. (N.C. Gen. Stat. §130A-148)
Enforcing agency:
Human Relations Commission
121 West Jones Street
Raleigh, NC 27603
919-733-7996

North Dakota

Race, color, religion, gender, national origin, age (if between ages 40 and 70), marital status, status with regard to public assistance or physical or mental disability and participation in lawful activity off your premises during non-working hours. (N.D. Cent. Code §14.02.4-03)
Enforcing agency: None

Ohio

Race, color, religion, gender, national origin, ancestry, age or physical or mental disability. Civil Rights Act (Ohio Rev. Code Ann. §4112.02)
Age, if 40 years old or over. (Ohio Rev. Code Ann. §4107.17)
Enforcing agency:
Civil Rights Commission
220 Parsons Avenue
Columbus, OH 43266-0543
614-466-5928

Oklahoma

Race, color, religion, gender, national origin, age (if age 40 or older) or physical disability. Applies if you employ more than 20 people. Civil Rights Act (Okla. Stat. Ann. tit. 25 §1302)
Enforcing agency:
Human Rights Commission
2101 North Lincoln Boulevard, Room 480
Oklahoma City, OK 73105
405-521-2360

Oregon

Race, color, religion, gender, national origin, marital status, age (if age 18 or older) or because of a juvenile record that has been expunged. Protection is also extended to persons who associate with members of the protected groups. Fair Employment Act (Or. Rev. Stat. §659.030)
Physical or mental disability. (Or. Rev. Stat. §659.400)
Enforcing agency:
Civil Rights Division
Bureau of Labor & Industry
800 NE Oregon Street, Box #32
Portland, OR 97232
503-731-4075

Pennsylvania

Race, color, religion, gender, national origin, ancestry, age (if between ages 40 and 70), physical or mental non job-related handicap or disability or the use of a guide or support animal because of blindness, deafness or physical handicap. Human Relations Act (43 Pa. Cons. Stat. Ann §954)
Enforcing agency:
Human Relations Commission
Uptown Shopping Plaza
2971-E North 7th Street
Harrisburg, PA 17110-2123
717-787-4410

Rhode Island

Race, color, religion, gender, ancestry, age (if between ages 40 and 70), sexual orientation or physical or mental disability. Fair Employment Practices Act (R.I. Gen. Laws §28-5-7)
AIDS condition or the perception of it. (R.I. Gen. Laws §23-6-22)
Enforcing agency:
Commission for Human Rights
10 Abbott Park Place
Providence, RI 02903-3768
401-277-2661

South Carolina

Race, color, religion, gender, age (if age 40 or older), national origin. Human Affairs Law (S.C. Code §1-13-20)
Physical or mental disability. (S.C. Code §43-33-530)
Enforcing agency:
Human Affairs Commission
2611 Forest Drive, Suite 200
Columbia, SC 29204
803-253-6336

South Dakota

Race, color, religion, creed, gender, national origin, ancestry or physical and mental disability. Human Relations Act (S.D. Codified Laws Ann. §20-13-10)
Enforcing agency:
Commission on Human Relations
224 West 9th Street
Sioux Falls, SD 57102
605-339-7039

Tennessee

Race, creed, color, religion, gender, age (if age 40 or older), national origin. Fair Employment Practices Act (Tenn. Code Ann. §4-21-401)
Physical or mental disability. (Tenn. Code Ann. §8-50-103)
Enforcing agency:
Human Rights Commission
531 Henley Street, Suite 701
Knoxville, TN 37902
615-594-6500

Texas

Race, color, religion, gender, age (if between ages 40 and 70), national origin, or physical or mental disability. Commission on Human Rights Act (Vernon's Texas Code Ann. Labor §21.051)
Enforcing agency:
Commission on Human Rights
8100 Cameron Road, #525
Austin, TX 78754
512-837-8534

Utah

Race, color, religion, gender, age (if over age 40), national origin; pregnancy, childbirth or related medical conditions; or physical or mental disability. Anti-Discrimination Act (Utah Code Ann. §§34-35-1 and following)
Enforcing agency:
Anti-Discrimination Division of the Industrial Commission
160 East Third, South, 3rd floor
Salt Lake City, UT 84111
801-530-6801

Vermont

Race, color, religion, gender, national origin, ancestry, age (if age 18 or older), place of birth, sexual orientation, HIV positive condition or requiring a blood test for the presence of HIV or physical or mental disability. Fair Employment Practices Act (Vt. Stat. Ann. tit. 21, §§495 and 495a and tit. 3 §961)
Enforcing agency:
Attorney General's Office
Civil Rights Division
109 State Street
Montpelier, VT 05609
802-828-3657

Virginia

Race, color, religion, gender, national origin, age, marital status or physical or mental disability. Human Rights Act (Va. Code Ann. §2.1-714 and following)
Enforcing agency:
Council on Human Rights
1100 Bank Street
Richmond, VA 23219
804-225-2292

Washington

Race, color, creed, gender, age (if between age 40 and 70), national origin, marital status, or the presence of any sensory, physical or mental disability, or the use of any trained guide or service dog by a disabled person. (Wash. Rev. Code Ann. §49.60.180)
Enforcing agency:
Human Rights Commission
1511 Third Avenue, Suite 921
Seattle, WA 98101
206-464-6500

West Virginia

Race, religion, color, national origin, gender, age (if age 40 or older), physical or mental disability. Human Rights Act (W.V. Code §5-11-9)
Enforcing agency:
Human Rights Commission
1321 Plaza East, Room 106
Charleston, WV 25301
304-348-6880

Wisconsin

Race, color, religion, gender, age (if age 40 or older), national origin, sexual orientation, marital status, arrest or conviction record, or physical disability. Fair Employment Practices Act (Wis. Stat. Ann. §111.31)
Enforcing agency:
Department of Industry, Labor and Human Relations
Equal Rights Division
201 East Washington Avenue, Room 402
Madison, WI 53708
608-266-6860

Wyoming

Race, color, creed, gender, national origin, ancestry, age (if between ages 40 and 69), or physical or mental disability. Fair Employment Practices Act (Wyo. Stat. §27-9-105)
Enforcing agency:
Fair Employment Commission
6101 Yellowstone, Room 259C
Cheyenne, WY 82002
307-777-7262

Adapted from *Your Rights in the Workplace*, by Barbara Kate Repa (Nolo Press). ■

CHAPTER

9

WORKERS WITH DISABILITIES

Many employers are reluctant to hire people who have disabilities. They assume that an applicant with a disability won't be able to handle a particular job. This assumption may be correct for some applicants, but way off the mark for many others.

A. The Americans With Disabilities Act

To help eliminate discrimination against people with disabilities, Congress recently passed the Americans with Disabilities Act or ADA (29 U.S.C. §706 and following). One part of the ADA sets out rules for how businesses must deal with job applicants and employees. That part of the law, known as Title I, is explained in this chapter.

NUMBERS TELL THE STORY

- Two-thirds of Americans with disabilities between the ages of 16 and 64 aren't working.
- Fully 84% of people aged 16 to 44 who are not working say they'd like to have a job.
- Most adults with disabilities who are currently working or are willing and able to work—69% of them—don't need special equipment or technology to perform effectively at work.

Source: Poll by Louis Harris and Associates, commissioned by the National Organization on Disability, 1994.

The idea behind the employment provisions of the ADA is that it's unfair to write off every applicant who has a disability. Many people who have a disability are able to perform many specific jobs. Some may need an accommodation—special equipment, perhaps, or a simple adjustment in their working conditions—to help them get the job done.

Basically, the ADA states that in making hiring and employment decisions, it's illegal to discriminate against anyone because of a disability. If a person is qualified to do the work, or to do it once a reasonable accommodation is made, you must treat that person the same as all other applicants and employees. Although the concept is simple, the ADA requirements are immensely complicated—primarily because the statute is poorly drafted.

For employers, the ADA has perhaps its heaviest impact on the hiring process. You must, for example:

- write job descriptions to focus on the core tasks so that a person with a disability isn't eliminated from being considered for a job because he or she can't perform a marginal job duty
- avoid questions in job applications and interviews that focus on possible disabilities, and
- defer pre-employment medical exams and inquiries until after you've made a conditional offer of employment.

(These hiring requirements are discussed in Chapter 1.)

In addition to laying down rules for employment, the ADA spells out what a business must do to make its services and facilities accessible to customers and other visitors with disabilities. That part of the law, known as Title III, applies to a wide range of businesses that serve the public, including:

- places that serve food or drink—such as restaurants and bars
- businesses that sell or rent goods—such as bakeries, grocery stores and hardware stores
- service businesses—such as laundromats, drycleaners, barber shops, travel agencies, shoe repair services and doctors and lawyers offices, and
- recreational facilities—such as gyms, health spas and bowling alleys.

ADA COVERAGE IS BROAD

Under the ADA, you can't discriminate against a person with a disability in any aspect of employment, including:

- applications
- interviews
- testing
- hiring
- job assignments
- evaluations
- disciplinary actions
- training
- promotion
- medical exams
- layoffs
- firing
- compensation
- leave, and
- benefits.

In addition, you can't deny a job to someone or discriminate against an employee because that person is related to or associates with a person who has a disability. For example, you can't:

- refuse to hire someone because that person's spouse, child or other dependent has a disability
- refuse to hire someone because that person's spouse, child or other dependent has a disability that's not covered by your current health insurance plan or that may cause increased healthcare costs, or
- fire an employee because that employee has a roommate or close friend who has AIDS, or because the employee does volunteer work for people who have AIDS.

Businesses covered by Title III must take reasonable steps to remove barriers in existing buildings that can limit access by disabled people. Stricter rules apply to new buildings and those undergoing major renovation.

Portions of the ADA and the regulations affecting employment practices are printed in a publication called *A Technical Assistance Manual on the Employment Provisions (Title I) of the Americans with Disabilities Act.* It's available from the U.S. Government Printing Office, Superintendent of Documents, Mail Stop: SSOP, Washington, DC 20402-9328, at a cost of $25. The publication also contains a comprehensive explanation of the employment provisions from the perspective of the Act's enforcer, the U.S. Equal Employment Opportunity Commission.

For an explanation of the portions of the Act and the regulations covering the accessibility of a business's services and facilities, see *The Americans with Disabilities Act Title III Technical Assistance Manual,* also available from the Government Printing Office for $25.

B. Businesses That Are Covered

You're covered by the ADA if you have 15 or more employees working for you for 20 or more weeks during the current calendar year—or if you had that many for 20 or more weeks last year. Parttime employees are counted.

STATE LAWS PROHIBIT DISCRIMINATION, TOO

Your state may also have a specific law that protects disabled people from discrimination in the workplace. Many of these state laws apply to employers who have only a few workers—sometimes just one worker. If your business is covered by both the ADA and a state law protecting people with disabilities, you must meet the requirements of both laws. If one is stricter than the other, you must meet the more strict requirements.

For a copy of the requirements in your state, contact your state's civil rights commission or the local labor department. (See the Appendix for a listing of labor departments.)

C. Who Is Protected

The ADA protects "qualified individuals with disabilities." To be protected from job discrimination, a person must not only have a disability, but must also be qualified for a particular job.

1. People With Disabilities

The ADA's protections extend to the disabled—defined as a person who:
- has a physical or mental impairment that substantially limits one or more major life activities
- has a record of being substantially limited, or
- is regarded as being substantially limited.

Because this definition can take on unexpected twists, it's useful to look at each part of it.

a. Impairments limiting a life activity

The ADA broadly defines physical and mental impairments. A physical impairment, for example, can be any disorder, condition, cosmetic disfigurement or anatomical loss affecting any of the body systems. A mental impairment is any mental or psychological disorder.

The fact that a person can use medication or a helping device such as a prosthesis to substantially overcome the disability doesn't eliminate that disability for purposes of the ADA.

Example: Archie has epilepsy and uses medication to control his seizures. He has an impairment, according to the ADA, even though the medicine reduces the impact of his impairment.

Example: Melanie walks with the aid of an artificial leg. She, too, has an impairment under the ADA even though her prosthesis helps her be freely mobile.

Once you determine that an applicant or employee has a physical or mental impairment, you must then determine whether the impairment substantially limits one or more major life activities.

Under the ADA, major life activities include:

- walking
- speaking
- breathing
- performing manual tasks
- seeing
- hearing
- learning
- taking care of oneself
- working
- sitting
- standing
- lifting, and
- reading.

It's not enough, for purposes of the ADA, that the impairment affects or touches on one of these major life activities; it must substantially limit the activity. For example, a person with mild asthma who occasionally becomes short of breath, but remains able to perform other daily tasks, will not be considered impaired under the ADA. However, a person with a more serious respiratory problem may be considered to have a disability—in which case it may be necessary for you to provide a smoke-free workplace under the ADA. (For more on smoking restrictions, see Chapter 7, Section G.)

Some impairments, such as blindness or deafness, may substantially limit all who are afflicted. Other impairments may limit some people and not others.

Example: Erwin has cerebral palsy. Cerebral palsy is a disorder that often restricts major life activities such as speaking, walking and performing manual tasks. In Erwin's case, however, the cerebral palsy is very mild and only slightly interferes with his ability to speak; it doesn't affect his other major life activities. Erwin isn't a person with a disability under the ADA definition. Joselyn, on the other hand, has a severe form of cerebral palsy that severely restricts her ability to walk and perform manual tasks; she is a person with a disability under the ADA.

In determining whether an impairment substantially limits a person, you must look at the effect of the impairment on that person's activities.

Example: Millie, a receptionist, injures her back. The resulting pain permanently restricts her ability to walk, sit, stand, drive, care for her home and engage in sports. Because her problems are permanent and substantially limit her life activities, Millie has a disability.

Example: Reginald, a general laborer, injures his back and recovers well. After a short period of rehabilitation, he is able to continue an active life, including recreational sports. He finds a new job as a security guard. Reginald doesn't have a disability under the ADA definition.

OBESITY: NO VERDICT YET

It's not yet clear whether extreme obesity is a disability under the ADA. The issue is still being debated in the courts.

The EEOC takes the position that someone who is 100% over normal weight—morbidly obese, in medical terms—has a disability whether or not disease caused the overweight condition. For less obese people such as someone who is 50 pounds overweight, the EEOC maintains that the person may have a disability if the obesity was caused by disease.

At least one court has held that extreme obesity can be a disability if the overweight person is perceived as being disabled—and so within the protections of the ADA. (For more on perceived disabilities, see subsection c below.)

In interpreting state laws granting rights to disabled workers, most state courts have held that excess poundage doesn't by itself constitute a disability—but it may in conjunction with a physical disorder such as diabetes, high blood pressure or heart disease.

Example: Toni, a five foot four inch tall woman who weighs 305 pounds, applies for a job at Community Foods, a health food store. Despite her food store experience, Toni doesn't get the job. She sues Community Foods, claiming she was discriminated against because of a disability—too much weight. The court dismisses the case because Toni can't prove her weight is caused by a physical condition. (*Cassista v. Community Foods, Inc.,* 5 Cal. 4th 1050 (1993).)

b. Record of impairment

The ADA also protects people who have a history of a disability—cancer or heart disease, for example—whose illnesses are either cured, controlled or in remission. And it protects people with a history of mental illness.

If a person has a record of disability and you rely on that record to reject that person for a job, that's a violation of the ADA if the person is currently qualified to do the work.

Example: Beatrice, who has a learning disability, applies for a job as a secretary-receptionist. Records from a previous employer state that she is mentally retarded. Still, her resume shows that she meets all requirements for the secretary-receptionist job. The new employer doesn't interview her because he doesn't want to hire a mentally retarded person. Relying on the records from the prior employer violates the ADA.

In this situation, it's best to determine the applicant's ability through practical tests that measure the skills needed for the job—for example, handling phone calls, taking messages, greeting customers, sorting mail and doing light typing.

c. Regarded as impaired

Some job applicants are not severely limited by a disability—yet, employers perceive them to have such a limitation. And, acting on these false perceptions, employers discriminate against these people.

There are several circumstances in which false assumptions violate the protections of the ADA.

A person may have an impairment which is at most a minor inconvenience, but the employer treats the impairment as if it's highly limiting.

Example: Ed has high blood pressure which is controlled by pills. His condition doesn't affect his work activities. Just the same, Ed's employer reassigns him to a less strenuous job with a lower salary because of a baseless fear that Ed may suffer a heart attack if he stays in his present job.

A person may have an impairment that's a problem mostly because of the other peoples' attitudes.

Example: Vern, an experienced assistant manager of a convenience store, has a prominent facial scar. Vern's employer passes him over for promotion to store manager, instead promoting a less experienced parttime clerk in the belief that customers and vendors won't want to look at Vern.

A person may have no impairment at all, but the employer regards the person as having being substantially limited.

Example: Jill is fired because of a false rumor that she has HIV. She has no impairment, but is being treated by her employer as if she does.

In considering whether to hire an applicant or to demote or fire an employee who has a disability, you may be concerned about productivity, safety, insurance, liability or attendance. Or you may worry that your business will have to spend money to accommodate a supposed disability or that co-workers and customers won't accept the applicant or employee. The best way to avoid problems under the ADA is to get the facts before you act; you must base all employment decisions on legitimate, non-discriminatory reasons.

2. People Who Are Qualified for the Job

To be protected by the ADA, a person must not only have a disability; he or she must also be qualified to do a particular job. This emphasizes a key point about the ADA: You don't have to hire or retain anyone who's not qualified to perform a job.

To figure out if a disabled person is qualified for a job in your business, go through two steps.

Step 1: Qualified to work. Determine whether the person is qualified for the job by education, work experience, training, skills, licenses, certificates and other job-related requirements—good judgment, for example, or the ability to work with other people.

Example: Trudy, an bookkeeper who has cerebral palsy, applies for a job as a bookkeeping manager. If the company's policy is that all managers must have at least three years of experience working with the company and Trudy has worked there only two years, she's not qualified for a management position. Therefore, she's not protected by the ADA.

Requirements used to screen out candidates must be job-related and based on business needs.

Step 2: Essential job functions. Determine if the person can perform what the ADA deems the essential functions of the job.

The ADA puts a lot of weight on two words: essential functions. The reason is that historically, many disabled people who were able to perform the basic tasks necessary for a job were denied employment because they couldn't do things only marginal to the job.

Example: The job description for a file clerk at Stony Creek Corporation states that the job includes answering the phone. In fact, most time on the job is spent filing and retrieving written materials; other employees usually answer the phone. A hearing impaired person may have trouble handling phone calls, but may be perfectly qualified to file and retrieve papers. Under the ADA, Stony Creek shouldn't disqualify a hearing impaired applicant for the file clerk job because answering the phone isn't an essential job function.

If you can write an accurate job description that identifies the essential functions of a job, you'll have an easier time deciding whether a person with a disability is qualified for the job. (See Chapter 1, Section B for more on essential functions.) This emphasizes the importance of periodically reviewing your job descriptions and keeping them current.

D. Exceptions to Coverage

Certain people and conditions aren't protected under the ADA.

1. Illegal Drug Use

People can't claim they're disabled and entitled to ADA protection because they illegally use drugs. This includes people who use prescription drugs illegally as well as those who use illegal drugs. Applying this part of the ADA becomes tricky, since the law may protect people who have been rehabilitated after drug use or who are in a drug or alcohol rehab program. (See Chapter 1, Section F5.)

2. Gay and Lesbian Workers

Homosexuality and bisexuality are not considered disabilities under the ADA, although many state laws prohibit discrimination based on sexual orientation. (See Chapter 8, Section F.)

3. Sexual and Behavioral Disorders

The term "disability" doesn't include the following sexual and behavioral disorders:
- transvestitism, transsexualism, pedophilia, exhibitionism, voyeurism, gender identity disorders not resulting from physical impairments, or other sexual behavior disorders
- compulsive gambling, kleptomania or pyromania, and
- psychoactive substance use disorders resulting from current illegal use of drugs.

4. Physical and Psychological Characteristics

Under the ADA, simple physical characteristics—eye or hair color, left-handedness, or height or weight within a normal range—are not treated as disabilities. Nor are personality traits such as poor judgment or quick temper. Also, environmental, cultural or economic disadvantages—such as lack of education or a prison record—are not disabilities.

Example: Rita can't read because she has dyslexia, a learning disability; Rita has an impairment under the ADA. Sonny can't read because he dropped out of school; his lack of education isn't a legal disability.

You don't have to hire or retain an employee who would pose a direct threat to his or her health or safety—or that of other employees. But be careful. You can't deny employment to a person with a disability because of a slightly increased risk. If you turn down an applicant or fire someone you've already employed, you must be prepared to show there is or would be a significant risk and a high probability of substantial harm if that person remained part of the workforce.

Example: Carlita has Parkinson's Disease, which restricts her manual dexterity. An employer can't assume that Carlita can't work in a lab because she'd pose a risk of breaking bottles that contain dangerous chemicals. The employer must evaluate Carlita's specific abilities and limitations.

Sometimes, you can get rid of or reduce the health or safety risk through a reasonable accommodation—a legal concept discussed at greater length in Section D. If an employee were to contract tuberculosis, for example, a reasonable accommodation might be to grant the employee a two-week leave of absence. With proper medication, the employee would no longer be contagious at the end of the two-week period.

Psychological behavior is more difficult to evaluate. However, if an employee is violent, aggressive or destructive, or makes threats, this can be good evidence that he or she may pose a direct threat to the safety of others. Still, before you make an employment decision based on such behavior, you may want to protect your legal position by having a psychologist or other mental health professional evaluate the behavior and the potential for harm.

E. Providing Reasonable Accommodations

The ADA requires you to accommodate the physical or mental limitations of a qualified applicant or employee who has a disability. However, you're excused from this requirement if it would be unreasonable for you to do so—for example, if it would place an undue hardship on your business. (For more on what constitutes undue hardship, see Section 2 below.)

The idea of a reasonable accommodation is quite simple: you may have to make some changes to help a disabled person do a job. This can take a number of forms, such as changing the job, an employment practice or the work environment. And you need not be psychic. Generally, the person with the disability needs to ask an employer to make the reasonable accommodation. (See Section 3 below.)

1. When Accommodations Are Required

You may have to make a reasonable accommodation for any part of the employment process—from completing the application, conducting the interview and testing the applicant, through changing workplace conditions and promoting the worker.

Job applications. Someone using a wheelchair may need an accommodation if the hiring office or interview site isn't wheelchair accessible; you may need to move the interview to a place that is accessible by wheelchair. A person with bad eyesight may need help in filling out an application; you may need to provide the needed assistance at company expense. (See Chapter 1, Section D.)

Job performance. Someone with poor hearing may need a special telephone that amplifies voices to perform a job. You may need to provide such a telephone at company expense. (See subsection 4, below.)

Access to benefits. Employees with disabilities must have unrestricted access to lunchrooms, lounges, restrooms, meeting rooms, and other services such as health programs, transportation and social events. You may need to modify existing your existing facilities or schedules.

2. Undue Hardship

The ADA doesn't require you to accommodate a disabled applicant or employee if it would place an undue hardship on the business—that is, if it would require significant difficulty or expense. Many of the legal battles involving the ADA are likely to be waged over this imprecise language.

Whether something is an undue hardship is decided on a case-by-case basis. What's easily managed by a large company may be very difficult for a small or mid-sized business. The law takes this into account by focusing on your business, not businesses in general. Under EEOC guidelines, several factors are considered in determining whether an accommodation would place an undue hardship on your business.

The net cost of the accommodation. The cost of accommodating an employee may be less than it first appears. You may qualify for a tax credit or deduction, and there are sources of funding to help pay for some accommodations. (See Section F.)

The size of the business and its financial resources. Obviously, larger and wealthier businesses are better able to put money into accommodations.

The structure of the business. A small facility that's part of a larger company may have access to funds from the home office. If so, the total resources become part of the equation.

The impact of the accommodation on business operations. An accommodation may be affordable, but would change the nature of the business—in which case it would be an undue hardship.

Example: Flo, who has an eyesight problem, applies for a waitress job at Rendezvous Night Club. The club keeps its lights dim to create an intimate setting. Flo requests bright lighting so that she can see to take orders. Rendezvous doesn't have to accommodate her; to do so would seriously affect the nature of the business. If Flo were applying for a bookkeeping position at the same nightclub, and would work in a poorly lit office away from customer areas, the employer could be required to provide brighter lighting as a reasonable accommodation.

Similarly, you wouldn't be required to raise the workplace temperature to accommodate a disabled employee if to do so would make it uncomfortably hot for other employees or customers. That solution would be unduly disruptive—but you could be required to provide a small space heater.

3. Deciding What Accommodations Are Needed

Figuring out viable accommodations usually requires cooperation between the employer and the applicant or employee with a disability. If a disabled person asks for an accommodation, chances are excellent that he or she will be able to explain his or her functional limitations to you. But if the person isn't articulate or is medically unsophisticated, it may take a letter from a doctor or psychologist to clarify the nature of the problem.

You may have your own creative ideas about an appropriate accommodation, but don't overlook the person with a disability as a good source of ideas. In fact, the EEOC recommends that you consult with the disabled person to identify potential accommodations and assess how effective each would be in enabling the person to do the job. Such consultation gets the relationship started on a positive note since you and the disabled person are working together to solve a problem. Moreover, this cooperative approach can yield dollar-and-cents benefits to your business; a person with a disability is often able to suggest a cost-effective accommodation that you wouldn't have considered.

Example: Tandex Company, a small manufacturer, believes that to hire Chester, a prospective employee who uses a wheelchair, it will be necessary to install a special lower drinking fountain. Chester, however, points out that he can use the existing fountain if Tandex simply provides paper cups next to the fountain.

Sometimes, there are several accommodations that would enable a person with a disability to handle a job. The EEOC recommends that you consider the preference of the disabled person. Still, under the ADA, you're free to make the final choice—for example, selecting an accommodation that's cheaper or easier to provide.

Help From The Job Accommodation Network

The Job Accommodation Network (JAN) is a federally funded service that provides free information and advice on making reasonable accommodations for employees with disabilities.

For a telephone consultation, call 800/526-7234; in West Virginia, call 800/526-4698.

4. Improving Accessibility

Under the ADA, you may be required to make your facilities accessible to job applicants and employees. This is a confusing area of the law for businesses—in part because the ADA covers more than equal employment opportunities for people with disabilities. As mentioned, it also requires businesses to make their facilities accessible to members of the general public. To further complicate matters, the accessibility requirements for existing facilities differ from the requirements for facilities that are being renovated or are under construction.

As an employer, you must make it possible for an individual applicant to apply for a job, which may include moving the interview site for him or her. You must also provide access to the job for an individual employee with a disability. This includes access to a building, to a worksite, to needed equipment and to all facilities used by the employee. You must provide such access unless it would cause an undue hardship.

a. Existing facilities

The ADA doesn't require you to change existing facilities until a particular applicant or employee with a particular disability needs an accommodation. Then the modifications should meet that individual's work needs. You don't have to make changes to provide access in places or facilities that won't be used by that person.

Here are alterations you can make to the workplace so a disabled employee can work there:

- Install a ramp at the entrance to your building.
- Remove raised thresholds.
- Reserve wide parking spaces close to the worksite for people in wheelchairs.
- Provide accessible toilet stalls, sinks, soap and towels in rest rooms.
- Rearrange office furniture and equipment.
- Make drinking fountains accessible.
- Provide clear paths to copying machines, meeting and training rooms, lunchrooms and lounges.
- Remove potential hazards from the path of blind people.
- Add flashing lights to alarm bells to alert hearing-impaired people in an emergency.

b. Renovation or new construction

As an employer, you must meet more extensive requirements for accessibility if you renovate your facilities or start new construction. The EEOC claims that remodeled buildings can usually be made to meet accessibility requirements at minimal additional cost.

Renovation and new construction requirements are described in the ADA Accessibility Guidelines which are part of the Department of Justice Title III regulations. For technical assistance and publications, call the Architectural and Transportation Barriers Compliance Board at 800/USA-ABLE.

c. Access to goods and services

If your business is a place of public accommodation—for example, a retail store, theater, hotel or restaurant—Title III of the ADA requires you to make your goods and services accessible to everyone. You're required to remove architectural barriers if this is structurally possible and can be done at reasonable expense. Be aware, too, that state and local building codes may require that existing commercial buildings be modified to be made accessible to people with disabilities.

To learn what is practical and affordable for existing facilities, you'll need the advice of an architect or other expert who knows the ins and out of the ADA requirements.

5. Other Types of Accommodation

Not all accommodations involve physical changes to the workplace. There are other things you can do to help qualified people with disabilities work effectively. You might, for example, restructure a job by transferring marginal or non-essential functions to another employee. Or you might modify work schedules. You could permit a worker with a mental disability to take off time for twice-a-week visits to a psychiatrist. Or you could assign a fixed shift to a diabetic employee who needs to eat on a regular schedule and take insulin at set times each day—departing from your usual practice of requiring employees to rotate their shifts.

Similarly, a reasonable accommodation might consist of having a flexible leave policy. You don't have to give additional paid leave, but consider allowing employees to use accrued leave or leave without pay to get needed rest or medical treatment. Or you may decide that it's better to reassign an employee to a different job. But be careful in choosing this option. To avoid discriminating against other employees on the job, you must reassign the disabled worker to a position that is vacant, and for which he or she is qualified.

Often you can buy equipment—or modify existing equipment—to accommodate an employee. Some examples of equipment and devices that may be used include:

- TDDs (Telecommunication Devices for the Deaf) that enable people with hearing or speech impairments to communicate over the phone
- telephone amplifiers, useful for people with hearing impairments
- software to enlarge print or convert print documents to spoken words for people with vision or reading disabilities
- telephone headsets and adaptive lights for people with cerebral palsy or other manual difficulties, and
- speaker phones, effective for people who are amputees or have other mobility impairments.

SOLUTIONS THAT DON'T COST A BUNDLE

As noted earlier, the Job Accommodation Network (JAN) is a free service funded by federal government. Its consultants can offer practical suggestions for accommodating disabled workers. You can reach JAN by calling 800/526-7234; in West Virginia call 800/526-4698.

Many examples from JAN and other sources for accommodating people with disabilities are contained in *A Technical Assistance Manual on the Employment Provisions (Title I) of the Americans with Disabilities Act,* prepared by the U.S. Equal Employment Opportunities Commission.

Some examples of low-cost accommodations are noted here.

- A timer with an indicator light allowed a medical technician who was deaf to perform laboratory tests.
  Cost: $27

- A clerk with limited use of her hands was provided a rotating file holder that enabled her to reach all materials needed for her job.
  Cost: $85

- A groundskeeper who had limited use of one arm was provided a detachable extension arm for a rake. This enabled him to grasp the handle on the extension with the impaired hand and control the rake with the functional arm.
  Cost: $20

- A desk layout was changed from the right to left side to enable a data entry operator who is visually impaired to perform her job.
  Cost: $0

- A telephone amplifier designed to work with a hearing aid allowed a plant worker to retain his job and avoid being transferred to a lower paying job.
  Cost: $24

F. Financial Assistance

There may be financial help available to assist you in complying with the ADA.

1. Tax Credit for Small Businesses

If your business has gross receipts of $1 million or less for the tax year, or if you have 30 or fewer employees, you can take a tax credit of up to $5,000 a year for accommodations you make to comply with the ADA. You can take this credit for one-half the cost of certain access expenses, including removing physical barriers and providing interpreters or readers. The credit applies to expenses that are more than $250, but not more than $10,250.

Example: ABC Company spends $10,250 to widen doorways to accommodate employees in wheelchairs. The company gets a tax credit of $5,000 ($10,250 minus $250, divided by 2).

To be eligible, you must meet the ADA Accessibility Guidelines. Contact a local IRS office for more details.

2. Tax Deduction for Removing Barriers

Any business can deduct up to $15,000 a year for the cost of removing specified architectural and transportation barriers—including steps, narrow doors and inadequate parking spaces, toilet facilities and vehicles. If your business meets the size and income requirements for the tax credit described in Section 1, it can take both the tax credit and the tax deduction. Contact a local IRS office for more details.

Example: CompuWay Corporation, a company with gross receipts of $950,000, spends $24,000 to widen its parking spaces and to add wide bathroom stalls that are more accessible to workers with disabilities. CompuWay can take the $5,000 tax credit for the first $10,250 and may deduct the remaining $13,750 from its taxable income.

3. Targeted Jobs Tax Credit

Your business may also be eligible for a tax credit if you hire specific people with disabilities who were referred to you by a qualifying governmental agency, such as a state or local vocational rehabilitation agency, state commission on the blind or the U.S. Department of Veteran Affairs. These workers must be certified by a state employment service.

If you hire such an employee, you can take a tax credit of 40% of the first $6,000 of his or her first-year salary. Congress authorizes this program on a year-to-year basis. For more information, or to check the current status of this credit, check with the office in your state that helps place employees.

Additional sources of funding are described in the *Technical Assistance Manual* described earlier in this chapter. The manual includes an ADA Resource Directory that's quite extensive.

TEN TIPS ON COMMUNICATING WITH PEOPLE WHO HAVE DISABILITIES

1. When talking with a person who has a disability, speak directly to that person rather than through a companion or sign language interpreter who may be present.
2. When introduced to a person with a disability, it is appropriate to offer to shake hands. People with limited hand use or who wear an artificial limb can usually shake hands. It's perfectly acceptable to greet people by shaking hands with the left hand.
3. When meeting a person who is blind or has partial sight, always identify yourself and others who may be with you. When conversing in a group, remember to identify the person to whom you are speaking.
4. If you offer assistance, wait until the offer is accepted. Then listen to or ask for instructions.
5. Treat adults as adults. Address people who have disabilities by their first names only when extending that same familiarity to all others present. Never patronize people who use wheelchairs by patting them on the head or shoulder.
6. Leaning or hanging on a person's wheelchair is similar to leaning or hanging on a person and is generally considered annoying. The chair is part of the personal body space of the person who uses it.
7. Listen attentively when you're talking with a person who has difficulty speaking. Be patient and wait for the person to finish, rather than correcting or speaking for the person. If necessary, ask short questions that require short answers, a nod, or a shake of the head. Never pretend to understand if you are having difficulty doing so. Instead, repeat what you have understood and allow the person to respond. The response will clue you in and guide your understanding.
8. When speaking with a person who uses a wheelchair or crutches, position yourself at eye level in front of the person.
9. To get the attention of a person who is deaf or hard of hearing, tap the person on the shoulder or wave your hand. Look directly at the person and speak clearly, slowly and expressively to establish if the person can read your lips. Not all people with a hearing impairment can lip-read. For those who do lip-read, be sensitive to their needs by facing the light source and keeping hands, cigarettes and food away from your mouth when speaking.
10. Relax. Don't be embarrassed if you happen to use accepted, common expressions, such as "See you later" or "Did you hear about this," that seem to relate to the person's disability.

Source: Adapted by Karen Meyer for United Cerebral Palsy Associations, Inc.

G. Health and Safety Standards

The ADA doesn't stop you from establishing standards ensuring that a workplace is safe and that workers are qualified and competent. You're free to set minimum requirements based on education, skills and work experience—and to specify physical and mental standards needed for job performance, health and safety. And you're able to hire the best qualified person for a job. However, so that you don't exclude people with disabilities from jobs they can perform, the ADA requires that your standards and selection criteria for workers be job-related and consistent with real business needs.

Don't Forget the Reasonable Accommodation Rule

If your job standards are job-related and consistent with your business needs, you must also consider whether a disabled person could meet the standards through a reasonable accommodation—such as a modified workstation or special equipment. (See Section E.)

As part of the standards for a job, you can set out that a person must not pose a direct threat to his or her health or safety, or to the health or safety of others. But if you use such a standard, be sure it applies to all applicants for that job.

Example: Alex applies for a position at The Wood Works—a custom cabinet manufacturer—that requires employees to operate power saws and other dangerous power tools. Alex is disabled by narcolepsy; he frequently and unexpectedly loses consciousness. Since the job poses a specific risk to Alex and the risk can't be reduced by reasonable accommodation, The Wood Works may drop Alex from its list of job prospects without violating the ADA.

The ADA requirements for exempting job candidates on health or safety grounds are intentionally tough—designed to prevent employers from acting on a stereotype or patronizing assumptions about people with disabilities. If you plan to exclude someone from consideration for a particular job on health or safety grounds, be sure you have evidence of specific risk to that person or others.

SPECIAL RULES FOR FOOD HANDLERS

The ADA recognizes that people with certain infectious or communicable diseases may be a direct threat to the health or safety of others if they're handling food. Each year, the U.S. Department of Health and Human Services and its Center for Disease Control update a list of contagious diseases that may be transmitted through food handling—diseases such as hepatitis and salmonella poisoning. The list also describes the methods by which these diseases are transmitted.

The list is short—and, in conformance with medical opinion, doesn't include AIDS or HIV virus.

The list emphasizes that the greatest danger of food-transmitted disease comes from infected animals and contamination in food processing. If someone with a listed disease applies for a food handling job, the usual rules apply: consider whether there's a reasonable accommodation that would eliminate risks to the health of others. In the case of an employee who becomes infected with one of the diseases on the list, see if you can reassign the person to a job that doesn't require food handling. Be sure that the person is qualified, the job is vacant and the reassignment wouldn't pose an undue hardship.

H. Medical Exams

The strict ADA rules that govern medical inquiries and exams during the hiring process are described in Chapter 1. After you hire someone, the rules are even tougher. Any medical exam or medical inquiry about the employee must be job-related and justified by business necessity. You may order an exam if you learn of a problem related to job performance or safety, but again, the exam must be related to job performance. In the case of a physically demanding job, you may order an exam to find out if employees continue to be fit to perform the work.

   Example: Nelson is a warehouse laborer. He has a back impairment that affects his ability to lift objects. Nelson's employer can require that he be examined by an orthopedic surgeon—but can't require Nelson to submit to an HIV test. Such a test isn't related to either the job or to Nelson's impairment.

   You can, however, order a medical exam or make medical inquiries if:

- an employee is having difficulty performing his or her job effectively
- an employee becomes disabled
- the exam is needed for you make a reasonable accommodation to an employee's disability, or
- exams, screening or monitoring are required by other laws.

   You can conduct medical exams and tests as part of wellness and health screening programs—but only if they are voluntary.

I. Enforcement

The U.S. Equal Employment Opportunity Commission (EEOC) enforces the employment provisions of the ADA. The Commission investigates charges of discrimination and attempts to resolve any discrimination it finds. If those attempts don't succeed, the EEOC may sue on its own or—more likely—may issue a right to sue letter to the person who filed the charge.

   The EEOC has acknowledged that disputes about ADA requirements are often the result of misunderstandings between employers and disabled people. It emphasizes that those who have a conflict should try to resolve these disputes through informal negotiation or mediation if possible. (See Chapter 8, Section A for more on enforcement procedures.)

If an ADA case goes through the formal enforcement procedures and your business is found to have discriminated against a disabled person, you may be ordered to take a number of steps, including: hiring, reinstating or promoting the disabled person; giving back pay or front pay; making reasonable accommodation; or taking other actions. Your company may also have pay for lawyers' fees, expert witness fees and court costs. What's more, if you're found to have discriminated intentionally, your company may have to pay compensatory and punitive damages to the individual.

The following sources can provide additional information about the ADA.

Information about Employment Provisions
Equal Employment Opportunity Commission
1801 L Street, NW
Washington, DC 20507
(202) 663-4900

Information about Public Accommodation Provisions
Office on the ADA
Civil Rights Division
U.S. Department of Justice
P.O. Box 66738
Washington, DC 20035-6738
800/514-0301

Architectural and Transportation Barriers Compliance Board
1331 F Street, NW
Suite 1000
Washington, DC 20004-1111
800/872-2253 ■

CHAPTER

10

TERMINATION

Firing an employee has always been an uncomfortable task, but it used to be clearcut—and relatively free of legal complications. You simply paid the former employee for accrued wages plus any earned but unused vacation time to which the employee was entitled.

Things are more complicated now. Firing someone—even a person who is demonstrably incompetent—can be a risky endeavor. Do it for the wrong reason or in the wrong way and you can be obligated to pay substantial money in damages, or to rehire the worker.

In firing employees, you must beware of potential legal sticking points. For example, a former employee who believes that he or she was fired in retaliation for reporting a workplace hazard to OSHA may have legal grounds for filing a claim against you. And, in some situations, an employee who asserts that your employee handbook amounted to a contractual guarantee of job security may be found to have a valid claim.

As a result of these and other exceptions to the at will principle, lawsuits by former employees against their former employers have increased. And despite the fact that many employees have been fired for valid reasons, some of them have won cases based on illegal firing simply because the employer was sloppy in terminating the employment relationship.

A. Wrongful Discharge Cases

Cases in which former employees claim they were terminated for an improper reason or that an employer bungled the process are known as wrongful discharge cases—and they're based on a number of legal theories. You can better avoid being sued for wrongful discharge if you grasp these theories.

Because state laws and court decisions vary in this area, not all of the legal theories for wrongful discharge will be available to all former employees. Also, since the law can change—and many recent changes favor workers, not employers—you need to keep up to date on the specific rules in your state.

Many state trade associations publish newsletters or magazines to help keep their members informed of changes in employment law. Your state chamber of commerce may also have helpful publications on this subject. (For more suggestions on doing your own legal research, see Chapter 13, Section D.)

1. Statutes

If you discriminate illegally in firing an employee, a statute may give him or her the right to base a wrongful discharge case against you on that ground. Other statutes prohibit firing an employee for specified reasons, unrelated to discrimination. The main statutes that employees rely upon in asserting wrongful discharge claims are described here.

a. Race, color, religion and national origin discrimination

Under federal law—and many state statutes as well—it's illegal to discriminate against workers based on race, color, religion or national origin. (See Chapter 8.)

b. Age, gender and pregnancy discrimination

Additional federal and state statutes bar discrimination based on age, gender and pregnancy. (See Chapter 8.) And discrimination based on sexual orientation is also prohibited in a growing number of states and local ordinances.

c. Sexual harassment

Sexual harassment is a form of illegal discrimination covered primarily by statutes prohibiting sex discrimination. (See Chapter 8.)

d. Disability discrimination

The Americans With Disabilities Act bars discrimination against people with physical or mental disabilities. (See Chapter 9.)

e. Refusal to submit to lie detector test

A federal law, the Employee Polygraph Protection Act, makes it illegal to fire an employee for refusing to take a lie detector test. Many state laws also set out strong prohibitions against using lie detector tests in employment decisions. (See Chapter 1, Section F.)

f. Alien status

The Immigration Reform and Control Act requires you to verify that an employee is eligible to work in the United States. But you can't use alien status as a reason to fire a worker who is legally eligible to work here. (See Chapter 1, Section K.)

g. Complaining about safety or health conditions

Under the Occupational Safety and Health Act, you can't fire someone for complaining that working conditions fall short of complying with state or federal safety and health rules. (See Chapter 7.)

2. Court Decisions

Wrongful discharge lawsuits are not always based on statutes. Many courts have awarded wrongful discharge damages to former employers for non-statutory or common law reasons. The main ones are discussed here.

a. Breach of contract

Employers sometimes make promises to job applicants to entice them to become employees. And some employers may also dangle inducements in front of current employees to discourage them from leaving. A number of judges have ruled that if a person relies on such promises, an enforceable contract of employment has been created. An employer may be held liable for wrongful discharge if the employee is fired in violation of that contract.

Example: Betty, a diligent worker at AutoTec, is offered a job by a rival employer. She declines the job after AutoTec's president tells her she'll have a job for life at AutoTec if she continues to effectively manage her workload. Three years later, AutoTec fires Betty even though she has kept up with her work. Betty sues for wrongful discharge, claiming AutoTec violated its employment contract with her by firing her.

Specific promises of job security—either written or oral—are not always necessary for a judge to rule that an employee can't be fired arbitrarily. Some judges have allowed fired employees to collect damages or be reinstated to jobs because the employer created a legitimate expectation that employees wouldn't be fired without good cause. The typical focus in these cases is on inferences of job security made by the employer in a written document such as an employee handbook. It, too, may be enforced as a contract. (See Chapter 2, Section B, for tips on how to avoid this pitfall.)

Example: After six months on the job, Tom is fired from his job at Syspro, a small software house. He sues for wrongful discharge, claiming that Syspro's employee handbook led him to believe that he'd only be fired for good cause—and that, in fact, Syspro fired him without a good reason. The judge agrees that it was reasonable for Tom to conclude, after reading the employee handbook, that his job was secure. The court rules that the employer's wording of the handbook constituted an implied contract.

b. Breach of good faith and fair dealing

A few wrongful discharge cases have been based on the premise that every employment relationship includes an automatic commitment by the employer to deal fairly and in good faith with the employee. Applying this doctrine, judges have held that a discharge was wrongful when an employer has dealt arbitrarily with an employee. Almost all of these cases have involved long-time employees who were fired as they neared retirement age.

Example: Rita has worked for Jones Enterprises for nearly 25 years. The company fires her just three months before her retirement benefits are to become permanent. In a wrongful discharge case against Jones, the judge finds that the company fired Rita to save itself the expense of paying her the full benefit of her retirement program. The judge rules in Rita's favor because the firing breached the implied covenant of good faith and fair dealing.

c. Violation of public policy

Judges sometimes rule that a firing was wrongful because it was against the best interests of the public. Most courts do not allow an employer to fire an employee, for instance, because he or she was trying to correct a potentially harmful business practice.

Example: Clinical Lab Center, a small company that processes blood tests for doctors, fires Joe, a medical technician, because he has twice complained to management that the inadequate testing of blood samples by other technicians has led to many inaccurate test results. A judge rules that Joe's firing was wrongful because it violated public policy. Workers, the judge notes, should be free to speak up about sloppy practices they find on the job—especially those affecting public health or safety.

Courts have held that it's against public policy to fire a worker for refusing to file phony reports with a state environmental agency, bribe public officials, commit perjury or engage in industrial espionage.

B. Guarding Against Legal Claims

Given the many legal weapons that a disgruntled fired worker can aim at you under the rubric of a wrongful discharge lawsuit, you can understand the danger in blithely carrying on as The Boss, believing in your unfettered right to fire any employee. Consider, too, that juries are often sympathetic to fired workers, regarding them as underdogs—sometimes in the face of considerable evidence to the contrary.

1. Having a Valid Reason

The safest approach any time you fire someone is to be sure you have a legitimate business reason—a reason that you have thought out and documented. If challenged on a particular firing, you should be able to show, for example, that the employee did not adequately perform specific job duties or violated a clearly stated company policy.

Example: The Mail Shoppe employs two men and one woman, Virginia, in its packaging department. One Friday afternoon, the owner fires Virginia. She then files a lawsuit claiming she's been discriminated against because of gender. In court, The Mail Shoppe's owner is able to show that Virginia frequently put too little postage on packages and often neglected to insert the bubble wrap as instructed, causing breakage and numerous customer complaints. The owner also shows that three written warnings were given to Virginia over a six-week period. The judge dismisses the gender discrimination complaint.

In addition to bolstering your legal position, using an open and consistent policy for disciplining and firing employees will usually help improve worker morale. It's reassuring to hard-working, competent employees to know that they won't be fired on a whim. They'll also respect you for knowing who's getting the job done and who isn't—and they'll likely feel relieved when sloths and incompetent workers are let go.

2. Safely Handling Layoffs

Generally, you're free to lay off or terminate employees because business conditions require a reduction in the workforce. But if you do cut back, don't leave your business open to claims that the layoffs were really a pretext for getting rid of employees for illegal reasons. If your layoff primarily affects black workers, or women or older employees, someone may well question your motives. So if you need to drop employees, be sensitive to how your actions may be perceived. Spread the pain around; don't let the burden of a reduction in force fall on just one group of employees.

If you're a larger employer, you must comply with the Worker Adjustment and Retraining Act or WARN (29 U.S.C. §2101 and following). The law covers your business if:

- you have 100 or more fulltime employees, or
- you have 100 or more employees whose total work amounts to 4,000 or more hours a week, not counting overtime hours.

To comply with WARN, you must notify employees if you plan to:

- close an employment site, causing 50 or more fulltime employees at the site to lose their jobs, or
- lay off at least one-third—but not less than 50—of the fulltime employees at a site.

In those situations, you must notify each employee—or the employee's union representative—in writing 60 days before you close the site or lay off the employees. You must also send written notice to the state's dislocated worker unit and the chief elected officer of the municipality where the closing or layoff will take place. But you needn't give a full 60 days' notice if a closing or layoff is caused by unforeseen business circumstances or a natural disaster.

If you fail to give the required notice, your employees can sue you for backpay and benefits. You may also have to pay penalties if you don't give timely notice to the local government.

For more information, get the pamphlet, "A Guide to Advance Notice of Closings and Lay offs." Write to the U.S. Department of Labor, Employment and Training Administration, Office of Work-Based Learning, Room N-4469, 200 Constitution Avenue, NW, Washington, DC 20210. Or call (202) 219-5577.

C. Guidelines for Firing Employees

Even though your motives in firing someone are completely honorable and legitimate, the action may remain legally risky business. But there are several steps you can take to greatly reduce the chances of a former employee suing your business and being awarded a judgment against you.

1. Contractual Commitments

Before you fire an employee, check into whether you've made an oral or written contractual commitment that may limit your right to fire. Consider the following:

- Is there a written or oral contract that promises the employee a job for a fixed period of time?
- When you hired the employee, did you make any oral commitments about job security?
- Have you assured the employee that you'd only fire him or her for good cause?
- Have you listed causes for termination—in a contract, employee handbook or elsewhere—in a way that limits you to those specified causes?
- Does your employee handbook or other written policy or memo make any promises about job security?
- Does your company have written or customary procedures that must precede firing?

Your answers to these questions will help you identify whether you've limited your ability to fire the individual.

Written employment contracts can be a two-way street. While they may limit your right to fire an employee, the flipside is that they usually spell out the employee's obligations to your business. If the employee isn't performing well, chances are that he or she is in breach of the contract, giving you the legal right to terminate the relationship. Because the interpretation of contract terms can involve legal subtleties, consider having a brief conference with a lawyer before firing an employee who has a written contract.

SAY WHAT YOU MEAN AND MEAN WHAT YOU SAY

The words you use in hiring someone and in writing an employee handbook can create a contractual commitment that you didn't anticipate. Your employee handbook and similar documents should reserve your right to terminate employees at your discretion. (See Chapter 2, Section B.) While you may also wish to list some specific types of conduct that will result in termination, such as dishonesty or excessive absenteeism, those shouldn't be stated in a way that implies they are the only ways to end the relationship. Also, your handbook and other communications with employees should not make any promises about long-term job security. If they do, it's time for a rewrite.

2. Lawful Reasons for Firing

To head off the possibility that an employee may try to base a wrongful termination action on alleged illegal conduct or motives in your workplace, be prepared to show the real reason for the firing.

Reasons that may support a firing include:
- performing poorly on the job
- refusing to follow instructions
- abusing sick leave
- being absent excessively
- being tardy habitually
- possessing a weapon at work
- violating company rules
- being dishonest
- endangering health and safety
- engaging in criminal activity
- using alcohol or drugs at work
- behaving violently at work
- gambling at work, and
- disclosing company trade secrets to outsiders.

Depending on the nature of your business, you may have other legitimate reasons to fire employees as well. Whatever reasons you use as a basis for firing people, it's absolutely essential that you treat your employees evenhandedly. That is, if you regularly let some employees engage in prohibited conduct, you'll be on shaky legal ground if you claim good cause for firing others for the same reason.

Example: Andrew, a black patient attendant, is a half-hour late for work three days in a row. His employer, a medical clinic, fires him. In suing for wrongful discharge based on illegal discrimination, Andrew shows that two white attendants had been similarly tardy in recent weeks, but received only a verbal warning to shape up. Even though excessive tardiness is a valid business reason for firing someone, the jury awards damages to Andrew because the employer applied the rules unevenly and unfairly.

Getting Help Before Firing a Violent Employee

Almost always, if an employee behaves violently or makes threats in the workplace, that will constitute a valid reason to fire him or her. After all, you need to protect other employees as well as customers and others likely to come into contact with the violent person. Yet, judges in a few cases have suggested that a violent or threatening employee may be entitled to some latitude or accommodation if the violent behavior stems from a mental or emotional disorder.

On balance, it's generally best to proceed decisively and fire the violent employee—as humanely as possible, of course. You may, however, want to confer in advance with an experienced employment lawyer to reduce the likelihood of later legal entanglements.

3. Independent Review

Avoid giving an employee's direct supervisor the sole authority to hire and fire. The supervisor may be too close to the picture to make an objective decision. Since firing is such a drastic and traumatic step—and one having potentially serious legal consequences—consider having an independent review made within your business before anyone is fired, although this may not be practical in small companies.

Any independent review should verify that:

- the firing wouldn't violate anti-discrimination or other statutes
- the firing wouldn't be a breach of contract, including oral assurances of job security or statements made in an employee handbook
- your company has given the employee adequate and documented warnings that he or she faced being fired—except where the conduct would clearly warrant immediate firing
- you have followed your stated personnel practices, and
- you have followed the same procedures in similar situations involving other employees.

D. Investigating Complaints Against Workers

The need to discipline or fire an employee is often revealed to you in a complaint from a co-worker, a manager, or even a customer or other outsider. This is particularly likely in complaints for sexual harassment or dishonesty.

Investigating the facts can be tricky. The law doesn't require you to learn the truth with absolutely certainty—or even beyond a reasonable doubt. But to protect yourself legally, your safest course is to investigate complaints quickly, thoroughly, fairly and as confidentially as is possible under the circumstances—before you penalize or fire an employee.

1. The Investigation

It's usually best to have private interviews with each witness and the accused employee. Listen carefully and take good notes. Don't show any bias for or against the accused. Further investigate any evidence that surfaces, such as a claim that another employee is aware of facts that will shed light on the complaint. Have good reasons for whatever conclusions you reach. If you follow reasonable procedures and reach a reasonable result, you can't be faulted even though another person may have reached a different conclusion.

After an employee files a complaint, it's a good idea to keep him or her informed about the general steps you're taking to investigate. The complaining employee needs to know that you're taking the matter seriously. But that doesn't mean the employee is entitled to know all the details of what you're finding. If you give out information too freely, you could easily step on the toes of other employees.

2. Hiring Investigators

If you have qualms about your ability to investigate a complaint, consider hiring an experienced employment consultant or someone else who knows the ropes. Far better to lay out some cash to do it right than risk the consequences of a clumsy investigation. For example, if there's an issue of

employee dishonesty or criminal conduct, look into companies that specialize in corporate security.

Similarly, if someone charges sexual harassment because a manager has displayed offensive cartoons or photos in a work area, consider hiring a consultant experienced in sexual harassment issues to review your entire workplace and recommend a course of action. Bringing in an outsider may also help to defuse tensions between workers which you might only worsen if you simply rip down the offending material.

LOCATING A GOOD INVESTIGATOR

When you suspect an employee of dishonesty or criminal conduct, a private investigator may help sort out the facts. The job of interviewing witnesses, analyzing documents, watching for misconduct and preserving evidence isn't easy. The investigator must follow procedures that respect the accused employee's legal rights. If a court later finds that you trampled an employee's due process rights during an investigation, your business may have to pay for that violation.

It's crucial to find an investigator who's experienced in conducting internal investigations for businesses. There are many people who have recently hung out their shingles as consultants, but don't really have training or experience.

This is sensitive work and the stakes are high. No matter where you find names of possible investigators—from phone book listings, management newsletters, trade associations or other businesspeople— ask for references. Look for positive feedback from at least two or three other businesses before you hire an investigator.

E. Alternatives to Firing

Sometimes, firing a troublesome employee is the best course of action. You owe it to your business and to diligent, conscientious employees to get rid of a troublemaker who can't be turned around. But occasionally, there are good alternatives to firing a worker—alternatives that can help you avoid the risk of a wrongful discharge lawsuit at the same time you provide a person with a chance to better use his or her skills.

One possibility is to redesign the employee's job to eliminate the problem areas. Or you may assign the employee to another job. For example, an employee who has a tendency to quarrel with customers, but is otherwise organized and efficient, might do an excellent job working alone in the warehouse. Of course, you must be careful not to unload work unfairly on other employees who are already working at peak efficiency.

If yours is a slightly larger business, and there's a personality clash between an employee and a supervisor, you may be able to assign the employee to a different supervisor. Where the conflict is between two employees, neither of whom is a supervisor, you may be able to assign them to separate work areas. If a personal problem is at the root of an otherwise good employee's difficulties, you might offer to pay for at least a limited amount of counseling—or offer the employee a leave of absence to get help with the problem.

Sometimes you and an employee can come to an understanding that the working relationship isn't a good fit for either of you and that the employee is expected to move elsewhere in the near future. Allowing the employee to look for a new job during regular working hours may be one rational way to handle such a situation.

F. The Firing Process

Where possible, give employees ongoing feedback about job performance, conduct formal job evaluations once or twice a year and impose progressive discipline. (See Chapter 2.) Ideally, a firing shouldn't come suddenly or as a surprise.

When you've reached the point where firing an employee is the best or only option, you must mind some legal strictures as you carry out the firing.

Speedy Action is Sometimes Appropriate

There can be situations in which moving quickly to fire someone—without a warning—may be the best course. For example, if your delivery truck driver is convicted of drunk driving, it makes sense to get rid of the driver. Similarly, you shouldn't feel it necessary to give advance warning to a bookkeeper who has embezzled money from your company. In general, use your judgment and err on the side of giving an employee a chance to correct a problem. But in extreme circumstances, don't hesitate to act quickly.

1. Severance Packages

Many employers and employees wrongly believe that every fired employee is legally entitled to severance pay. The truth is that you must only give severance pay when it's required by a contract with the employee. Still, in some cases, you may wish to offer severance pay and other benefits to help cushion the impact of a firing—and alleviate ill will.

If you're inclined to offer a severance package, it makes sense to be more generous with long-time employees than with those who have been with you just a year or two. For a short-term employee—someone who's worked for you for two years, for example—you might offer one month's pay plus payment of health insurance premiums for 90 days. For an employee who's been on your payroll for 15 years, it would be reasonable to offer six months of salary plus one year's worth of paid health insurance premiums.

You can be creative in putting together a severance package. The benefits you may wish to consider include:
- severance pay
- continuation of employee benefits, such as payment of health insurance premiums for a limited time
- a favorable letter of reference if your normal policy is to give only a former employee's position and term of employment
- releasing the employee from special obligations such as a covenant not to compete
- allowing the employee to keep any advance of expense funds or commissions that otherwise would be repayable to your business
- allowing the employee to keep the desk, chair, computer, cellular phone or tools that he or she has been using
- agreeing not to contest the employee's right to unemployment compensation
- paying for outplacement services, and
- promising to pay an employee's moving expenses, up to a stated limit.

Also, consider paying the employee for unused vacation time that the employee would otherwise lose. Normally, the conditions under which an employee will be compensated for unused vacation time are a matter of policy to be set by an employer—but you can bend that policy to benefit a departing employee.

Example: Alpine Ski Shop pays its employees for two weeks of vacation time each year, but states in its employee's handbook: "You must take your vacation during June, July or August and while you are on Alpine's payroll. Vacation time not used during that period will be forfeited unless you secure prior approval." Employee Kurt takes one week of his vacation in July and doesn't ask for permission to take the second week later. In October, Alpine fires Kurt because of an attitude problem. As part of a severance package, Alpine pays Kurt for the unused week of vacation time.

Paying for Vacation Time May be Mandatory

In some states, the law doesn't allow an employer to set a policy forcing employees to forfeit unused vacation or sick time once it has accrued. In such states, the accrued vacation or sick time is treated as wages and must be included in an employee's final paycheck. The key legal issue is whether the vacation time has accrued. Check with the state department of labor to learn how much latitude you have regarding payment for vacation and sick time. (See the Appendix for contact details.)

2. Preparing the Paperwork

Before you fire an employee, prepare a letter describing the severance package you intend to offer. And if you want the employee to waive possible legal claims against your business to qualify for the severance benefits, consider preparing a severance agreement as well.

a. Termination letter

To soften the shock of a firing, you may wish to present the employee with a letter such as the following during the termination meeting.

SAMPLE TERMINATION LETTER—NO RELEASE REQUIRED

Dear _____ :

Your employment with XYZ Company is being terminated at
5 p.m. _____ 19XX.

You will receive a paycheck covering the wages you have earned
and for your accrued vacation time. In addition, you will receive the
following severance benefits:

1. Four weeks of additional pay.

2. Payment of your health insurance premiums for six months (or
   until you begin work at a new job, if that occurs sooner).

3. You will be allowed to keep the $500 advanced to you for job-
   related expenses.

4. In addition, the Company will not contest your right to receive
   unemployment compensation.

I wish you well in your further endeavors.

Date: _____ 19XX

_____

President, XYZ Company

Use such a letter if you're not requiring the employee to sign a release
waiving possible legal claims against your business to qualify for the
severance package.

b. Release of claims

You may wish to provide a severance package to a terminating employee
only if the employee agrees to waive all potential legal claims—a reasonable
condition in many situations. If so, consider a letter and severance agreement such as the following.

SAMPLE TERMINATION LETTER—RELEASE REQUIRED

Dear _____ :

Your employment with XYZ Company is being terminated at
5 p.m. _____ 19XX.

You will receive a paycheck covering the wages you have earned and for your
accrued vacation time.

In addition, we are prepared to provide the following severance benefits:

1. Eight weeks of additional pay.

2. We will release to you all rights to the inventory software program that you
    developed while working here.

3. You will be allowed to keep the computer, printer and cellular phone that we
    provided for your use as an employee.

4. In addition, if you move from the area within six months, we will reimburse you
    for your moving expenses, up to $2,500.

Please sign the attached severance agreement acknowledging that you are accepting
these benefits as a final settlement of any claims you may have against XYZ Company. You may wish to have a lawyer look over the severance agreement before you
sign it since it affects your legal rights.

If you want additional time to think about the severance benefits and the agreement,
you need not return the agreement to me with your signature until _____,
19XX. The terms offered here will become void if you haven't signed it and returned it
to me by that date. You will be given a copy for your records.

Date: _____ 19XX

_____

President, XYZ Company

SAMPLE SEVERANCE AGREEMENT

XYZ Company (Company) and _____ (Employee) agree as follows:

1. Employee's employment was terminated on _____ , 19XX. Company and Employee wish to resolve all possible claims pertaining to Employee's employment and termination.

2. In consideration of Employee's signing this agreement, Employee will receive the following severance benefits:

   a. Eight weeks of pay beyond Employee's termination date.

   b. Company will release to Employee all rights to the inventory software program that Employee developed while employed by Company.

   c. Company will transfer to Employee full ownership of the computer, printer and cellular phone that Company provided for Employee's use while employed by Company.

   d. In addition, if Employee moves from the area within six months from the date of termination, Company will reimburse Employee for moving expenses, up to $2,500.

3. Employee releases Company and its employees from all claims in connection with Employee's employment and termination, including contract and tort claims and claims based on the Age Discrimination in Employment Act of 1967, 29 U.S.C. §621. This release applies to all claims that Employee has or may believe he or she has against Company or its employees.

4. Employee signs this Agreement freely and voluntarily and acknowledges that he or she has been advised to consult a lawyer and has had the opportunity to do so.

5. Employee has __ days from _____ , 19XX to accept this Agreement. After accepting it, Employee has __ days to revoke the Agreement by giving Company written notice of revocation. If Employee does not revoke the Agreement during that period, it will be deemed accepted.

Date: _____ 19XX

_____   _____
Employee   President, XYZ Company

For a release to be enforceable, you must offer the employee something of value in exchange for giving up his or her possible claims against your business. The severance package in the sample agreement satisfies this legal requirement.

Also, give the employee a reasonable time—three or four business days, for example—to decide whether to accept your severance package and sign the severance agreement containing a release of claims. A coerced release is legally worthless.

Special rules apply if the employee is releasing claims under the Age Discrimination in Employment Act. If you present a release to an individual employee who's 40 years old or older, you must give the employee a fixed period of time in which to decide on signing the waiver. That period must be at least 21 days if the waiver has been presented to the employee alone. If you've presented the waiver to a group or class of employees, you must give each worker at least 45 days to decide whether or not to sign. In either case, a worker has seven days after agreeing to such a waiver to revoke his or her decision. (See Chapter 8, Section C2 for details.)

For more information on severance agreements, see "Using Releases in Employment Termination Cases" by Nancy E. Sasamoto and Stephen M. Proctor, *The Practical Lawyer,* June 1994. A single issue of *The Practical Lawyer* costs $7.75. An annual subscription, consisting of eight issues, costs $35. Call (215) 243-1640 or write 4025 Chestnut Street, Philadelphia, PA 19104-3099.

3. Return of Property

In planning for the termination meeting, make a list of all company property that has been given to the employee. Be prepared to get back these items from the employee either at the meeting or within a reasonable time afterward. Items to think about include:

- automobiles
- computers, cellular phones and beepers
- confidential manuals and other documents
- keys, credit cards, uniforms, ID badges, and
- parking permits.

Don't overlook any expense account funds you advanced to the employee. You may be entitled to deduct such advances from the employee's final paycheck. (See Section H for more legal rules on final paychecks.)

4. The Termination Meeting

Call the employee into a private office or meeting room and inform him or her of your decision. Be honest and direct in stating your reasons for ending the employment. If you've given the employee ongoing feedback, the firing shouldn't come as a complete shock. Make it clear that this is a final decision and that you're not going to change your mind. Unless the employee is likely to be a menace in the workplace, allow a day or so—but no longer—to clear out his or her desk and say goodbye to co-workers.

Go over any severance package the employee will receive—and explain the severance agreement if you require one to be signed. (See Section 2 above.)

Then give the employee a reasonable chance to vent his or her feelings about the discharge. Just listen and don't argue. Don't insult or abuse the employee no matter how angry, bitter or insulting he or she is to you. Typically, the employee's anger and disappointment will fade with time.

COMMON SENSE CAN HELP AVERT VIOLENCE

You may have zeroed in on scary newspaper headlines about disgruntled former employees who open fire on former employers. The actual incidence of such violence is quite low. Still, it pays to be prudent.

Violence following a firing is most apt to occur in a workplace where there are high levels of stress, autocratic and unpredictable managers, poor communication and employees who feel powerless.

Be especially careful if you're firing an employee for performing poorly—a charge that may be emotionally loaded. Some workers who are fired without warning can go over the edge because they feel there was nothing they could do to control the situation. In giving feedback before a firing, let workers know if their performances are below par—and focus on the specific ways in which job performance falls short of the mark. Warn workers that they may lose their jobs if they don't improve.

At a termination meeting with a potentially volatile employee, confine your discussion to the specific behavior about which the employee was warned. Never attack the worker personally. Remind the worker that he or she was given fair warning and an ample opportunity to change work habits.

Let the fired employee know that you won't be discussing the reasons for the firing with his or her former co-workers and that you're prepared to give a neutral letter of recommendation to prospective employers who inquire. This will help preserve the employee's self esteem, making violence unlikely.

Troubled employees often exhibit behavioral clues that you shouldn't ignore: high absenteeism, known substance abuse, chronic tardiness, and harassing and threatening others. If you're about to fire someone who appears to have a potential for violence, consider consulting first with a psychologist who specializes in workplace issues.

G. Heading Off Trouble

As noted, there are many ways to fortify your legal position so that an employee will be less likely to succeed in a claim against you for wrongful discharge. Some additional steps can help keep the goodwill of an employee who's being terminated, making it less likely that you'll even be sued.

1. Offering a Chance to Resign

Permitting the employee to resign gives him or her the opportunity to save face—so the employee may be less bitter about the termination and less hostile to your business. Be aware, however, that if you give the employee a stark choice between resigning and being fired, it's probably not legally considered a voluntary termination. The employee likely will be eligible for unemployment compensation benefits. (See Section J.) And a forced resignation may be treated the same as a firing if the employee does decide to sue for wrongful discharge.

2. Offering a Favorable Reference

If you would be willing to give a former employee a positive reference, tell him or her as soon as possible. Knowing that her or she will get a favorable recommendation can help temper a worker's ire over a termination. Obviously, such a reference isn't always possible. But quite often, an employee who wasn't a good fit at your business will do well elsewhere and you won't have a difficult time emphasizing the employee's good qualities.

When other employers call, follow through and accentuate the positive. Keep in touch with the former employee by phone and by sending copies of any letters in which you state positive things.

Glowing Recommendations Can Backfire

You must weigh the possibility of future legal problems that a favorable reference can create. The fired employee may use the favorable reference in court as evidence that he or she was really doing a great job for you and shouldn't have been terminated.

3. Help With Finding a New Job

You may be able to inform an employee of openings elsewhere that would be better suited to his or her skills and personality. Or, if it's a longtime senior employee to whom you feel a lot of loyalty, you may even consider footing the bill to have a personnel agency assist the employee in finding another job. Another possibility is to give an employee paid time off to find a new job—using your phone, if necessary, to call prospects.

H. Final Paychecks

Most states have a law specifying when you must give a final paycheck to a terminated employee. Most of these laws set different deadlines for employees who have quit and those who have been fired. (See the following chart.) If you don't give a final paycheck on time, you may have to pay damages to the employee and perhaps a penalty to the state as well.

Note that in many states, the law requires that the final paycheck include accrued vacation pay and anything else owed to an employee who's covered by the law. If you have additional questions about final paychecks, contact the wage and hour division of your state's labor department to doublecheck your state law. (See the Appendix for contact details.)

STATE LAWS THAT CONTROL FINAL PAYCHECKS

The laws listed here specify how soon a final paycheck must be given to an employee under the laws of the state in which your busines is located.

Alabama	No applicable law.
Alaska	Within 3 days. (Alaska Stat. §23.05.140)
Arizona	If you are fired: within 3 days or next scheduled payday. If you quit: next scheduled payday. (Ariz. Rev. Stat. Ann. §23-353)
Arkansas	If you are fired: within 7 days after your demand. If you quit: no applicable law. (Arkansas Code §11-4-405)
California	If you are fired: immediately—or within 72 hours for employees of the seasonal industries. If you quit: within 72 hours, or immediately if you have given 72 hours notice. (Cal. Labor Code §§201 and 202)
Colorado	If you are fired: immediately. If you quit: next scheduled payday. (Colo. Rev. Stat. Ann. §8-4-104)
Connecticut	If you are fired: next business day. If you quit: next scheduled payday. (Conn. Gen. Stat. Ann. §1-71c)
Delaware	Next scheduled payday. (Del. Code Ann. §19-1103)
District of Columbia	If you are fired: next business day. If you quit: next scheduled payday or 7 days, whichever is sooner. (D.C. Code §36-103)
Florida	No applicable law.
Georgia	No applicable law.
Hawaii	If you are fired: next business day. If you quit: next scheduled payday. (Hawaii Rev. Stat. §388-3)
Idaho	Next scheduled payday or within 10 business days, whichever is sooner. If written request made for earlier payment, within 48 hours. (Idaho Code §45-606)
Illinois	Next scheduled payday. (820 Ill. Cons. Stat. 115/5)
Indiana	Next scheduled payday. (Ind. Code §§22-2-9-2 and 22-2-5-1)
Iowa	Next scheduled payday. (Iowa Code Ann. §91A.4)
Kansas	Next scheduled payday. (Kan. Stat. Ann. §31-315)
Kentucky	If you are fired: next scheduled payday or within 14 days, whichever is later. If you quit: no applicable law. (Ky. Rev. Stat. Ann. §337.055)
Louisiana	Within 3 days of your date of discharge or resignation. (La. Rev. Stat. Ann. §§23-631)

Maine	Next scheduled payday or within 2 weeks after demand, whichever is earlier. (Me. Rev. Stat. Ann. tit. 26 § 626)
Maryland	Next scheduled payday. (Md. Labor & Employment Code Ann. §3-505)
Massachusetts	If you are fired: immediately. If you quit: next scheduled payday. (Mass. Ann. Laws ch. 149 §148)
Michigan	As soon as amount can be determined with due diligence. (Mich. Stat. Ann. §17.277(5))
Minnesota	If you are fired: within 24 hours of demand. If you quit: within 5 days, or within 24 hours if you have given at least 5 days notice. (Minn. Stat. §§181.13 and 181.14)
Mississippi	No applicable law.
Missouri	If you are fired: within 7 days after you make a written demand. If you quit: no applicable law. (Mo. Ann. Stat. §290.110)
Montana	If you are fired for cause: immediately; otherwise, within 3 days. An extension of 3 additional days is given to the employer if its payroll checks come from outside the state. (Mont. Code Ann. §39-3-205)
Nebraska	If you are fired: next scheduled payday or within 2 weeks, whichever is sooner. If you quit: no applicable law. (Neb. Rev. Stat. §48-1230)
Nevada	If you are fired: immediately. If you quit: next scheduled payday or within 7 days, whichever is earlier. (Nev. Rev. Stat. §608.020 and 608.030)
New Hampshire	If you are fired: within 72 hours. If you quit: next scheduled payday; or if you give at least one pay period's notice, within 72 hours of end of work. (N.H. Rev. Stat. Ann. §275:44)
New Jersey	Next scheduled payday. (N.J. Stat. Ann. §34:11-4.3)
New Mexico	If you are fired: within 5 days. If you quit: no applicable law. (N.M. Stat. Ann. §§50-4-4 and 50-4-5)
New York	If you are fired: next scheduled payday. If you quit: no applicable law. (N.Y. Labor Laws §191)
North Carolina	Next scheduled payday. (N.C. Gen. Stat. §95.25.7)
North Dakota	If you are fired: within 24 hours of the time of separation at employer's place of business or within 15 days or on the next scheduled payday, whichever comes first. If you resign: next scheduled payday by certified mail to an address designated by the employee. (N.D. Cent. Code §34-14-03)
Ohio	No applicable law.
Oklahoma	Next scheduled payday. (Okla. Stat. Ann. tit. 40, §165.3)

Oregon	If you are fired: immediately. If you quit: within 48 hours. (Or. Rev. Stat. §652.140)
Pennsylvania	Next scheduled payday. (Pa. Stat. Ann. tit. 43, §260.5)
Rhode Island	Next scheduled payday under normal circumstances; within 24 hours if the employer is going out of business, merging or moving out of state. (R.I. Gen. Laws §28-14-4)
South Carolina	Within 48 hours or next scheduled payday, which may not be more than 30 days after written notice is given. (S.C. Codified Laws §41-11-170)
South Dakota	If you are fired: within 5 days after you have returned anything belonging to the employer. If you quit: next scheduled payday after you have returned anything belonging to the employer. (S.D. Codified Laws §§60-11-10 and 60-11-11)
Tennessee	No applicable law.
Texas	If you are fired: within six days. If you quit: next regularly scheduled payday. (Tex. Civ. Stat. Art. 5155)
Utah	If you are fired: within 24 hours. If you quit: within 72 hours, or immediately if you have given at least 72 hours notice. (Utah Code Ann. §34-28-5)
Vermont	If you are fired: within 72 hours. If you quit: next scheduled payday or, if no scheduled payday exists, the next Friday. (Vt. Stat. Ann. tit. 21, §342)
Virginia	Next scheduled payday. (Va. Code §40.1-29)
Washington	Next scheduled payday. (Wash. Rev. Code §49.48.010)
West Virginia	If you are fired: within 72 hours. If you quit: next regular payday. (W. Va. Code §21-5-4)
Wisconsin	If you are fired: within 3 days. If you quit: within 15 days. (Wis. Stat. Ann. §109.03)
Wyoming	If you are fired: within 24 hours. If you quit: within 72 hours. (Wyo. Stat. Ann. §27-4-103)

I. Continuing Health Insurance

If you have 20 or more employees and you offer a group health insurance plan, a federal law called the Consolidated Omnibus Budget Reconciliation Act or COBRA requires you to offer former employees the option of continuing their coverage for some time after their employment ends. (For more on COBRA, see Chapter 4, Section A.)

J. Unemployment Compensation

Employees who are terminated because of cutbacks or because they are not a good fit for a job are generally entitled to unemployment benefits under state unemployment insurance programs. Employees who are fired for serious misconduct—stealing or repeated absenteeism, for example—or who voluntarily leave a job without good cause are not entitled to unemployment payments.

Applying these categories to a particular termination isn't always easy. For example, suppose you and an employee get into an argument and she leaves shortly afterward. If she has quit, benefits are not legally due. If she was fired, however, she's entitled to unemployment benefits absent truly bad conduct such as selling illegal drugs in the workplace. It's sometimes difficult to discern whether a termination is a quitting or a firing.

1. The Claims Process

Although the details of unemployment compensation vary in each state, some general principles apply in most cases. As a private employer, you contribute a relatively small amount to an unemployment insurance fund in your state. Your rate is normally based on the size of your payroll and the amount of unemployment benefits paid from your account. Employers with smaller payrolls and low levels of unemployment claims will, over time, pay lower taxes.

An unemployment claim will typically proceed through a number of steps.

a. Filing the claim

The former employee files a claim with the state unemployment program. You receive written notice of the claim and can file a written objection—usually within seven to 10 days. If you want to file an objection, don't miss this deadline. If you do, you may be cut off from raising your objection.

b. Eligibility determined

The state agency makes an initial determination of whether the former employee is eligible to get unemployment benefits. Usually there's no hearing at this stage.

c. Referee's hearing

You or the former employee can appeal the initial eligibility decision and have a hearing before a referee—a hearing officer who is on the staff of the state agency. Normally conducted in a private room at the unemployment office, this airing of the situation is the most important step in the process. At the hearing, you and the former employee each have your say. In addition, you're entitled to have a lawyer there and to present witnesses and any relevant written records such as employee evaluations or warning letters.

Before the hearing, ask to see the agency's complete file on the claim. This will give you a chance to be prepared to refute inaccurate statements. Bring all pertinent employment records to the hearing. Also, line up witnesses who can give first-hand testimony about why the former employee was guilty of misconduct, quit voluntarily or is otherwise ineligible for benefits.

It may be too expensive to hire a lawyer to handle an unemployment compensation hearing. In some states, you have the alternative of hiring an experienced nonlawyer specialist to oppose claims at a fraction of what lawyers charge. A clerk in the referee's office may know who performs these services in your area. But since the procedures in the hearing are purposely simple and nontechnical, you probably won't need any hired help.

Serious Charges May be Raised

The referee's decision sometimes influences what happens in a related civil lawsuit. For example, if the referee rules that the employee quit because he or she was being sexually harassed, that ruling may be decisive in a later case that the employee brings against your business. Consult a lawyer if you anticipate that complicated legal issues—such as sexual harassment, illegal discrimination or retaliation for complaining about a workplace hazard— may surface at the hearing.

d. Administrative appeal

Either side can appeal the referee's decision to an administrative agency such as a board of review. At this stage, it's advisable to hire a lawyer. This appeal usually is based solely on the testimony and documents recorded at the referee's hearing, although in some states, the review board can direct that additional evidence be taken. While the review board is free to draw its own conclusions from the evidence and overrule the referee, more often than not it goes along with the referee's ruling.

e. Judicial appeal

Either side can appeal to the state court system, but this is rare. Typically, a court will overturn the agency's decision only if the decision is contrary to law or isn't supported by substantial evidence.

For more information, see *Employer's Unemployment Cost Control Handbook,* published by the National Foundation for Unemployment Compensation and Workers' Compensation, 1331 Pennsylvania Avenue, NW; 1500 North Tower, Washington, DC 20004-1703; telephone: 202-682-1517. The cost is $20. While the book recommends taking a more aggressive stance in fighting claims than may be prudent, it is full of good information.

DOING YOUR OWN RESEARCH

Many states keep records of decisions of the review board. These are gathered and bound together—allowing you to see how cases similar to yours were decided. This can be a helpful resource if you represent your business in an administrative appeal. Your state's unemployment agency can tell you if and where such decisions are kept for public inspection.

Similarly, when an unemployment case is reviewed by a state appeals court, the written decision becomes a public record and is placed in bound books alongside other court decisions. To locate court decisions dealing with unemployment law, start with the annotated version of your state's statutes—often called an annotated code. It should be available at larger public libraries.

Look up the unemployment compensation law and you'll find short summaries of each case in which an appeals court interpreted the law. Then look up the full decision which will be in the case reports—the books that collect all appeals court decisions in your state. (For more on how to do your own legal research, see Chapter 13, Section D.)

2. Saving Money

In theory, at least, you'll save money if you recognize and successfully oppose questionable claims. But this isn't always true. First, lots of claims you think are questionable probably are allowed under unemployment compensation laws, which are deliberately lenient to give unemployed workers a transitional source of income. Unless there's strong evidence that the employee pilfered from the company or engaged in other fairly extreme conduct, he or she will usually win in a claims contest.

Second, fighting a claim can be time consuming, emotionally draining and costly for you—especially when balanced against the fact that a few unemployment claims spread over several years are unlikely to greatly increase your insurance rate. Third, fighting an unemployment claim will guarantee an angry former employee—a person far more likely to file a lawsuit or harm you or your business in some other way. This might happen anyway. But your challenge to the employee's right to receive unemployment benefits may be the irritant that prompts the former employee to strike back.

Balance the benefits of saving on unemployment taxes against the trouble it takes to fight the claim and the risk of inviting a lawsuit against your business.

In addition to challenging questionable claims, there are other ways you may be able to reduce the costs of unemployment benefits.

Doublecheck the information your state unemployment agency uses to compute your tax rates and to compute benefits paid to former employees. Make sure the agency's records don't indicate that your business has had more claims filed against it than it really did have. Clerical errors can be costly.

Also, keep in mind that a former employee may be eligible for benefits at first, but later become ineligible. For example, three weeks after being fired, a claimant may decide to return to school fulltime, meaning that he or she is unavailable to take a new job. Or a former employee may receive retirement or vacation pay that means he or she is no longer eligible for unemployment benefits or that the amounts should be reduced. Or you may hear that the employee is working for another business, but being paid under the table so as to keep getting unemployment benefits. If you learn any such information, notify the state agency promptly.

K. Protecting Your Business Information

Some employees have access to sensitive business information or trade secrets. When these employees leave—either because they quit or because you've fired them—you may be concerned that they'll use this information to their personal advantages. For example, a former employee may open a business that competes with yours or may go to work for a competitor.

Chapter 1, Section A5, discusses how you can protect yourself by having certain employees sign covenants not to compete and agreements not to divulge or use trade secrets. This section covers what to do if a former employee begins to compete unfairly with your business in violation of such a covenant or agreement.

1. Enforcing Noncompete Agreements

You may assume it would be difficult to learn whether a former employee is competing with you. However, many businesses are fairly public, making it difficult for a former employee to hide. Also, there's a good chance that you'll be contacted by your loyal customers who have been approached by the former employee. The lure of a lower price offered by the former employee often isn't enough to win over a customer who suspects the former employee of unfairly competing with you and using inside information.

If the former employee's conduct violates a valid noncompete agreement and your business will suffer immediate damage, you can seek a court order to put a legal stop to the unfair activities. You'll probably need to hire a lawyer to help. (See Chapter 13, Section A.)

Fortunately, the procedures for getting a ruling from a judge in this situation are fairly fast and efficient. A lawyer will likely ask the judge assigned to your case to set an early hearing to decide whether to issue a preliminary injunction—an order that prohibits the former employee from unfairly competing with you while the case is pending. A judge who's convinced that the threat of damage to your business is great may even grant a temporary restraining order forbidding the former employee from taking any action until the initial hearing can be held.

A restraining order or injunction is a powerful legal weapon. If a former employee violates such an order, he or she can be found in contempt of court. The punishment for contempt is a fine, imprisonment—or both.

WEIGHING YOUR CHANCES OF SUCCESS

Whether a judge will enforce a covenant not to compete is always an iffy question. The legal system puts a high value on a person's right to earn a living. Covenants not to compete won't be enforced if they're found to be unreasonable. A covenant may be held unreasonable because it covers too wide a geographic area or lasts for too long a time.

Example: Walt—a veterinarian who operates three animal hospitals in Anderson County—hires Fred, another veterinarian, to work for him. Fred signs an employment contract which states that for three years after his employment ends, he won't practice veterinary medicine within 15 miles of any veterinary practice operated by Walt. Together, the three prohibited areas embrace nearly all of Anderson County, plus parts of several adjoining counties. The contract also states that Fred will pay $30,000 in damages if he violates the covenant.

Fred quits his job and begins a mobile veterinary practice in Anderson County, bringing his work within the restricted areas. Walt sues Fred for $30,000 but the court holds the covenant can't be enforced because it's unreasonably broad. (*Stringer v. Herron*, 424 S.E.2d 547 (1992).)

A covenant may also be held unreasonable because the information revealed to the worker isn't all that sensitive, so the restriction doesn't serve a valid business purpose.

Example: Image Supplies Inc., a printing supply company in Chicago, hires John as a salesman. John signs a covenant stating that for one year after his job ends, he won't compete with Image Supplies within 100 miles of Image Supplies' headquarters. John resigns and goes to work for a competitor in the Chicago area.

Image Supplies seeks an injunction—a court order prohibiting John from working for the competitor—because John has the names and locations of its customers and the prices charged to each customer. The court refuses to grant an injunction. It holds that Image Supplies has no protectable business interest in the information that John has. The names of firms in the printing business are easily found in the phone book and trade publications, and anyone can learn about prices by asking the customer. (Image Supplies Inc. v. Hilmert, 390 N.E.2d 68 (1979).)

Judges are more likely to enforce restrictive covenants against high-level managers who truly are given inside information. Such former employees are in a position to do real harm.

2. Protecting Trade Secrets

A trade secret is information that gives you a competitive advantage because it isn't generally known and can't be readily learned by other people who could benefit from it. It can be a formula, pattern, compilation, program, device, method, technique or process that you've made reasonable efforts to keep secret.

A judge may order the employee not to use the information even if he or she didn't sign a secrecy agreement—but you must show that what the employee took is truly a trade secret. This often involves establishing two things: that the information was not readily obtainable elsewhere, and that you took precautions to keep it secret. For example, if you developed a unique plant fertilizer that you manufacture and distribute, you should be able to establish that you created the fertilizer through extensive trial and error and then made sure that employees learned the formula on a strict need-to-know basis.

Similarly, if you put together a valuable customer list that includes your customers' buying history and buying habits, you should be able to show that you painstakingly built up the list over several years and that you only allowed a limited number of employees to see it. (For more on trade secret protection, see Chapter 1, Section A.)

L. Handling Post-Employment Inquiries

One of your knottiest dilemmas after an employee quits or has been fired is what to tell other businesses that inquire about the former employee. You may be tugged in several directions.

- You want to tell the truth—good, bad or neutral—about the former worker.
- You may want to help the former worker find another job for which he or she is better suited.
- You may fear that if you do say anything negative, you'll be sued for libel or slander.
- You may feel that the best way to head off a possible lawsuit or complaint by an angry employee is to help him or her find another job.
- You don't want to overpraise a marginal employee and risk the anger of the new employer.

The law doesn't require you to completely clam up about a former employee. If you follow some basic legal guidelines, you can disclose significant information about the former employee without risking a lawsuit.

1. Legal Requirements

The key to protecting yourself is to stick to the facts and act in good faith.
It's when you go beyond the facts or are motivated by a desire to harm the
former employee or cover up the truth that you can find yourself in deep
trouble.

Former employees who feel maligned can sue for defamation—called
slander if the statements were spoken or libel if they were written. To win a
defamation case, a former employee must prove that you gave out false
information and that the information harmed his or her reputation. If you
can prove that the information you gave out was true, the defamation
lawsuit will be dismissed.

And employers in most states are entitled to limited protection in
defamation cases, even if the information they provide is untrue. This is
based on a legal doctrine called "qualified privilege." To receive the benefit
of this protection, you must show that:

• you made the statement in good faith
• you and the person to whom you disclosed the information shared a
  common interest, and
• you limited your statement to this common interest.

The law recognizes that a former employer and a prospective employer
share a common interest in the attributes of an employee. To get the
protection of the qualified privilege, your main task is to stick to facts that
you've reasonably investigated and to lay aside your personal feelings about
the former employee.

If you can establish that you're protected by the qualified privilege, the
only way a former employee can succeed in a defamation lawsuit is to prove
that you knew the information was false but you passed it on anyway, or
that you acted recklessly in sorting out the facts.

Speaking Candidly

In a trend designed to encourage fuller disclosure in responding to reference checks, states have begun passing laws allowing you to be more candid about former employees. Generally, these laws expand on the common law principles that protect you if you act in good faith. A Kansas law, for example, says you're presumed to be acting in good faith when you respond to a reference check.

Under that law, to collect damages for a bad reference, the former employee must prove by "clear and convincing evidence" that you acted in bad faith. If your state has a similar law, you can rest a bit easier when discussing former employees.

2. Deciding What to Say

A practical policy—and one that gives you a high degree of legal protection—is simply not to discuss an employee with prospective employers if you can't say something positive. Just tell the person inquiring that it's not your policy to comment on former workers.

Where an employee's record is truly mixed, it's usually possible to accent the positive while you try to put negative information into a half-way favorable, or at least less negative, perspective.

Example: Madeline, a copywriter for your ad agency, started working for you right out of college. She was a creative writer with lots of clever ideas, but never really caught on to how to manage the production details for the mail order catalogs that are the bread and butter of your business. After a year, you concluded that this was just not a good fit and you reluctantly gave Madeline 60 days to find a slot elsewhere—hopefully with an agency looking for the dazzling, witty prose that was Madeline's forte.

Possible approach to inquiries: Emphasize that Madeline is so full of creative energy and enthusiasm that she gets bored when it comes to tracking mundane details. Suggest that Madeline would do best in a spot where creative writing and initiative are required and where new and clever ideas are needed.

Stick to known, provable facts and scrupulously avoid passing along speculation or rumor.

Example: Joan worked for your company for a year as your bookkeeper and manager of your checking accounts. After suspecting some shortages of funds, you hired a CPA to review the books and bank records. The CPA reported in writing that there were indeed some serious irregularities. You confronted Joan with the CPA's report and she quit her job in a huff, denying any involvement. Because Joan always seemed to be sniffling, you suspected that she had been taking money to support a cocaine habit.

Possible approach to inquiries: Describe the CPA's written report and the fact that Joan left just after it was issued, but avoid voicing your unconfirmed suspicions about Joan's drug addiction. A safer course is to say nothing at all, since no dishonesty or drug usage was actually proven.

Example: Norm drove a delivery van for your business. In a six-month period, he had two accidents with the van as a result of speeding. You're convinced that on one occasion he'd been drinking, although he wasn't charged with drunk driving. In the second accident, a pedestrian was seriously injured. You fired Norm.

Possible approach to inquiries: Give the facts about the two accidents, but don't speculate about Norm's suspected drunk driving.

Example: Oscar, a salesman for your company, has an explosive temper. You received reports from several customers that Oscar had lost his cool and shouted obscenities at them. In one instance, he was nose-to-nose with the customer. In another case, he grabbed the customer's shoulder. You were about to discuss these incidents with Oscar when he quit to move to another city. The scuttlebutt around the office was that Oscar would often drink three martinis at lunch.

Possible approach to inquiries: Describe Oscar's strong selling skills and then tell of documenting customer complaints, but refrain from repeating gossip you overheard about Oscar's drinking.

It also pays to watch your tongue in informal settings. Don't let down your guard at trade meetings or at places where you're chatting socially with others. If a fired employee was with your business for a while, a supplier or customer may ask, "Where's John these days?" If you reply in a vindictive way, describing all your grievances that led you to fire John, word will likely spread. And John may wind up being blackballed in your field or town. This can lead to legal complications for you and your business.

BE CAREFUL WITHIN YOUR BUSINESS

Usually, when a former employee sues for defamation, it's because the old employer has gone overboard in giving information to a prospective employer. But you can also get in trouble if you're not discreet in what you say about the former employee within your own company.

To help avoid liability, follow a few common sense policies.

- Disclose the reasons for a firing strictly on a need-to-know basis—for example, to an employee who handles unemployment compensation claims for your business.
- Avoid discussing firings at meetings and employee gatherings—and never post the details on a bulletin board. Limit announcements to something non-committal: "Bob has left the company as of last Friday. His position is being filled by Rita."
- Be sure your personnel files reflect fairness, objectivity and good faith. A former employee who sues you will certainly subpoena his or her employment records. These must be free of unprovable gossip or your whole case may be jeopardized. ■

CHAPTER
11
INDEPENDENT CONTRACTORS

Many businesses hire independent contractors rather than employees to perform at least some of their work. There are often advantages to such an arrangement—but there can be a downside, too. If you mistakenly classify a worker as an independent contractor rather than an employee, you face potentially serious legal problems—particularly when it comes to taxes. The IRS prefers to have a worker classified as an employee rather than an independent contractor if there's doubt about the worker's status.

The main difference between independent contractors and employees is that independent contractors have the right to control not only the outcome of a project, but also the means of accomplishing it. Problems arise because some workers fall into a gray area, creating the danger of misclassification. To avoid such problems, it pays to become familiar with the analytic tools that IRS examiners use to sort out complicated cases. (See Section B.)

A small or midsized business may hire several types of workers as independent contractors. Common examples are a lawyer or accountant, a painter who spruces up your office, or a computer consultant who installs specialized software at your store and teaches your employees how to use it. Typically—but not always—independent contractors have special skills that you need to call upon only sporadically.

Hiring Independent Contractors, by Stephen Fishman (Nolo Press) provides clear and comprehensive guidance that will help you avoid a collision with the IRS over how you classify a worker.

A. Comparing Employees and Independent Contractors

Sometimes, your company has needs that can be filled equally well by an employee or an independent contractor.

In choosing which route to take, there are several factors worth considering.

1. Tax Obligations

Employee. You must make an employer's contribution for the worker's Social Security and Medicare taxes. You're also responsible for withholding federal and state income taxes and the worker's share of Social Security and Medicare taxes, and for keeping records and reporting on these items to the federal and state governments. Each year, you must send the employee a Form W-2 showing how much he or she earned and how much was withheld. (See Chapter 5, Sections B and C for details on tax responsibilities.)

Independent Contractor. When you hire an independent contractor, you're not required to withhold taxes from the amount you pay the worker, and you don't have to pay any portion of the worker's Social Security and Medicare taxes. Your only tax responsibility is to complete a Form 1099-MISC at the end of the year if you paid the independent contractor $600 or more during the year. You must send copies of this form to both the IRS and the employee.

2. Workers' Compensation

Employee. You must carry workers' compensation insurance for an employee. The workers' compensation system provides replacement income and medical expenses to employees who are injured or become ill as a result of their jobs. (See Chapter 7, Section E.)

Independent Contractor. Generally, an employer does not pay for workers' compensation for an independent contractor.

3. Unemployment Compensation

Employee. You must contribute to an unemployment insurance fund in your state and pay a federal unemployment tax. An employee who is laid off or is fired for a reason other than serious misconduct is entitled to unemployment benefits from the state fund. (See Chapter 10, Section J.)

Independent Contractor. Generally, an employer does not make contributions to a state unemployment fund or pay the federal unemployment tax for an independent contractor.

4. Job Benefits

Employee. An employer usually provides job benefits for an employee, such as paid vacations, sick leave and holidays, health insurance and a retirement plan. (See Chapter 4.)

Independent Contractor. An independent contractor is paid only for time spent working—and is responsible for paying for his or her own health insurance and retirement savings plan.

PENALTIES LURK IF YOU MISCLASSIFY A WORKER

If you weigh both possibilities and conclude it's in your company's best interests to hire and classify a worker as an independent contractor rather than an employee, fine. But be sure he or she really qualifies for this status under the IRS rules. If you classify a worker as an independent contractor when the worker should have been treated as an employee, you can be required to pay:

- the employer's and employee's share of Social Security and Medicare contributions
- income tax that should have been withheld from the employee's wages, and
- federal unemployment tax.

You may also be liable for the employee's state income taxes that should have been withheld, as well as unemployment compensation taxes. And if the worker is injured on the job, you may have to pay workers' compensation benefits because you didn't cover the employee under your company's workers' compensation policy.

5. Workspace

Employee. An employer provides workspace and equipment for an employee—meaning the employer pays for rent, maintenance, property insurance and utilities, as well as for tools, computers, furniture and vehicles, depending on the type of business.

Independent Contractor. An independent contractor usually—but not always—pays for his or her own workspace and equipment.

6. Firing the Worker

Employee. If you become unhappy with an employee's work and he or she doesn't improve, you will likely have to fire the worker—often a traumatic and legally hazardous course of action. (See Chapter 10.)

Independent Contractor. The emotional and legal bonds with an independent contractor are typically looser. An independent contractor is usually hired for a set assignment to be completed by a fixed deadline. If the independent contractor isn't satisfactory, you can simply turn to another independent contractor for future work. And if the independent contractor will be doing a series of projects over a long period, a written contract allowing you or the worker to cancel on two weeks notice can simplify termination.

7. Cost

Employee. The hourly rate of an employee may be relatively low—but the true cost must reflect the money you pay for taxes, insurance, job benefits, workspace and equipment.

Independent Contractor. The hourly rate of an independent contractor may be relatively high because the worker must earn enough to cover business expenses and taxes.

8. Governmental Regulations

Employee. An employer is subject to a wide range of governmental regulations intended to protect employees. There are, for example, laws dealing with wages and hours (see Chapter 3), employee benefits (see Chapter 4), family and medical leave (see Chapter 6), workplace health and safety (see Chapter 7) and illegal discrimination (see Chapters 8 and 9).

Independent Contractor. A company's relationship with an independent contractor—if the worker has been properly classified as such—is subject to fewer legal restrictions. For example, you needn't pay an independent contractor time and a-half for overtime hours, and you're not responsible for monitoring health and safety conditions at an independent contractor's own home, shop or office.

9. Liability for Worker's Actions

Employee. An employer generally is legally liable for an employee's negligence. If, for example, an employee carelessly injures a customer while at work or damages someone's property, the employer can be held responsible.

Independent Contractor. If you hire an independent contractor, your company generally won't be liable for the negligence of that person. Be aware, however, that in some situations, your company may be liable for the actions of an independent contractor—especially if he or she was acting as your agent.

10. Liability for Injury to Worker

Employee. An employer is responsible for medical treatment for an employee hurt on the job and for paying money to partially cover the employee's lost wages. This is generally handled through workers' compensation insurance. These payments are required whether or not your company was at fault for the employee's injuries. (See Chapter 7, Section E.)

Independent Contractor. If an independent contractor is injured because of some dangerous situation at your business premises, he or she can recover medical bills and lost income from your business, as well as money for pain and suffering. But first, the independent contractor must show that you were negligent. You're not liable for injuries the independent contractor receives elsewhere while working for you—unless you truly had control over those premises.

Consider Leasing Workers

If you need extra workers for peak periods, a leasing service may be the answer. Leasing services hire workers as their employees, taking care of all the normal employer responsibilities—payroll, taxes and insurance. You pay the leasing service to provide qualified workers to you for short-term assignments. Obviously, the leasing service must make a profit, so the cost to you is higher than if you hired the workers directly. The advantage to you is the convenience—and the fact that you're not going to be hassled by the IRS for possibly misclassifying a worker.

11. Worker's Preferences

Employee. A worker may prefer to be an employee because that status promises a steady, predictable salary, paid vacations, medical care and other job benefits at the employer's expense—and freedom from worry about the paperwork and recordkeeping required of people who are in business for themselves. What's more, an employee usually doesn't have to invest in tools and equipment. If an employee incurs business expenses, he or she will usually be reimbursed by the employer. If not, the employee can take a tax deduction to the extent such expenses exceed 2% of his or her adjusted gross income.

Independent Contractor. A worker may prefer to be an independent contractor to have greater control over working hours and conditions, and to maintain the freedom to work for several businesses. Some like the fact that there's no withholding of taxes; they feel that they have a better cash flow, even though they're ultimately responsible for paying their taxes. Workers may also see benefits in being treated as independent contractors because they're able to deduct their business expenses from their gross incomes, including money spent on cars, home offices, and even for some travel and entertainment.

12. Employer's Preferences

Employee. An employer may prefer to hire a worker as an employee because the business has that worker's undivided loyalty and can better control the worker's hours and methods of doing the job.

Independent Contractor. An employer may prefer to hire a worker as an independent contractor because it allows more flexibility to adjust to fluctuating needs. For example, if an employer anticipates a two-month crunch on a project, farming out the extra work to an independent contractor may involve less workplace disruption than hiring an employee, providing workspace and then laying off the employee.

B. The IRS Rules

To determine whether someone is an employee or an independent contractor, the IRS looks at the degree of control you have over the worker. If you control—or can control—not only what is to be done but also how it's done, the worker is an employee.

Other Tests May Apply

The IRS tests for independent contractor status are emphasized here because the IRS is the agency with which you're most likely to have a problem. Be aware, however, that in dealing with other agencies and laws, slightly different tests may be used. For example, a different test is used to determine if a person is an independent contractor under the Fair Labor Standards Act. (See Chapter 3, Section A1.) And other tests may apply under state laws dealing with workers' compensation insurance and unemployment compensation. (See Section D below.)

The IRS doesn't care what label you apply to a worker. You can designate someone as a partner, co-venturer, agent or independent contractor. But if the person legally qualifies as an employee, the IRS insists that you withhold income taxes and the employee's share of Social Security and Medicare contributions—and pay the employer's share of those contributions.

In deciding whether a person is an employee or an independent contractor, the IRS used to rely on a list of 20 factors cobbled together from various court decisions. The IRS, however, didn't spell out what weight it accorded to any one factor, which led to inconsistent rulings and considerable confusion.

Because a worker's status often remained unclear after applying the traditional test, it was easy for the IRS to classify the worker as an employee—an IRS preference grounded in the assumption that the government stands to collect more tax revenue if a worker is classified as an employee rather than as an independent contractor.

Although the IRS hasn't formally repealed the 20-factor test, it has decidedly moved away from that test by publishing in late 1996 the worker classification training materials it now uses for indoctrinating IRS examiners. For employers trying to figure out where they stand on independent contractor issues, the training materials are a vast improvement over the old 20-factor test. The training materials provide welcome guidance on the weight given to various factors.

For a free copy of the worker classification training materials, call 202/622-5164, or write to: IRS Freedom of Information Office, Freedom of Information Reading Room, P.O. Box 795, Ben Franklin Station, Washington, DC 20444. You can also get the training materials on the Internet at www.irs.ustreas.gov.

To determine whether you should classify a worker as an employee rather than as an independent contractor, IRS examiners are instructed to look primarily at three categories:

- **Behavioral control.** Do you have the right to direct or control how the worker performs the specific task for which he or she is hired?
- **Financial control.** Do you have the right to direct or control how the business aspects of the worker's activities are conducted?
- **The relationship.** How do you and the worker perceive your relationship? The following sections discuss these categories in more detail.

1. Behavioral Control

The type of instruction or training you give a worker helps show the extent to which you retain the right to control the worker's method of getting the job done. IRS examiners may check on other types of behavioral control as well.

a. Instruction

The IRS recognizes that you'll probably impose some form of instruction on all workers—whether they're independent contractors or employees. For example, you might require that the job be performed within a specified time period. The big question is how far you go in instructing the worker on how the job gets done rather than just indicating the end result. Giving a worker autonomy in making decisions is evidence that you're not controlling the worker's behavior.

Example: Star Brite Manufacturing Company hires Lou Ann as a management consultant for its sales department. She is to ensure that the department is fully staffed and that sales brochures are stocked and available. She is also to review all sales contracts. Star Brite requires Lou Ann to get prior approval before she hires or fires anyone in the sales department, purchases additional sales materials or accepts any sales contract.

The IRS views the requirement of prior approval as evidence that Star Brite controls Lou Ann's behavior in the performance of her services. If Star Brite were not to require these prior approvals but were to leave matters to Lou Ann's discretion, this would be evidence of her autonomy in doing the work and, therefore, consistent with independent contractor status.

The IRS distinguishes between telling a worker what is to be done and how it is to be done. A worker can be an independent contractor even though you indicate what the job entails.

Example: Jim is an independent truck driver. Young Industries, Inc. calls him to make a delivery run from the Gulf Coast to the Texas Panhandle. Jim accepts the job and agrees to pick up the cargo the next morning. Upon arriving at the warehouse, Jim is given an address to which to deliver the cargo and is advised that the delivery must be completed within two days. The IRS treats this as a direction of what is be done—not how it is to be done—and therefore consistent with independent contractor status.

On the other hand, if you give too much instruction on how the work is to be done, you may have to classify the worker as an employee.

Example: Tess, a truck driver, does local deliveries for Zancor. She reports to Zancor's warehouse each morning. The warehouse manager tells Tess what deliveries have to be made, how to load the cargo in the truck, what route to take and the order in which the cargo is to be delivered. This is instruction on how the work is to be performed—consistent with employee status, in the eyes of the IRS.

b. Training

If you provide periodic or ongoing training to a worker, it's usually strong evidence of an employer-employee relationship. That's not true, however, of training that merely informs a worker about your policies, a new product line or applicable governmental regulations. Similarly, the IRS won't imply an employer-employee relationship from programs a worker attends voluntarily and without compensation.

c. Suggestions

Mere suggestions to a worker don't constitute control over the worker's behavior. So suggesting that a worker avoid Main Street because of traffic congestion is consistent with the worker's status as an independent contractor.

d. Business identification

In the past, requiring a worker to identify himself or herself with your business was evidence of employment status. For example, if you required a worker to wear a uniform bearing your company's name or to paint your logo on his or her truck, that would have been an indication that the worker was an employee.

Today, the IRS recognizes that there are concerns about safety; people often want reassurance about who's coming to their homes or workplaces. The result: if there's a valid security reason for requiring a uniform or logo, the requirement is now a neutral fact in analyzing whether an employment relationship exists.

2. Financial Control

The IRS looks at whether your business has the right to direct or control the economic aspects of the worker's activities.

a. Significant investment

Although it's not necessary for a worker to buy or rent costly equipment to be considered an independent contractor, evidence of such an investment does help to establish independent contractor status. There are no precise dollar guidelines on what constitutes a significant investment.

There can be a significant investment even if you're selling or leasing the equipment to the worker—but the worker must pay the full market value or full rental value. Otherwise, the evidence may be insufficient to establish a significant investment.

Example: Cal operates a backhoe for Yorba Distributing Company. He leases the backhoe from Yorba at less than its fair rental value and can turn it in at any time without liability for further payments. Yorba pays for liability insurance and regular maintenance on the backhoe. Although Cal is paying something to rent the backhoe, the facts here don't establish that he's made a significant investment.

b. Business expenses

The extent to which a worker chooses to incur expenses and be responsible for them can affect the worker's potential to make a profit or sustain a loss. A worker's unreimbursed business expenses can be evidence that the worker has the right to control the financial side of his or her business operations—helping to show independent contractor status.

But there are limits to this principle. If the unreimbursed expenses are minor, this isn't evidence of an independent contractor relationship. The same is true of heavier expenses that are customarily borne by an employee in a particular line of business, such as an auto mechanic's tools.

c. Advertising and visibility

An independent contractor is generally free to seek out business opportunities. The fact that a worker advertises or maintains a visible business location to attract new clients is evidence that the worker is an independent contractor. On the other hand, neither advertising nor having a visible business location is a requirement for independent contractor status. A worker with special skills who gets jobs through word of mouth can qualify as an independent contractor.

In addition, the IRS recognizes that a person who has negotiated a long-term contract may find advertising unnecessary and may even be unavailable to work for others for the duration of the contract—and that will not affect the person's status as an independent contractor. Other independent contractors may find that a visible business location doesn't produce enough business to justify the expense.

In short, the IRS treats the absence of advertising or a visible business location as well as the temporary inability to work for others as neutral factors.

Example: Unicorn Ventures engages Cindy to mow the lawn weekly and trim the hedges yearly at Unicorn's headquarters. Cindy advertises in the Yellow Pages that she does landscaping. The advertising indicates that Cindy is available to perform services to the relevant market. This is evidence that she is an independent contractor.

Example: Cindy negotiates a long-term contract with Unicorn to maintain all of Unicorn's business locations. Cindy decides to drop her Yellow Pages advertising, although she continues to be available to other businesses. The lack of advertising doesn't automatically change her independent contractor status.

d. Method of payment

A worker who's paid hourly, weekly or by another unit of time is guaranteed a return for labor. This is generally evidence of a employer-employee relationship, even when a commission is also paid. However, in some fields, such as law, it's typical to pay independent contractors on an hourly basis, so the hourly payment can be a neutral factor.

Paying a worker a flat fee is generally evidence of an independent contractor relationship, especially if the worker incurs expenses in performing the job. When you pay the worker—daily, weekly or monthly—isn't relevant.

A person who's paid solely on a commission basis can be either an independent contractor or an employee. The worker's status may depend on his or her ability to realize a profit or incur a loss in performing services.

e. Profit or loss

A worker's ability to earn a profit or incur a loss is probably the strongest evidence that the worker controls the business aspects of the work. The four economic factors discussed above all relate to the worker's potential for profit or loss. A key question is whether the worker can make decisions that affect his or her bottom line. These might, for example, be decisions involving ordering inventory, investing money or purchasing or leasing equipment.

A worker's ability to decide whether to work longer hours to earn more money or to work fewer hours and take less money is a neutral factor.

3. The Relationship

The IRS considers how you and the worker view your relationship. Your perceptions and those of the worker may suggest what the two of you intend regarding the all-important issue of control.

a. Written contract

The IRS focuses on the substance of the contract—not on labels. Calling the worker an independent contractor isn't enough. Key clauses are those dealing with the method of compensation, payment of expenses and, most crucial, the rights and obligations of you and the worker regarding how work is to be performed.

b. Form W-2

Filing a Form W-2 usually indicates that the worker is an employee—but the IRS may find independent contractor status despite it.

c. Incorporation

If a worker has formed a corporation and you hire the corporation to do the work, the IRS will almost always treat the worker as an employee of his or her own corporation—not as an employee of your business.

SIDESTEP IRS PROBLEMS BY CONTRACTING WITH CORPORATIONS

If you want to hire someone as an independent contractor but you're not convinced that the worker will pass IRS muster as an independent contractor, the easiest solution is to require the worker to form a corporation.

One-person corporations are simple to create. After the worker incorporates, your business signs a contract with the corporation in which the worker's corporation agrees to provide the needed services. You pay the corporation as specified in the contract. The worker receives a paycheck—and possible bonuses as well—from his or her corporation, which is the employer.

The IRS will recognize this arrangement except in cases of clear abuse—and independent contractor status will no longer be an issue. Presumably, you can reach the same result if a worker forms a limited liability company instead of a corporation, although the IRS hasn't addressed this yet.

d. Employee benefits

Providing a worker with benefits traditionally associated with employee status can be evidence that the worker is an employee. If you give the worker paid vacation days, paid sick days, health insurance, life or disability insurance or a pension, that's some evidence of employee status. The evidence of employee status is strongest if you provide benefits under a tax-qualified retirement plan, a 403(b) annuity or a cafeteria plan.

If you exclude a worker from a benefit plan because you don't consider the worker to be an employee, that's relevant but not conclusive evidence that the worker's an independent contractor.

e. Discharge or termination

The IRS may look at the conditions under which you or the worker can terminate the working relationship. It's clear, however, that the IRS regards this as a complicated legal question and doesn't usually treat it as a decisive factor in deciding if a worker has been properly classified.

f. Permanency

If you and the worker arranged for work to be done with the expectation that the relationship would continue indefinitely rather than for a specific project or period, that's generally evidence that the two of you intended to create an employment relationship. That's different, however, than simply setting up a long-term relationship, which is consistent with either employee or independent contractor status. The IRS recognizes that your relationship with an independent contractor may be long-term because that's what your work agreement requires. It can also be long-term because you renew the agreement regularly due to superior service, competitive prices or lack of competition.

For these reasons, if a relationship is long-term but not indefinite, the IRS disregards this as a factor in looking at the worker's status. The IRS also treats the temporary nature of a relationship as being neutral.

g. Regular business activity

The IRS may look at whether the services performed by a worker are a key aspect of your company's regular business. This can be a bit subtle.

The mere fact that a service is desirable, necessary or even essential to your business doesn't mean that the service provider is an employee. If you have an appliance store, for example, you need workers to install electricity and plumbing in your building. This work can be done equally well by employees or independent contractors. The IRS examiner focuses on the fact that the work of the electricians and plumbers isn't part of your regular business.

By contrast, the work of an attorney or legal assistant is part of the regular business of a law firm. It's likely that a law firm will direct or control the work of a lawyer or legal assistant it hires since the firm's name will go on documents the worker produces. In this situation, the IRS will probe for further facts showing the firm's right to direct and control the worker.

4. Facts of Less Importance

In addition to the three primary categories of evidence listed above, the IRS looks at other facts—but gives them less weight.

a. Parttime or fulltime work

Whether a worker performs services on a fulltime or parttime basis is a neutral fact. The same is true for whether a worker performs services for one business or several.

b. Place of work

Whether work is performed on your premises or somewhere you select often has no bearing on worker status. Usually it's only relevant as part of the IRS inquiry into your right to control how the work is to be done.

In many cases, services can only be performed at one location. To repair a leaky pipe, for example, a plumber a must go to the site where the pipe is located. Similarly, a camera operator must shoot a commercial where the director and actors are located. These requirements aren't evidence of the right to direct and control how the work is to be performed.

Sometimes, work can be performed at many different locations. Off-site work is consistent with independent contractor or employee status. If a worker has his or her own office or business location, this can be evidence of an independent contractor relationship—but the IRS gets into this as part of its examination of the worker's investment, unreimbursed expenses or opportunity for profit or loss.

c. Hours of work

The IRS generally considers hours of work when it looks at the extent of the instructions you give the worker. As with work location, some work, by its nature, must be performed at a specific time; the photographer must shoot the commercial at the time scheduled for the director and actors to be present.

Flexible workhours are not given much importance by the IRS, being consistent with either employee or independent contractor status.

SEEKING A SAFE HARBOR

Despite the strict IRS rules, a business that wrongly classifies a worker as an independent contractor may escape the usual harsh consequences.

In theory at least, you're protected by the safe harbor language of the tax law if you had a reasonable basis for classifying a worker as an independent contractor—for example:

- You relied on court rulings, IRS rulings, or advice given to you by the IRS.
- You were audited by the IRS and weren't assessed for employment taxes for workers holding jobs similar to the one held by the misclassified worker.
- You followed a longstanding and recognized practice of your industry.

But theory is one thing—and the real world experience of challenging the IRS is another. If you seek the protection of the safe harbor provisions, the IRS won't give up without a fight. Be prepared for a furious legal battle.

C. Workers Automatically Classified as Employees

In most situations, the status of a worker is determined by the factors already explained. (See Sections B1 and B2.) Certain workers, however, fall into special categories, and the usual IRS criteria don't apply to them. For example, the federal tax law says that certain workers are automatically employees—in legal lingo, statutory employees—including:

Delivery drivers. Drivers who deliver meat, vegetables, fruits, bakery products, or beverages other than milk, or who pick up and deliver laundry or dry cleaning. These drivers are employees if they're legally agents of a company and are paid on a commission. An agent is someone who's authorized by another to act on his or her behalf.

Example: Rachel, a bread truck driver, sells on commission to a customer route for Barry's Bakery and no other bakeries; under the federal law, she's a statutory employee of the bakery. But Allen, a restaurant supply distributor who buys bread from Barry's Bakery at wholesale prices and resells it at a profit, is neither an agent nor a statutory employee of Barry's Bakery.

Insurance agents. Insurance sales agents whose main job is selling life insurance or annuity contracts, or both, primarily for one life insurance company.

Home workers. People who work at home according to a company's specifications on materials or goods that are supplied by a company and must be returned to that company or to someone the company designates.

Business-to-business salespeople. People whose main job is to sell for a company and turn in orders to that company from wholesalers, retailers, contractors, hotels, restaurants or other business establishments. The goods sold must be merchandise for resale or supplies for use in the buyer's business, rather than goods bought for home consumption.

Federal tax law also provides that licensed real estate agents and door-to-door salespeople are generally treated as "non-employees" or "exempt employees," but they may be treated as employees for the purpose of liability and workers' compensation.

D. State Laws

The IRS list of factors for differentiating between employees and independent contractors is similar to the standards followed in most states for state taxes and unemployment compensation, but there can be some differences. For example, in deciding whether a worker is an employee for purposes of workers' compensation coverage or unemployment compensation benefits, a state may use a simple economic reality test.

If you plan to hire independent contractors, check first with the labor department in your state to see what rules are in effect. (See the Appendix for contact details.)

E. The Risks of Misclassification

There are at least three ways for the IRS to learn about your hiring and classification practices. First, the IRS may look into the affairs of an independent contractor who hasn't been paying his or her income taxes. Second, disgruntled employees may complain to the IRS if they think independent contractors are getting favored treatment. Third, during tax audits, the IRS routinely checks to see if workers have been misclassified as independent contractors.

The presumption is that the worker is an employee unless proven otherwise. If the IRS questions the status of a worker, it's up to you to prove that the worker is an independent contractor rather than an employee.

If the IRS determines that an employee was misclassified, the cost to your business will be heavy. You'll be responsible for paying the employee's Social Security tax, federal income tax and federal unemployment insurance for up to three years. In addition, the IRS can add penalties and interest to the tally you must pay.

State government officials are also interested in businesses that misclassify employees as independent contractors. A state employment office may audit your business to see if there's been any misclassification. The audit can be the result of a spot check by the state employment office or a request by an independent contractor for unemployment or workers' compensation benefits. You may wind up owing money to a state unemployment insurance fund.

THE IRS CAN BE TOUGH

The IRS has been aggressively cracking down on employers that have misclassified workers as independent contractors. Underlying this crackdown is a belief that tax revenue is slipping through the cracks because independent contractors aren't reporting all of their income.

Also, IRS officials know that potential tax revenue is lost because even independent contractors who do report their full income can deduct a wide range of business expenses—deductions that employees have difficulty taking.

Fighting the IRS can be expensive. Raleigh Air Cargo Express learned that the hard way. For years, the company hired college students and retirees to make occasional freight runs using rented trucks. Because of the sporadic nature of the work, the small North Carolina company paid these workers as independent contractors.

Eventually, Raleigh shifted these workers to employee status—a move that ironically triggered an IRS audit and a demand that Raleigh pay some $47,000 in back taxes, plus interest and penalties. It took Raleigh nearly three years and $27,000 in legal and accounting fees, but the tenacious company eventually got a fair hearing from a sympathetic IRS appeals officer who canceled the IRS claim. And not a moment too soon. Fighting the IRS nearly put Raleigh out of business.

Moral of the story: The fate of your business can hang on something as tenuous as getting the right IRS person on the right day to listen to you.

F. Hiring Independent Contractors

There are several things you can do to help establish that a worker is properly classified as an independent contractor right from the start of the relationship. (See Chapter 1 for a detailed discussion of hiring employees.)

Sign a contract with the independent contractor clearly spelling out his or her responsibilities and how payment is to be determined for each job. (See sample contract below.) The contract should allow the independent contractor to hire his or her own assistants—and should specifically state that the contractor will carry his or her own insurance, including workers' compensation. In addition to helping satisfy the federal or state government that a worker is truly an independent contractor, a good written contract will reduce disputes with the independent contractor about the details of the relationship.

Require the independent contractor to supply all or most of the tools, equipment and material needed to complete the job and to pay for his or her own liability insurance.

Give the independent contractor the maximum possible freedom to decide how to perform the work.

Avoid a commitment to reimburse the independent contractor for his or her business expenses; have the independent contractor assume that responsibility.

Arrange to pay a flat fee for the work rather than an hourly or weekly rate, if that's feasible to do.

Don't provide employee-type benefits such as paid vacation days, health insurance or retirement plans.

Make it clear that the independent contractor is free to offer services to other businesses.

Keep a file containing the independent contractor's business card, stationery samples, ads and employer identification number. These items can help show that the contractor has an established business.

Finally, consider asking the independent contractor to incorporate. Then, sign a contract with the corporation instead of the individual. As explained in Section B3 above, this is probably your most effective means of avoiding a shoot-out with the IRS over the proper classification of a worker.

Trade Secrets Need Special Protection

In some situations, you may disclose trade secrets of your business to an independent contractor. If so, include a clause in the agreement prohibiting the independent contractor from disclosing or making any other unauthorized use of the trade secrets. (See Chapter 1, Section A5.)

Sample Contract With an Independent Contractor

AGREEMENT

This agreement made on _____ , 19____ between

_____
CLIENT

of _____
BUSINESS ADDRESS

and _____
CONTRACTOR

of _____ .
BUSINESS ADDRESS

1. Services To Be Performed. Contractor agrees to perform the following services for Client:
    [DESCRIPTION OF SERVICES]

2. Time For Performance. Contractor agrees to complete the performance of these services
    on or before _____ , 19____.

3. Payment. In consideration of Contractor's performance of these services, Client agrees to
    pay Contractor as follows:
    [DESCRIPTION OF HOW PAYMENT WILL BE COMPUTED]

4. Invoices. Contractor will submit invoices for all services performed.

5. Independent Contractor. The parties intend Contractor to be an independent contractor in
    the performance of these services. Contractor shall have the right to control and deter-
    mine the method and means of performing the above services; Client shall not have the
    right to control or determine such method or means.

6. Other Clients. Contractor retains the right to perform services for other clients.

7. Assistants. Contractor, at Contractor's expense, may employ such assistants as Contractor
    deems appropriate to carry out this agreement. Contractor will be responsible for paying
    such assistants, as well as any expense attributable to such assistants, including income
    taxes, unemployment insurance and Social Security taxes, and will maintain workers'
    compensation insurance for such employees.

8. Equipment and Supplies. Contractor, at Contractor's own expense, will provide all
    equipment, tools and supplies necessary to perform the above services, and will be
    responsible for all other expenses required for the performance of those services.

_____
CONTRACTOR

_____
CLIENT

Source: The Legal Guide for Starting and Running a Small Business, *by Fred S. Steingold (Nolo Press).* ∎

CHAPTER

12

UNIONS

Only 11% of U.S. workers in the private sector belong to unions—and most of them work in larger businesses. The figure is expected to drop to 7% by the year 2001. Why membership is declining is open to debate. Perhaps unions are less necessary today because of the growing array of laws that protect workers. Perhaps the changing nature of work plays a role.

The effect on small and midsized businesses is clear: if your business isn't unionized now, it's unlikely that it ever will be. Still, workers do have the legal right to form unions and, despite the odds, a union could be formed in your workplace. So you need a basic understanding of workers' rights as well as your own.

This chapter discusses the legal highlights of the relationship between employers and workers who choose to unionize. If your workplace is already unionized or if workers decide to form a union, it's wise to consult a lawyer experienced in labor law. (See Chapter 13, Section A.)

A. The National Labor Relations Act

The National Labor Relations Act or NLRA (29 U.S.C. §151 and following) is the most sweeping law regulating the formation of unions. It establishes the right of most—but not all—workers to organize into unions and, through union representatives, to negotiate an employment contract covering all members of the union.

Private sector employees who are not covered by the NLRA include:

- managers and supervisors
- confidential employees—such as company accountants
- farm workers

- members of an employer's family
- most domestic workers, and
- workers in certain industries—such as the railroad industry—that are covered by other labor laws.

The National Labor Relations Board (NLRB) administers the law and interprets its provisions. The role of the NLRB in overseeing the unionizing of a workplace is discussed in Section B, Section 3.

B. Unionizing a Workplace

Workers who choose to form or join a union usually believe that they'll have more bargaining clout than they would if they dealt with their employer one-on-one. They feel that the union can get them better pay, benefits and working conditions than they could obtain on their own—and that, through structured grievance procedures, the union can get them a fairer shake in resolving workplace disputes.

And just as business trade associations may offer attractive services and products to employers, larger unions may provide valuable enticements to workers—for example, low interest credit cards, home mortgage programs, free or reduced rate legal services, low cost prescription plans and competitive car insurance.

1. The Bargaining Unit

Employees can form their own union or can choose to affiliate with a national union. Either way, the employees must be part of a proper bargaining unit—a group of employees who perform similar work and logically have similar concerns about issues such as pay rates, workhours and working conditions.

A workplace may have several bargaining units—each represented by a different union—and some workers in such a workplace may not be represented by any union.

Example: Offices Unlimited sells office equipment and supplies. The check-out clerks have formed one bargaining unit and the warehouse workers another. Other workers, such as the sales assistants, are not represented by a union.

If a majority of workers in a bargaining unit authorize a union to represent them, the union becomes the sole representative of all the employees in that unit to bargain over wages, hours and other working conditions. This is what is known as collective bargaining.

2. Authorization Cards

Workers express their wishes to be represented by a union by signing authorization cards. If you receive authorization cards signed by a majority of the workers in a bargaining unit, you can voluntarily recognize the union as the sole representative of the unit—but you don't have to do so.

If you don't voluntarily recognize the union, the workers can ask for an election to be conducted by the NLRB.

3. NLRB Elections

If 30% or more of the workers in a proposed bargaining unit have signed authorization cards, the union can petition the NLRB to hold a secret election to determine if a majority of the workers support the union. The union's petition will include the a description of what group of workers the union would like to have included in the bargaining unit.

Then the NLRB will conduct an election to determine whether or not the workers in the bargaining unit want to be represented the union. If a majority of them vote for the union, it's officially certified as the sole bargaining agent for the unit.

VOICING YOUR OPPOSITION

You may have good reasons to refuse to recognize a union. For example, you may object that it includes workers who have managerial duties. Or you may suspect that some signatures indicating a wish to unionize were not truly voluntary, but the result of intimidation.

Employers' most common challenge is to question the union's description of the bargaining unit. One basis for a challenge is that the workers included by the union don't do similar work. You may also be able to exclude from the bargaining unit any employee who has authority to:

- assign work or direct employees
- evaluate work
- grant time off
- schedule work hours
- discipline employees
- hire or fire
- keep time records, or
- adjust grievances.

An employee can be excluded, too, if he or she can effectively recommend action on any of these tasks.

4. Negotiating a Contract

After a union is voluntarily recognized as the official representative of the bargaining unit or is certified by the NLRB, the representatives of the union and the employer negotiate a contract—a collective bargaining agreement. A contract typically covers wages, benefits, work breaks, overtime, holidays, vacation and sick time, seniority for promotions and safety rules. Often, there's a grievance procedure under which workers bring their complaints to the union and the union takes the problems to the employer. Employees represented by the union pay monthly dues—often through a payroll deduction called a checkoff.

Since negotiating a labor contract is governed by special rules that don't apply to ordinary business contracts, it's wise to consult a labor lawyer who's experienced in labor negotiations. (See Chapter 13, Section A.)

VARIATIONS ON A THEME

Unionized workplaces come in three basic varieties.

Union shops. In a union shop, all workers in the bargaining unit must join the union. A collective bargaining agreement may provide that any worker who doesn't join the union within a specified time—typically, within 60 days of employment—will be fired. In practice, the union is unlikely to insist that you fire a worker who doesn't join as long as he or she pays the union's regular fees or dues.

Agency shops. In an agency shop, workers can join the union or not—but all workers in the bargaining unit must pay union dues and other fees. The union must protect nonmembers if there's a labor problem, but doesn't have to give nonmembers the benefits of the broader protections and disciplinary processes that may be included in a union contract.

Open shops. A worker in the bargaining unit can't be required to join the union or pay dues to it. The union must fairly represent all workers in the unit—including nonmembers. Open shops are required by right to work laws adopted by nearly half of the states.

C. Employer Rights and Limitations

If you are an employer facing unionization efforts in your workplace, the law shapes how you may and may not voice any objections.

1. What Is Permitted

You can try to dissuade employees from forming or joining a union. You can, for example, use letters, posters, brochures and speeches to tell employees that they currently enjoy many job benefits and that their wages and benefits compare favorably to those of other workers in your industry. Be able to document your claims.

You're legally allowed to state that your door is open to hear complaints and that you will attempt to take appropriate action. You can explain that you prefer to settle complaints with employees personally rather than through union agents.

Pointing out potentially negative features of union representation is also permitted. For example, you might emphasize that workers will be paying dues and fees if they unionize, and will be under the control of union rules and regimentation.

You can explain, too, that those signing authorization cards aren't bound to vote for the union in the secret balloting conducted by the NLRB and that they don't have to stand for undue pressure by the union. Depending on the composition of your workforce, you might mention that the union's emphasis on seniority may put newer workers at a disadvantage.

2. What Is Not Permitted

Some actions in opposing a union are off limits. Most courts have ruled that under the NLRA you may not:

- ask employees for their thoughts on union matters or how they plan to vote
- attend union meetings or spy on employees
- grant or promise employees a promotion, pay raise, desirable work assignment or other special favors if they oppose unionizing efforts
- close down a worksite or transfer work or reduce benefits to pressure workers not to support unionization
- dismiss, harass, reassign or otherwise punish or discipline workers—or threaten to—if they support unionization, or
- refuse to bargain collectively with the employees' union representative.

Sometimes the distinctions between what you can and can't do are subtle. Before acting to oppose a union, consult a lawyer who knows the ropes. (See Chapter 13, Section A.)

D. Employee Rights and Limitations

Generally, courts have ruled that the NLRA gives workers the right to:

- discuss union membership and distribute union literature during nonwork time in nonwork areas such as an employee lounge
- use your bulletin board to post union notices
- sign a card asking you to recognize the union and bargain with it
- sign petitions and grievances concerning employment terms and conditions
- ask co-workers to sign petitions and grievances, and
- display pro-union sentiments by wearing message-bearing items such as hats, pins and T-shirts on the job.

But workers have no right to threaten or intimidate other workers to gain their support for a union. And union organizers who are not employed by your business have no right to be on your premises. But don't rush to call the police to have outside organizers ejected as trespassers—especially if their activities are not disrupting your business. Such an approach may alienate employees. It's better to emphasize to workers the advantages of staying union-free. (See Section E.)

E. Making Unions Unnecessary

Unions usually gain a foothold because employees are dissatisfied with some aspects of their worklife. Contented workers don't generally seek to unionize, as it entails some degree of regimentation and workplace politics.

Be sensitive to what's going on the workplace and make reasonable changes if required. Encourage employees to come to you with their workplace complaints—and listen carefully to what they're saying. If there's a health or safety problem, fix it. If a workplace procedure is annoying or seems unfair to workers, look into changing it.

Be fair and consistent in enforcing work rules and disciplining employees. They need to know what to expect and they can become frustrated and angry if you act arbitrarily.

To the extent possible, give employees some control over how they perform their jobs. In almost any job position, it's possible to allow some degree of worker autonomy. Employees who have some freedom to put their imprints on their work tend to be most content on the job. Periodically survey what similar businesses are paying their workers—and make sure that the wages and benefits you provide are competitive. Offer incentives for excellent performance.

Try to keep your workforce steadily employed. Hiring employees for seasonal overloads and laying them off when the work levels off creates feelings of insecurity. Consider hiring temporary workers for seasonal increases in the workflow. ■

CHAPTER
13
LAWYERS AND LEGAL RESEARCH

When you own or run a business, you need lots of legal information on employment issues. For example, you may need to learn how an anti-discrimination law is being interpreted by the EEOC or whether an agreement with a departing employee will be enforced by a court. Lawyers, of course, are prime sources of this information. But if you bought all the needed information at the rates they charge—$150 to $250 an hour—you'd quickly empty your bank account. Fortunately, for an intelligent employer, there are a number of other ways to acquire a good working knowledge of the legal principles and procedures necessary to handle employment and other issues.

How frequently you'll need a lawyer's help will depend on the nature of your business, the number of employees you hire, how many locations you have and the kinds of problems you run into with employees and governmental agencies. Your challenge isn't to avoid lawyers altogether, but to use them cost-effectively.

Lawyers aren't the only source for legal help. The U.S. Department of Labor, the Internal Revenue Service, the U.S. Equal Employment Opportunity Commission, the U.S. Department of Justice and other federal agencies offer publications at little or no cost explaining federal laws and regulations that affect employers. Many are referred to in this book. Similarly, many state agencies have helpful printed materials available. And representatives of federal and state agencies can help explain how the laws they administer are interpreted.

And keep in mind that professionals who charge less than lawyers—for example, accountants and workplace consultants—can also help you within their areas of expertise.

A. Getting Help From a Lawyer

Ideally, you should find a lawyer who's willing to help you educate yourself. Then you can often do the preliminary work on your own, turning to your lawyer from time to time for advice and fine-tuning.

In working with a lawyer, remember that you're the boss. A lawyer, of course, has specialized training, knowledge, skill and experience in dealing with legal matters. But that's no reason for you to abdicate control over legal decision-making and how much time and money should be spent on a particular legal problem. You have an intimate knowledge of your business and are in the best position to call the shots—even though a lawyer may be willing or even eager to do it all for you.

Since you almost surely can't afford all the services a lawyer might offer, you need to set priorities. When thinking about a legal problem, ask yourself: "Can I do this myself?" "Can I do this myself with some help from a lawyer?" "Should I simply put this in my lawyer's hands?"

1. Getting Leads

Of the close to 800,000 lawyers in America today, probably fewer than 50,000 have sufficient training and experience in small business law to be of real help to you. And even fewer have significant experience in employment law.

Don't expect to locate a good employment lawyer by simply looking in the phone book, consulting a law directory or reading an advertisement. There's not enough information in those sources to help you make a valid judgment. Almost as useless are lawyer referral services operated by bar associations. Generally, these services make little attempt to evaluate a lawyer's skill and experience. They simply supply the names of lawyers who have listed with the service, often accepting the lawyer's own word for what types of skills he or she has.

A better approach is to talk with people in your community who own or operate excellent businesses. These people are likely to have ferreted out the best lawyers. Ask them who their lawyers are and a little about their experiences. Ask them about other lawyers they've worked with and what led them to make a change. If you talk to half a dozen employers, chances are you'll come away with several leads on good, experienced business lawyers.

Other people who provide services to the business community may also help you identify lawyers you might consider hiring. For example, speak with your banker, accountant, insurance agent and real estate broker. These people come into frequent contact with lawyers who represent employers and are in a position to make informed judgments. Friends, relatives and business associates within your own company can also provide names of possible lawyers. But ask them specifically about lawyers who have had experience working for employers; a good divorce lawyer would likely make a poor employment advisor, for example.

There are several other sources to which you can turn for possible candidates in your search for a lawyer.

- The director of your state or local chamber of commerce may know of several employment lawyers who have the kind of experience that you seek.

- Articles about employment law in trade magazines and newspapers are often written by lawyers. Track down these authors and call them. Most will be flattered to help or provide other referrals.

- The director of your state's continuing legal education (CLE) program— usually run by a bar association, a law school or both—can identify lawyers who have lectured or written on employment law for other lawyers. Someone who's a "lawyer's lawyer" presumably has the extra depth of knowledge and experience to do a superior job for you—but may charge more, unfortunately.

- The chairperson of a state or county bar committee for business lawyers may be able to point out some well-qualified practitioners in your vicinity.

Once you have the names of several lawyers, a good source for more information about them is the *Martindale-Hubbell Law Directory*, available at most law libraries and some local public libraries. This resource contains biographical sketches of most practicing lawyers and information about their experience, specialties, education and the professional organizations to which they belong. Many firms also list their major clients in the direc-tory—an excellent indication of the types of problems with which they've had experience. Be aware, however, that lawyers purchase the space for their biographical sketches, so don't be overly impressed by long biogra-phies.

In addition, almost every lawyer listed in the directory, whether or not he or she has purchased space for a biographical sketch, is rated AV, BV or CV. These ratings come from confidential opinions that Martindale-Hubbell solicits from lawyers and judges.

The first letter is for Legal Ability, which is rated as follows:

A—Very High to Preeminent

B—High to Very High

C—Fair to High

The V part of the rating stands for Very High General Recommenda-tion—meaning that the rated lawyer adheres to professional standards of conduct and ethics. But the V part is practically meaningless, because lawyers who don't qualify for it aren't rated at all. *Martindale-Hubbell* prudently cautions that such absence shouldn't be construed as a reflection on the lawyer, since there many reasons for the absence of a rating. Some lawyers, for example, ask that their rating not be published and others are too new to a community to be known among the local lawyers and judges who are the sources for ratings.

Don't make the rating system your sole criterion for deciding on a potential lawyer for your business. But you can be reasonably confident that a lawyer who gets high marks from other business clients and an "AV" rating from *Martindale-Hubbell* will have experience and expertise.

Computer buffs can reach Martindale-Hubbell online at: http://www.martindale.com. The online listings contain everything except the ratings. Another excellent source of information about lawyers is the West's Legal Directory, which you'll find at http://www.wld.com.

2. Shopping Around

After you get the names of several good prospects, shop around. Most lawyers will be willing to speak with you for a half hour or so at no charge so that you can size them up and make an informed decision about whether to hire them. Look for experience and for the ability to listen and communicate. These characteristics may be apparent almost immediately—but, in some cases, may take longer to evaluate. So even after you've hired a lawyer who seems right for you, keep open the possibility that you may have to make a change later.

Pay particular attention to the rapport between you and your lawyer. No matter how experienced and well-recommended a lawyer is, if you feel uncomfortable with that person during your first meeting or two, you may never achieve an ideal lawyer-client relationship. Trust your instincts and seek a lawyer whose personality is compatible with your own.

Your lawyer should be accessible when you need legal services. Unfortunately, the complaint logs of all legal regulatory groups indicate that many lawyers are not. If every time you have a problem there's a delay of several days before you can talk to your lawyer on the phone or get an appointment, you'll lose precious time, not to mention sleep. And almost nothing is more aggravating to a client than to leave a legal project in a lawyer's hands and then wait weeks or even months while nothing happens.

You want a lawyer who will work hard on your behalf and follow through promptly on all assignments. Unfortunately, it's usually difficult to tell at the outset how attentive the lawyer will be later on. But it can be helpful to ask how the lawyer intends to keep in touch with you. Perhaps you can exact a promise that you'll receive a status report at least monthly.

B. Paying a Lawyer

When you hire a lawyer, have a clear understanding about how fees will be computed. And as new jobs are brought to the lawyer, ask specifically about charges for each. Many lawyers initiate fee discussions, but others forget or are shy about doing so. Bring up the subject yourself. Insist upon a written explanation of how the fees and costs will be paid.

COSTS CAN MOUNT UP

In addition to the fees they charge for their time, lawyers often bill for some costs as well—and these costs can add up quickly. When you receive a lawyer's bill, you may be surprised at both the amount of the costs and the variety of the services for which the lawyer expects reimbursement. These can include charges for:

- long distance phone calls
- photocopying
- faxes
- overnight mail
- messenger service
- witness fees
- court filing fees
- process servers
- work by investigators
- work by legal assistants or paralegals
- deposition transcripts
- online legal research, and
- travel.

You'd think that a lawyer would absorb the cost of many of these items as normal office overhead—part of the cost of doing business—but that's not always the case. So in working out the fee arrangements, discuss the costs you'll be expected to pay. Try to avoid being charged for long distance calls, photocopies and faxes—and negotiate an overall cap on costs, if possible.

1. Types of Fee Arrangements

There are four basic ways that lawyers charge, usually depending on the type of legal help you require.

a. Hourly fees

In most parts of the United States, you can get competent services for your business for $150 to $250 an hour.

b. Flat fees

Sometimes, a lawyer quotes you a flat fee for a specific job. For example, a lawyer may offer to draw up an employment agreement for $300. Or to represent you in a labor department dispute for $3,000. You pay the same amount regardless of how much time the lawyer spends.

c. Contingent fees

This is a percentage (such as 33-1/3%) of the amount the lawyer obtains for you in a negotiated settlement or through a trial. If the lawyer recovers nothing for you, there's no fee. However, the lawyer does generally expect reimbursement for out-of-pocket expenses such as filing fees, long distance phone calls and transcripts of testimony. Contingent fees are common in personal injury cases, but relatively unusual in employment cases.

d. Retainer fees

You may be able to hire a lawyer for a flat annual fee, or retainer, to handle all of your routine legal business. You'll usually pay in equal monthly installments and, normally, the lawyer will bill you an additional amount for extraordinary services—such as representing you in a wrongful discharge lawsuit filed by a former employee. Obviously, the key to making this arrangement work is to have a written agreement clearly defining what's routine and what's extraordinary.

Comparison shopping among lawyers will help you avoid overpaying. But the cheapest hourly rate isn't necessarily the best. A novice who charges only $80 an hour may take three hours to review a consultant's work-for-hire contract. A more experienced lawyer who charges $200 an hour may do the same job in half an hour and make better suggestions. If a lawyer will be delegating some of the work on your case to a less experienced associate, paralegal or secretary, that work should be billed at a lower hourly rate. Be sure to get this information recorded in your initial written fee agreement.

2. Saving on Legal Fees

There are many ways to hold down the cost of legal services.

Be organized. It's important to gather important documents, write a short chronology of events and concisely explain a problem to your lawyer. Since papers can get lost in a lawyer's office, keep a copy of everything that's important.

Ask the lawyer to be your coach. Make it clear that you're eager to do as much work as possible yourself, with the lawyer coaching you from the sidelines. For example, you can write your own employee handbook, giving your lawyer the relatively inexpensive task of reviewing and polishing the document. In defending a wrongful discharge case, you can assemble needed documents and line up witnesses. But get a clear understanding about who's going to do what. You don't want to do the work and get billed for it because the lawyer duplicated your efforts. And you certainly don't want any crucial elements to fall through cracks because you each thought the other was attending to the work.

Read trade journals in your field. They'll help you keep up with specific legal developments that your lawyer may have missed. Send pertinent clippings to your lawyer—and encourage your lawyer to do the same for you. This can dramatically reduce legal research time.

Show that you're an important client. The single most important thing you can do to tell your lawyer how much you value the relationship is to pay your bills on time. Beyond that, let your lawyer know about plans for expansion and your company's possible future legal needs. And drop your lawyer a line when you've recommended him or her to your business colleagues.

Group together your legal matters. You'll save money if you consult with your lawyer on several matters at one time. For example, in a one-hour conference, you may be able to review with your lawyer the annual updating of your corporate record book, renew your lease and get final approval a non-competition agreement you've drafted for new employees to sign.

A TAX TIP

If you visit your lawyer on a personal legal matter (such as reviewing a contract for the purchase of a house) and you also discuss a business problem (such as a pending OSHA inspection), ask your lawyer to allocate the time spent and send you separate bills. At tax time, you can easily list the business portion as a tax-deductible business expense.

C. Resolving Problems With Your Lawyer

If you see a problem emerging with your lawyer, nip it in the bud. Don't just sit back and fume; call, or visit or write your lawyer. The problem won't get resolved if your lawyer doesn't even know there's a problem. An open exchange is essential for a healthy lawyer-client relationship.

Whatever it is that rankles, have an honest discussion about your feelings. Maybe you're upset because your lawyer hasn't kept you informed about what's going on in your case or has missed a promised deadline. Or maybe last month's bill was shockingly high or lacked any breakdown of how your lawyer's time was spent.

One good test of whether a lawyer-client relationship is a good one is to ask yourself if you feel able to talk freely with your lawyer about your degree of participation in any legal matter and your control over how the lawyer carries out a legal assignment. If you can't frankly discuss these sometimes sensitive matters with your lawyer, fire that lawyer and hire another one. Otherwise, you'll surely waste money on unnecessary legal fees and risk having legal matters turn out badly. Remember that you're always free to change lawyers and to get all important legal documents back from a lawyer you no longer employ.

Out With the Old—Then, In With the New

Be sure to fire your old lawyer before you hire a new one. Otherwise, you could find yourself being billed by both lawyers at the same time.

If you have a dispute over fees, the local bar association may be able to mediate it for you. And if a lawyer has violated legal ethics, the bar association can take action to discipline or even disbar the lawyer. Where a major mistake has been made—for example, a lawyer has missed the deadline for filing a case—you can sue for malpractice. Virtually all lawyers carry malpractice insurance.

YOUR RIGHTS AS A CLIENT

As a client, you have the following rights:

- to be treated courteously by your lawyer and the members of his or her staff
- to receive an itemized statement of services rendered and a full explanation of billing practices
- to be charged reasonable fees
- to receive a prompt response to phone calls and letters
- to have confidential legal conferences, free from unwarranted interruptions
- to be kept informed of the status of your case
- to have your legal matters handled diligently and competently, and
- to receive clear answers to all questions

D. Legal Research

Law libraries are chock full of valuable information—information that you can easily find on your own. All you need is a rudimentary knowledge of how that information is organized.

1. Finding a Law Library

Your first step is to find a law library that's open to the public. You may find such a library in your county courthouse or at your state capitol. Public law schools generally permit the public to use their libraries, and some private law schools grant access to their libraries—sometimes for a modest fee. The reference department of a major public library may have a fairly decent legal research collection. Finally, don't overlook the law library in your own lawyer's office. Most lawyers, on request, will gladly share their books with their clients.

There are a number of sources that provide good guidance in how to do your own legal research.

Legal Research: How to Find and Understand the Law, by Stephen Elias and Susan Levinkind (Nolo Press). This nontechnical book simply explains how to use all major legal research tools and helps you frame your research questions.

Legal Research Made Easy: A Roadmap through the Law Library Maze, by Robert C. Berring (Legal Star/Nolo Press). This is an entertaining videotape with a six-step strategy for legal research. If you really plan to do your own legal research, this is a must see. It's available from many public and law library video collections—or directly through Nolo Press.

The Plain-Language Law Dictionary for Home and Office, edited by Robert S. Rothenberg (Penguin Books). This paperback book defines over 6,500 technical words and phrases in easily understood language—a valuable resource if you don't speak legalese.

2. Federal and State Laws

Employment is governed by both federal law and state law. Federal statutes, for example, deal with wages and hours, continuation of health insurance coverage when an employee is terminated, withholding employee taxes and Social Security contributions, unpaid family and medical leave, illegal discrimination and workplace safety. State statutes often touch on many of these same topics, as well as unemployment compensation and workers' compensation. The law of wrongful discharge—except where it involves claims of illegal discrimination—is primarily a matter of state law, most of which comes from judges' decisions rather than from statutes.

3. Sources of Legal Research

In doing legal research, there are several sources you many find useful, broadly categorized as primary and secondary sources. You use primary sources to find out the current status of the law. They include:
- constitutions (federal and state)
- legislation (laws—also called statutes or ordinances—passed by congress, your state legislature and local governments)
- administrative rules and regulations (issued by federal and state administrative agencies charged with implementing statutes)
- case law (decisions of federal and state courts interpreting statutes—and sometimes making law, known as common law, if the subject isn't covered by a statute)

A small or midsized employer rarely gets involved in questions of constitutional law. You're far more likely to be concerned with law created by a federal or state statute, or by an administrative rule or regulation. At the federal level, that includes the Internal Revenue Code and regulations adopted by the Internal Revenue Service; regulations dealing with wages and hours adopted by the U.S. Department of Labor; and anti-discrimination statutes such as Title VII of the Civil Rights Act administered by the Justice Department and Equal Employment Opportunity Commission.

At the state level, you'll likely be interested in state statutes dealing with unemployment compensation and workers' compensation. You may also need to look into county and city ordinances addressing workplace issues such as tobacco smoke and discrimination.

4. How to Begin

Obviously, primary sources—statements of the "raw law"—are important. But most legal research begins with secondary sources—books that comment on, summarize, organize or describe the law.

It often makes sense to start with one of the two national encyclopedias, *American Jurisprudence 2d* (cited as Am. Jur. 2d) or *Corpus Juris Secundum* (cited as C.J.S.). If your state has its own encyclopedia, check that, too. These encyclopedias organize the case law and some statutes into narrative statements organized alphabetically by subject. Through citation footnotes, you can locate the full text of the cases and statutes.

It's also helpful if you can find a treatise on the subject you're researching. A treatise is simply a book or series of books that covers a specific area of law. You may want to look at:

- *Labor Law in a Nutshell*, by Douglas L. Leslie
- *Workers' Compensation and Employee Protection Law in a Nutshell*, by Jack B. Hood, Benjamin A. Hardy, Jr. and Harold S. Lewis, Jr., or
- *Sex Discrimination in a Nutshell*, by Claire Sherman Thomas.

  The entire series is published by West Publishing Company.

HOW TO READ A CASE CITATION

There are several places where a case may be reported. If it is a case decided by the U.S. Supreme Court, you can find it in either the United States Reports (U.S.) or the Supreme Court Reporter (S.Ct.). If it is a federal case decided by a court other than the U.S. Supreme Court, it will be in either the Federal Reporter, Second Series (F.2d) or the Federal Supplement (F. Supp.).

Most states publish their own official state reports. All published state courts decisions are also included in the West Reporter System. West has divided the country into seven regions—and publishes all the decisions of the supreme and appellate state courts in the region together. These reporters are:

A. and A.2d. Atlantic Reporter (First and Second Series), which includes decisions from Connecticut, Delaware, the District of Columbia, Maine, Maryland, New Hampshire, New Jersey, Pennsylvania, Rhode Island and Vermont.

N.E. and N.E.2d. Northeastern Reporter (First and Second Series), which includes decisions from New York,* Illinois, Indiana, Massachusetts and Ohio.

N.W. and N.W.2d. Northwestern Reporter (First and Second Series), which includes decisions from Iowa, Michigan, Minnesota, Nebraska, North Dakota, South Dakota and Wisconsin.

P. and P.2d. Pacific Reporter (First and Second Series), which includes decisions from Alaska, Arizona, California,* Colorado, Hawaii, Idaho, Kansas, Montana, Nevada, New Mexico, Oklahoma, Oregon, Utah, Washington and Wyoming.

S.E. and S.E.2d. Southeastern Reporter (First and Second Series), which includes decisions from Georgia, North Carolina, South Carolina, Virginia and West Virginia.

So. and So.2d. Southern Reporter (First and Second Series), which includes decisions from Alabama, Florida, Louisiana and Mississippi.

S.W. and S.W.2d. Southwestern Reporter (First and Second Series), which includes decisions from Arkansas, Kentucky, Missouri, Tennessee and Texas.

A case citation will give you the names of the people or companies on each side of a case, the volume of the reporter in which the case can be found, the page number on which it begins and the year in which the case was decided. For example:

Smith v. Jones Int'l, 123 N.Y.S.2d 456 (1994)

Smith and Jones are the names of the parties having the legal dispute. The case is reported in volume 123 of the New York Supplement, Second Series, beginning on page 456; the court issued the decision in 1994.

*All California appellate decisions are published in a separate volume, the California Reporter (Cal. Rptr.) and all decisions from New York appellate courts are published in a separate volume, New York Supplement (N.Y.S.).

Law reviews published by law schools and other legal periodicals may also contain useful summaries of the law. The *American Bar Association Journal* as well as the journal published by your state bar association should be available in the law library that you use. In these journals, you'll often find timely articles on legal issues that affect small businesses. You can locate law review and bar journal articles through *The Index to Legal Periodicals*. Be forewarned, however, that law school reviews contain articles by law professors and students, and are usually of more academic than practical interest.

One good periodical for background information is *The Practical Lawyer*, published by the Joint Committee on Continuing Legal Education of the American Law Institute and American Bar Association (ALI-ABA). Each edition contains half a dozen clear and practical articles—many of which address topics of interest to employers. The checklists and forms are superb. This resource is virtually unknown outside the legal profession. An annual subscription, consisting of eight issues, costs $35. Call (215) 243-1640 or write to: 4025 Chestnut Street, Philadelphia, PA 19104-3099.

Finally, practically every state has an organization that provides continuing legal education to practicing lawyers. Some of these organizations publish excellent books on business law subjects which focus on the law in your state and contain state-specific forms and checklists. You can also find a wealth of relevant information in the course materials prepared for continuing legal education seminars. To locate the organization that provides continuing legal education in your state, call the local or state bar association.

5. Online Research

For the computer savvy, online research is not only avant garde but, more to the point, can be speedy and inexpensive. The logical starting point is Nolo's *Law on the Net,* by James Evans. There you'll find an impressive overview of the World Wide Web and the Internet, followed by a mind-boggling array of sites you might want to visit in doing legal research.

Be sure to stop at Nolo's own site, http://www.nolo.com, where you'll discover valuable online information, including material on employment law.

Lawyers who do computer research rely primarily on two systems: Westlaw and Lexis. A small but growing number of public law libraries offer these services. Those that do offer them usually require a sizable advance or a credit card; you pay as you go. Ask a law librarian for details, but be prepared for sticker shock. You can end up paying as much as $300 an hour.

It's more practical to use other online sources that cost you nothing other than the usual charges for online access time.

For an introduction to the vast amount of information that's out there, you might sample these sites:

- Lawyers Weekly at: http://www.lweekly.com. Here you'll find up-to-date news on a wide range of legal topics. Check out the aptly named Treasure Chest of Important Documents for items you might want to download.
- The Thomas Legislative Information site at: http://thomas.loc.gov. Named for Thomas Jefferson, this site contains a wealth of information on bills pending in Congress and laws recently adopted.
- The Court TV Small Business Law Center at: http://www.courttv.com/legalhelp/business. Look for articles and forms on small business law in general and employment law in particular.
- Lectric Law Library at http://www.lectlaw.com. This is a good place to explore a wide range of business law issues. Many employment law topics are covered in reasonable depth.

TIPS FOR RESEARCHING EMPLOYMENT LAW

When looking up statutes, use the annotated versions. They typically come in multi-volume sets and contain the text of the laws plus references to court and administrative decisions interpreting the statutes and often to treatises and articles that discuss the law.

Statutes are frequently amended. Always check the supplement at the back of statute books to make sure you have the latest edition.

Most federal statutes and many state statutes are interpreted in regulations which have the force of law. For example, the U.S. Department of Labor has enacted many regulations concerning the Fair Labor Standards Act. (See Chapter 3.) Where regulations exist, they're an essential part of your research.

Use the Shepard Citation system to see if and where the court case you're looking at has been mentioned in a later case. This can expand your research—and also let you know if the law has changed recently. *Legal Research: How to Find and Understand the Law* by Stephen Elias and Susan Levinkind (Nolo Press) has a good, easy-to-follow explanation of how to use the Shepard's system.

A relatively unknown resource for quickly locating business laws in your state is the United States Law Digest volume of the *Martindale-Hubbell Law Directory*. It contains a handy summary of laws, including statutory citations, for each state. But you may need a magnifying glass: the print is minuscule. ■

APPENDIX

U.S. Department of Labor
200 Constitution Avenue, NW
Washington, DC 20210
(202) 219-6666

STATE LABOR DEPARTMENTS

Alabama
Labor Department
1789 Dickenson Drive, 2nd Floor
Montgomery, AL 36130
(205) 242-3460

Alaska
Labor Department
P.O. Box 21149
Juneau, AK 99802-1149
(907) 465-2700

Arizona
Labor Division
800 West Washington Street, Suite 102
Phoenix, AZ 85007
(602) 542-4515

Arkansas
Labor Department
10421 West Markham Street
Little Rock, AR 72205
(501) 682-4500

California
Industrial Relations Department
455 Golden Gate Avenue
P.O. Box 420603
San Francisco, CA 94142-0603
(415) 703-4281

Colorado
Labor Division
1120 Lincoln Street
Denver, CO 80203
(303) 837-3800

Connecticut
Labor Department
200 Folly Brook Boulevard
Wethersfield, CT 06109
(203) 566-4384

Delaware
Labor Department
820 North French Street; 6th Floor
Wilmington, DE 19801
(302) 577-2710

District of Columbia
Wage and Hour Office
950 Upshur Street, NW; 2nd Floor
Washington, DC 20011
(202) 576-6942

Florida
Labor Employment & Training Division
Atkins Building, Suite 300
Tallahassee, FL 32399-0667
(904) 488-7228

Georgia
Labor Department
148 International Blvd, NE, Suite 600
Atlanta, GA 30303
(404) 656-3011

Hawaii
Labor & Industrial Relations Department
830 Punchbowl Street
Honolulu, HI 96813
(808) 586-8842

Idaho
Labor & Industrial Services Department
277 North 6th Street
State House Mail
Boise, ID 83720
(208) 334-3950

Illinois
Labor Department
160 North LaSalle Street, 13th Floor
Chicago, IL 60601
(312) 793-2800

Indiana	Labor Department 402 West Washington, Room W-195 Indianapolis, IN 46204 (317) 232-2655
Iowa	Labor Services Commission 1000 East Grand Avenue Des Moines, IA 50319 (515) 281-8067
Kansas	Public Employee Relations Board 512 West 6th Topeka, KS 66603 (913) 296-3094
Kentucky	Labor Cabinet US Hwy. 127, South Building Frankfort, KY 40601 (502) 564-3070
Louisiana	Labor Department P.O. Box 94094 Baton Rouge, LA 70804-9094 (504) 342-3011
Maine	Labor Department 20 Union Street P.O. Box 309 Augusta, ME 04332-0309 (207) 287-3788
Maryland	Labor & Industry Division 501 Saint Paul Place Baltimore, MD 21202 (410) 333-4179
Massachusetts	Labor & Industries Department 100 Cambridge Street, Room 1100 Boston, MA 02202 (617) 727-3454
Michigan	Labor Department Victor Office Building 201 North Washington Square P.O. Box 30015 Lansing, MI 48909 (517) 373-9600

Minnesota	Labor & Industry Department 443 Lafayete Road St. Paul, MN 55155 (612) 296-2342
Mississippi	Employment Security Commission 1520 West Capitol P.O. Box 1699 Jackson, MS 39215 (601) 354-8711
Missouri	Labor & Industrial Relations Department 3315 West Truman Boulevard Jefferson City, MO 65109 (314) 751-4091
Montana	Labor & Industry Department 1327 Lockey Avenue P.O. Box 1728 Helena, MT 59624 (406) 444-3555
Nebraska	Labor Department P.O. Box 94600 Lincoln, NE 68509 (402) 471-9000
Nevada	Labor Commission 1445 Hot Springs Road, Suite 108 Carson City, NV 89710 (702) 687-4850
New Hampshire	Labor Department 95 Pleasant Street Concord, NH 03301 (603) 271-3171
New Jersey	Labor Department John Fitch Plaza, CN 110 Trenton, NJ 08625 (609) 292-2323
New Mexico	Labor & Industrial Division 1596 Pacheco Street Santa Fe, NM 87501 (505) 827-6808
New York	Labor Department State Campus, Bldg. 12 Albany, NY 12240 (518) 457-2741

North Carolina	Labor Department 4 W. Edenton Street Raleigh, NC 27601 (919) 733-7166
North Dakota	Labor Department 600 East Boulevard Bismarck, ND 58505 (701) 224-2660
Ohio	Industrial Relations Department 2323 West 5th Avenue P.O. Box 825 Columbus, OH 43216 (614) 644-2223
Oklahoma	Labor Department 4001 Lincoln Boulevard Oklahoma City, OK 73105 (405) 528-1500
Oregon	Labor & Industries Bureau 800 NE Oregon Portland, OR 97232 (503) 731-4200
Pennsylvania	Labor & Industry Department Labor & Industry Building Harrisburg, PA 17120 (717) 787-3756
Rhode Island	Labor Department 610 Manton Avenue Providence, RI 02909 (401) 457-1800
South Carolina	Labor Department P.O. Box 11329 Columbia, SC 29211-1329 (803) 734-9594
South Dakota	Labor Department 700 Governors Drive Pierre, SD 57501 (605) 773-3101
Tennessee	Labor Department 710 James Robertson Parkway, 2nd Floor Nashville, TN 37243-0655 (615) 741-2582

Texas	Licensing & Regulation Department P.O. Box 12157, Capitol Station Austin, TX 78711 (512) 463-5522
Utah	Labor Division 160 E. 300 South, 3rd Floor P.O Box 146630 Salt Lake City, UT 84114-6630 (801) 530-6921
Vermont	Labor & Industry Department National Life Building, Drawer 20 Montpelier, VT 05620-3401 (802) 828-2286
Virginia	Labor & Industry Department 13 South 13th Street Richmond, VA 23219 (804) 786-2377
Washington	Labor & Industries Department P.O. Box 44001 Olympia, WA 98504-4001 (206) 956-4213
West Virginia	Labor Division 1800 Washington Street E Charleston, WV 25305 (304) 558-7890
Wisconsin	Industry, Labor & Human Relations Department P.O. Box 7946 Madison, WI 53707 (608) 266-7552
Wyoming	Labor & Statistics Department U.S. West Building 6101 Yellowstone Road, Room 259C Cheyenne, WY 82002 (307) 777-7261

INDEX

A

Accommodations. *See* Americans With Disabilities Act (ADA)

Accounting methods, 5/15-16

Acquired Immune Deficiency Syndrome (AIDS), 7/37

ADA. *See* Americans With Disabilities Act (ADA)

ADEA. *See* Age Discrimination in Employment Act (ADEA)

Administrative employees
 and Equal Pay Act, 3/16
 and FLSA, 3/6-9

Adoption, as reason for unpaid leave, 6/4-5

Adoption assistance programs, 4/27

Advance notice
 of leave, 6/10-11
 of testing, 1/33

Advertisements for job openings, 1/20
 avoiding discrimination, 1/5

Affirmative action plans, 8/23

Age discrimination, 8/18-21
 avoiding claims, 8/19
 in wrongful discharge case, 10/4

Age Discrimination in Employment Act (ADEA), 4/21, 8/2, 8/18-19
 requirements for firing process, 10/24

Agency shops, 12/6

Agricultural jobs, and young workers, 3/34-35

Alcohol, and privacy rights, 1/6-7

Alcohol abuse, 7/39-40, 7/43
 and employee handbook, 2/12

Alcohol testing, state laws, 1/39-42

Aliens
 discrimination, 10/5
 documented. *See* Immigration Reform and Control Act (IRCA)
 undocumented, 1/17, 1/57

Americans With Disabilities Act (ADA), 8/2, 9/3-30
 accessibility requirements, 9/4-6, 9/16, 9/19-21
 accommodations, 9/16-23
 and AIDS or HIV, 7/37
 and alcoholism, 7/43
 and applicants, 1/25-27, 9/4
 aptitude testing, requirements, 1/33-34
 and behavioral disorders, 9/14
 businesses covered, 9/6
 definition of disabilities, 9/7-12
 and drug testing, 1/38, 1/43
 and employee files, 2/4-5
 enforcement, 9/29-30
 exceptions to coverage, 9/14-15
 financial assistance, 9/24-25
 and FMLA, 6/25
 food handlers, 9/28
 and gay and lesbian workers, 9/14
 and healthcare coverage, 4/6-8
 and hiring process, 9/4-6
 and history of disability, 9/10-11
 impairments, 9/8-12
 and job applications, 9/16
 and job descriptions, 1/18
 and job performance, 9/16
 medical exams, 9/28-29
 medical information in employee files, 2/4-5
 medical testing of applicants, 1/36-37
 obesity, 9/10
 and physical characteristics, 9/15
 and pre-employment questions, 1/26-27

and psychological characteristics, 9/15
 record of disability, 9/10-11
 and sexual disorders, 9/14
 skills testing, requirements, 1/32-33
 tax credit for targeted jobs, 9/25
 tax credits for small businesses, 9/24
 tax deductions for removing barriers, 9/24
 testing, requirements, 1/33
 undue hardship of accommodations, 9/17
 and wrongful discharge cases, 10/5

Anti-discrimination laws, 1/4-5
 exception for BFOQ, 1/19
 and job descriptions, 1/18

Applicants
 disabled, interview, 1/32, 9/16
 investigating, 1/27-28, 1/44-53
 privacy rights, 1/6-7, 1/11
 rejecting, 1/55
 testing, 1/32-43

Application for Employer Identification Number (EIN), Form SS-4, 1/56, 5/4-7

Application forms for job, 1/21-29
 and ADA, 1/25
 avoiding unlawful questions, 1/21-27
 legal effect, 1/27-29
 sample clause for at will employment, 1/8

Application fraud, 1/28

Apprentices
 and FLSA, 3/10
 and state laws, 3/10

Arbitration, 8/7

CATALOG
...more from Nolo Press

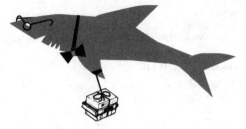

	EDITION	PRICE	CODE

BUSINESS

	EDITION	PRICE	CODE
The California Nonprofit Corporation Handbook	7th	$29.95	NON
The California Professional Corporation Handbook	5th	$34.95	PROF
The Employer's Legal Handbook	2nd	$29.95	EMPL
Form Your Own Limited Liability Company	1st	$24.95	LIAB
▣ Hiring Independent Contractors: The Employer's Legal Guide (Book w/Disk)	2nd	$29.95	HICI
▣ How to Form a CA Nonprofit Corp.—w/Corp. Records Binder & PC Disk	1st	$49.95	CNP
▣ How to Form a Nonprofit Corp., Book w/Disk (PC)—National Edition	3rd	$39.95	NNP
▣ How to Form Your Own Calif. Corp.—w/Corp. Records Binder & Disk—PC	1st	$39.95	CACI
How to Form Your Own California Corporation	8th	$29.95	CCOR
▣ How to Form Your Own Florida Corporation, (Book w/Disk—PC)	3rd	$39.95	FLCO
▣ How to Form Your Own New York Corporation, (Book w/Disk—PC)	3rd	$39.95	NYCO
▣ How to Form Your Own Texas Corporation, (Book w/Disk—PC)	4th	$39.95	TCOR
How to Handle Your Workers' Compensation Claim (California Edition)	1st	$29.95	WORK
How to Mediate Your Dispute	1st	$18.95	MEDI
How to Write a Business Plan	4th	$21.95	SBS
The Independent Paralegal's Handbook	4th	$29.95	PARA
Legal Guide for Starting & Running a Small Business, Vol. 1	3rd	$24.95	RUNS
Marketing Without Advertising	2nd	$19.00	MWAD
▣ The Partnership Book: How to Write a Partnership Agreement (Book w/Disk—PC)	5th	$34.95	PART
Sexual Harassment on the Job	2nd	$18.95	HARS
▣ Taking Care of Your Corporation, Vol. 1, (Book w/Disk—PC)	1st	$26.95	CORK
▣ Taking Care of Your Corporation, Vol. 2, (Book w/Disk—PC)	1st	$39.95	CORK2
Tax Savvy for Small Business	2nd	$26.95	SAVVY
Trademark: How to Name Your Business & Product	2nd	$29.95	TRD
Your Rights in the Workplace	3rd	$18.95	YRW

● Book with CD-ROM
▣ Book with disk

CALL 800-992-6656 OR USE THE ORDER FORM IN THE BACK OF THE BOOK

	EDITION	PRICE	CODE

CONSUMER

Title	EDITION	PRICE	CODE
Fed Up With the Legal System: What's Wrong & How to Fix It	2nd	$9.95	LEG
How to Win Your Personal Injury Claim	2nd	$24.95	PICL
Nolo's Pocket Guide to California Law	5th	$11.95	CLAW
Nolo's Pocket Guide to Consumer Rights	2nd	$12.95	CAG
Trouble-Free Travel...and What to Do When Things Go Wrong	1st	$14.95	TRAV

ESTATE PLANNING & PROBATE

Title	EDITION	PRICE	CODE
8 Ways to Probate (Quick & Legal Series)	1st	$15.95	PRO8
How to Probate an Estate (California Edition)	9th	$34.95	PAE
Make Your Own Living Trust	2nd	$21.95	LITR
🖥 Nolo's Will Book (Book w/Disk—PC)	3rd	$24.95	SWIL
Plan Your Estate	3rd	$24.95	NEST
The Quick and Legal Will Book	1st	$15.95	QUIC
Nolo's Law Form Kit: Wills	1st	$14.95	KWL

FAMILY MATTERS

Title	EDITION	PRICE	CODE
A Legal Guide for Lesbian and Gay Couples	9th	$24.95	LG
Child Custody: Building Parenting Agreements That Work	2nd	$24.95	CUST
Divorce & Money: How to Make the Best Financial Decisions During Divorce	3rd	$26.95	DIMO
Get A Life: You Don't Need a Million to Retire Well	1st	$18.95	LIFE
The Guardianship Book (California Edition)	2nd	$24.95	GB
How to Adopt Your Stepchild in California	4th	$22.95	ADOP
How to Do Your Own Divorce in California	21st	$24.95	CDIV
How to Do Your Own Divorce in Texas	6th	$19.95	TDIV
How to Raise or Lower Child Support in California	3rd	$18.95	CHLD
The Living Together Kit	8th	$24.95	LTK
Nolo's Pocket Guide to Family Law	4th	$14.95	FLD
Practical Divorce Solutions	1st	$14.95	PDS
Smart Ways to Save Money During and After Divorce	1st	$14.95	SAVMO

GOING TO COURT

Title	EDITION	PRICE	CODE
Collect Your Court Judgment (California Edition)	3rd	$24.95	JUDG
How to Seal Your Juvenile & Criminal Records (California Edition)	6th	$24.95	CRIM
How to Sue For Up to 25,000...and Win!	2nd	$29.95	MUNI
Everybody's Guide to Small Claims Court in California	12th	$18.95	CSCC
Everybody's Guide to Small Claims Court (National Edition)	6th	$18.95	NSCC
Fight Your Ticket ... and Win! (California Edition)	6th	$19.95	FYT
How to Change Your Name (California Edition)	6th	$24.95	NAME
Mad at Your Lawyer	1st	$21.95	MAD
Represent Yourself in Court: How to Prepare & Try a Winning Case	1st	$29.95	RYC
Taming the Lawyers	1st	$19.95	TAME

● Book with CD-ROM
🖥 Book with disk

| | EDITION | PRICE | CODE |

HOMEOWNERS, LANDLORDS & TENANTS

IMMIGRATION

MONEY MATTERS

PATENTS AND COPYRIGHTS

RESEARCH & REFERENCE

● Book with CD-ROM
☐ Book with disk

	EDITION	PRICE	CODE

SENIORS

	EDITION	PRICE	CODE
Beat the Nursing Home Trap	2nd	$18.95	ELD
Social Security, Medicare & Pensions	6th	$19.95	SOA
The Conservatorship Book (California Edition)	2nd	$29.95	CNSV

SOFTWARE

	EDITION	PRICE	CODE
California Incorporator 2.0—DOS	2.0	$47.97	INCI2
Living Trust Maker 2.0—Macintosh	2.0	$47.97	LTM2
Living Trust Maker 2.0—Windows	2.0	$47.97	LTWI2
Small Business Legal Pro—Macintosh	2.0	$25.97	SBM2
Small Business Legal Pro—Windows	2.0	$25.97	SBW2
Small Business Legal Pro Deluxe CD—Windows/Macintosh CD-ROM	2.0	$35.97	SBCD
Nolo's Partnership Maker 1.0—DOS	1.0	$47.97	PAGI1
Personal RecordKeeper 4.0—Macintosh	4.0	$29.97	RKM4
Personal RecordKeeper 4.0—Windows	4.0	$29.97	RKP4
Patent It Yourself 1.0—Windows	1.0	$149.97	PYWI
WillMaker 6.0—Macintosh	6.0	$41.97	WM6
WillMaker 6.0—Windows	6.0	$41.97	WIW6

● Book with CD-ROM
▣ Book with disk

SPECIAL UPGRADE OFFER

Get 25% off the latest edition of your Nolo book
It's important to have the most current legal information. Because laws and legal procedures change often, we update our books regularly. To help keep you up-to-date we are extending this special upgrade offer. Cut out and mail the title portion of the cover of your old Nolo book and we'll give you 25% off the retail price of the NEW EDITION of that book when you purchase directly from us. For more information call us at 1-800-992-6656.
This offer is to individuals only.

ORDER FORM

Name

Address (UPS to street address, Priority Mail to P.O. boxes)

Catalog Code	Quantity	Item	Unit Price	Total

Subtotal	
In California add appropriate Sales Tax	
Shipping & Handling: $6.00 for 1 item, $7.00 for 2 or more.	
UPS RUSH delivery $7.50-any size order*	
TOTAL	

UPS to street address, Priority mail to P.O. boxes

* Delivered in 3 business days from receipt of order. S.F. Bay Area use regular shipping.

METHOD OF PAYMENT

☐ Check enclosed   ☐ VISA   ☐ Mastercard   ☐ Discover Card   ☐ American Express

Account #   Expiration Date

Signature   Phone

FOR FASTER SERVICE, USE YOUR CREDIT CARD and OUR TOLL-FREE NUMBERS

ORDER 24 HOURS A DAY	1-800-992-6656
FAX US YOUR ORDER	1-800-645-0895
e-MAIL	cs@nolo.com
GENERAL INFORMATION	1-510-549-1976
CUSTOMER SERVICE	1-800-728-3555, Mon.-Fri. 9am-5pm, PST

Or mail your order with a check or money order made payable to:
Nolo Press, 950 Parker St., Berkeley, CA 94710

VISIT OUR OUTLETS

You'll find our complete line of books and software, all at a discount.
BERKELEY—950 Parker St., Berkeley, CA 94710 • 1-510-704-2248
SAN JOSE—111 N. Market Street, #115, San Jose, CA 95113 • 1-408-271-7240

VISIT US ONLINE on the **INTERNET** — www.nolo.com

*E*ducators, you can teach from these books.

Take advantage of Nolo's 25 years of experience in simplifying complex legal material and consider one or more of these Nolo Press titles for your primary or supplementary text(s).

NOLO'S PAPERBACKS FOR THE CLASSROOM • **Comprehensive** • **Easy-to-Read** • **Affordable**

To request a complimentary copy for course adoption consideration, please write us or FAX us on your school letterhead. LIMIT: 2 BOOKS. Ask us to send you our complete catalog, too.

*The Legal Guide for Starting
& Running a Small Business*
ISBN 0-87337-374-X, $24.95

Tax Savvy for Small Business
ISBN 0-87337-372-3, $26.95

Business Plans to Game Plans
ISBN 1-56343-071-1, $29.95

Mastering Diversity
ISBN 1-56343-102-5, $29.95

*How to Form A
Nonprofit Corporation*
ISBN 0-87337-333-2, $39.95

How to Write a Business Plan
ISBN 0-87337-184-4, $21.95

*Helping Employees Achieve
Retirement Security*
ISBN 1-885123-04-3, $16.95

*How to Finance a
Growing Business*
ISBN 1-56343-100-9, $24.95

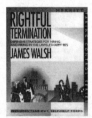

Rightful Termination
ISBN 1-56343-067-3, $29.95

Trademark
ISBN 0-87337-311-1, $29.95

*Taking Care of Your Corporation
Volume 1: Director & Shareholder
Meetings Made Easy*
ISBN 0-87337-223-9, $26.95

*Taking Care of Your Corporation
Volume 2: Key Corporate
Decisions Made Easy*
ISBN 0-87337-276-X, $39.95

NOLO

PRESS

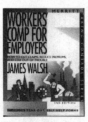

Worker's Comp for Employers
ISBN 1-56343-155-6, $29.95

Sexual Harassment on the Job
ISBN 0-87337-265-4, $18.95

Your Rights in the Workplace
ISBN 0-87337-346-4, $19.95

Nolo Press, 950 Parker St., Berkeley, CA 94710 Attn: Academic Sales • FAX 510-548-5902 • http://www.nolo.com